May 12, 1976

To ████████

In deep appreciation
of your teaching.

Charles, Muriel, Becky
Harmany

SACRED AND SECULAR
A Companion

SACRED
AND SECULAR

A Companion

Compiled by
Adam Fox and Gareth and Georgina Keene

WILLIAM B. EERDMANS PUBLISHING COMPANY
Grand Rapids

Published by Special Arrangement
with John Murray (Publishers) Ltd., London.
Printed in the United States.

Library of Congress Cataloging in Publication Data

Main entry under title:

Sacred and secular.

Includes index.
1.   Church year — Prayer-books and devotions —
English.   I.   Fox, Adam, 1883-   II.   Keene, Gareth,
1944-   III.   Keene, Georgina, 1948-
BV4812.A1S2   1975   242′.3   75-20224
ISBN   0-8028-3469-8

PREFACE

This book is designed to bring an element of the secular into religious devotion. Anyone who will read these Sequences, as we call them, will see how. Each sequence has a title which indicates the theme. Then (I) a passage giving a context to the title, (II) a passage from the Old Testament illustrating the theme, (III) a passage from the New Testament chosen with the same purpose, (IV) a brief quotation, which may serve as a transition from sacred to secular, (V) a passage from a non-biblical and most often a purely secular source to put the theme in a new light, (VI) a piece of poetry chosen for the same purpose, and (VII) an afterthought offering something to think or reflect upon.

We have sought to find a picture to go with each sequence. Print and paint can thus become partners. When the sequences have had their say, the pictures may say something more and in a different language.

It is a pity that it is not possible to bring music to the aid of devotion in the same way, seeing how close the connection between music and religion has always been, but we have offered a selection of musical titles in the hope that the reader may himself bring music to his aid by means of gramophone records, the radio or public performance.

The book is arranged within a framework provided by the Calendar in the Book of Common Prayer of 1662. An Appendix at the end of the book suggests how it may be fitted to the new Calendar now under consideration as an alternative. It can be used independently of either.

In a very few places we have deviated from the Authorized Version to that of the New English Bible, and from the Prayer Book of 1662 to that of 1928. The extracts from the Psalms are from the Version in the Book of Common Prayer, as being much the most familiar through their constant repetition in church and their use in quotation. It is the Version made in 1540 with some small alterations in 1562 and 1611.

CONTENTS

Acknowledgements   xii

Sequences:

I   THE FIRST SUNDAY IN ADVENT   I
      The house of prayer

2   THE SECOND SUNDAY IN ADVENT   7
      Distress of nations, with perplexity

3   THE THIRD SUNDAY IN ADVENT   12
      Stewards of the mysteries of God

4   THE FOURTH SUNDAY IN ADVENT   17
      The race that is set before us

5   CHRISTMAS-DAY   22
      The express image of his person

6   THE FIRST SUNDAY AFTER CHRISTMAS-DAY   28
      God with us

7   THE SECOND SUNDAY AFTER CHRISTMAS (BCP 1928)   33
      Jesus Christ was made in the likeness of men

8   THE EPIPHANY, OR THE MANIFESTATION OF
      CHRIST TO THE GENTILES   38
      The Gentiles should be fellow-heirs,
        and of the same body

9   THE FIRST SUNDAY AFTER THE EPIPHANY   43
      Sitting in the midst of the doctors

10 THE SECOND SUNDAY AFTER THE EPIPHANY   47
      Whatsoever he saith unto you, do it

11 THE THIRD SUNDAY AFTER THE EPIPHANY   52
      Stretch forth thy right hand to help and defend us

CONTENTS

12 THE FOURTH SUNDAY AFTER THE EPIPHANY 57
   The frailty of our nature

13 THE FIFTH SUNDAY AFTER THE EPIPHANY 61
   Psalms and hymns and spiritual songs

14 THE SIXTH SUNDAY AFTER THE EPIPHANY 65
   A great sound of a trumpet

15 THE SUNDAY CALLED SEPTUAGESIMA 69
   He had agreed with the labourers for a
   penny a day

16 THE SUNDAY CALLED SEXAGESIMA 75
   The mysteries of the kingdom of God

17 THE SUNDAY CALLED QUINQUAGESIMA 79
   Now we see through a glass, darkly

18 ASH-WEDNESDAY 83
   Acknowledging our wretchedness

19 THE FIRST SUNDAY IN LENT 88
   Having nothing, and yet possessing all things

20 THE SECOND SUNDAY IN LENT 93
   Evil thoughts which may assault and
   hurt the soul

21 THE THIRD SUNDAY IN LENT 98
   Awake, thou that sleepest

22 THE FOURTH SUNDAY IN LENT 102
   Jerusalem which now is—Jerusalem which is
   above

23 THE FIFTH SUNDAY IN LENT 107
   Good things to come

24 THE SUNDAY NEXT BEFORE EASTER: PALM SUNDAY 112
   The example of his patience

25 GOOD FRIDAY 117
   He said, It is finished

CONTENTS

26 EASTER–DAY 122
God, who through Jesus Christ hast
overcome death

27 THE FIRST SUNDAY AFTER EASTER 127
The first day of the week

28 THE SECOND SUNDAY AFTER EASTER 132
The Shepherd and Bishop of your souls

29 THE THIRD SUNDAY AFTER EASTER 137
Your joy no man taketh from you

30 THE FOURTH SUNDAY AFTER EASTER 142
The sundry and manifold changes of the world

31 THE FIFTH SUNDAY AFTER EASTER 146
Thy merciful guiding

32 THE ASCENSION–DAY 151
He was received up

33 SUNDAY AFTER ASCENSION–DAY 156
These things have I spoken unto you

34 WHIT–SUNDAY 161
Ye in me, and I in you

35 TRINITY–SUNDAY 166
A door was opened in heaven

36 THE FIRST SUNDAY AFTER TRINITY 170
The Saviour of the world

37 THE SECOND SUNDAY AFTER TRINITY 175
He laid down his life for us

38 THE THIRD SUNDAY AFTER TRINITY 179
An hearty desire to pray

39 THE FOURTH SUNDAY AFTER TRINITY 184
Things temporal—the things eternal

40 THE FIFTH SUNDAY AFTER TRINITY 189
Launch out into the deep

CONTENTS

41 THE SIXTH SUNDAY AFTER TRINITY   194
    The likeness of his resurrection

42 THE SEVENTH SUNDAY AFTER TRINITY   199
    Increase in us true religion

43 THE EIGHTH SUNDAY AFTER TRINITY   203
    Sons of God

44 THE NINTH SUNDAY AFTER TRINITY   208
    The children of this world

45 THE TENTH SUNDAY AFTER TRINITY   213
    The same Spirit

46 THE ELEVENTH SUNDAY AFTER TRINITY   217
    A measure of thy grace

47 THE TWELFTH SUNDAY AFTER TRINITY   222
    Trust

48 THE THIRTEENTH SUNDAY AFTER TRINITY   227
    True and laudable service

49 THE FOURTEENTH SUNDAY AFTER TRINITY   232
    Walk in the Spirit

50 THE FIFTEENTH SUNDAY AFTER TRINITY   237
    The lilies of the field

51 THE SIXTEENTH SUNDAY AFTER TRINITY   241
    God's help and goodness

52 THE SEVENTEENTH SUNDAY AFTER TRINITY   245
    Baptism

53 THE EIGHTEENTH SUNDAY AFTER TRINITY   251
    Enriched by God, in all utterance

54 THE NINETEENTH SUNDAY AFTER TRINITY   255
    Corrupt communication

55 THE TWENTIETH SUNDAY AFTER TRINITY   260
    Ready both in body and soul

56 THE TWENTY-FIRST SUNDAY AFTER TRINITY   265
       The whole armour of God

57 THE TWENTY-SECOND SUNDAY AFTER TRINITY   270
       The glory and praise of God

58 THE TWENTY-THIRD SUNDAY AFTER TRINITY   275
       Our conversation is in heaven

59 THE TWENTY-FOURTH SUNDAY AFTER TRINITY   280
       All patience and longsuffering with joyfulness

60 THE TWENTY-FIFTH SUNDAY AFTER TRINITY
       or THE SUNDAY NEXT BEFORE ADVENT (BCP 1928) 285
       Judgment and justice in the earth

61 THE PRESENTATION OF CHRIST IN THE TEMPLE   291
       commonly called
       THE PURIFICATION OF SAINT MARY THE VIRGIN
       2 February
          The Lord, whom ye seek

62 THE ANNUNCIATION OF THE BLESSED VIRGIN MARY   295
       25 March
          The message of an angel

63 THE TRANSFIGURATION (BCP 1928)   300
       6 August
          He was transfigured

    Selection of Music   305

    Illustrations   311

    Appendix: The Calendar and Lessons for the
       Church's Year (1968)   319

    Index of biblical references   325

    Index of non-biblical sources   331

ACKNOWLEDGEMENTS

The compilers wish to thank Simon Young for his patient help and unfailing encouragement during the preparation of this book. They are most grateful also to Roger Hudson and Herbert Rees for their expert assistance in finalizing the text, to Roger Gaunt and Philip Radcliffe for their advice in drawing up the list of musical suggestions and to George Guest for kindly scrutinizing and commenting upon the selection of music at a later stage.

We acknowledge with thanks permission to reprint the following copyright material: for "Church Going," *The Less Deceived* to Philip Larkin and The Marvell Press, England; from Louis Macneice's "Autumn Journal," *The Collected Poems,* edited by E.A. Dodds, © the Estate of Louis Macneice, 1966, and for Edwin Muir's "The Incarnate One" and "Nothing There but Faith," *Collected Poems 1921-1958,* © 1960 by Willa Muir, reprinted by permission of Oxford University Press, Inc.; from "The Country Clergy," *Poetry for Supper* to R.S. Thomas and Granada Publishing Ltd; for "Days of Endeavour," to the Society of Authors as the literary representative of the Estate of John Masefield; from John Masefield's *Gallipoli,* reprinted with the permission of Macmillan Publishing Co., Inc., © 1916, 1925 by Macmillan Publishing Co., Inc., renewed 1944, 1953 by John Masefield; from *Images of God* to A.C. Bridge and the publishers, Messrs. Hodder and Stoughton; from *The Christian Faith in Art* by Eric Newton and William Neil to Thames and Hudson Ltd ; from *Muted Joy* to the late Very Reverend W.R. Matthews; for "A Broken Image," *The Fourth Man,* to Thomas Blackburn and Granada Publishing Ltd ; from the Sixth Edition of J.L. Brierly's *The Law of Nations,* edited by Sir Humphrey Waldock (Oxford University Press, 1963), to the Clarendon Press, Oxford; to Sir John Wolfenden for one of his sayings; from *Teach your Child about Sex* to the late Julie Dawkins and the Hamlyn Publishing Group Ltd.; from Dietrich Bonhoeffer's *Letters and Papers from Prison,* from the revised-enlarged edition, 1971, © 1953, 1967, reprinted with permission of Macmillan Publishing Co., Inc., © 1953, 1967, 1971 by SCM Press Ltd.; for "On a Friend's Escape from Drowning off the Norfolk Coast" from *Collected Poems 1930-1965*, © 1957, 1962 and 1965 by George Granville Barker, reprinted by permission of October House, Inc.; from Rudyard Kipling's "When Earth's Last Picture," *The Seven Seas* to Mrs. George Bambridge, Methuen & Co., Ltd. and The Macmillan Company of Canada Ltd.; from Baron Friedrich von Hugel's *Selected Letters* and *Essays & Addresses on the Philosophy of Religion*, from George Santayana's *Spinoza's Ethics* and from F.J. Powicke's *The Cambridge Platonists* to J.M. Dent & Sons Ltd.; from "The Sirens: an Ode" to Mrs. Nicolette Gray and the Society of Authors on behalf of the Laurence Binyon Estate; for a saying by W.R. Lethaby to *The Times*; from J.M. Barrie's *Peter Pan* to Brockhampton Press Ltd.; from Michel Quoist's *Christ is Alive!* to Gill and Macmillan Ltd., Dublin; for "Awake!" to the Literary Trustees of Walter de la Mare and the Society of Authors as their representative; from Sir G. Arthur's *Life of Kitchener*, Armitage Robinson's *St. Paul's Epistle to the Ephesians* and William Temple's *Readings in St. John's Gospel* to Messrs. Macmillan, London and Basingstoke; from Pierre Teilhard de Chardin's *Le Milieu Divin*, translated by Bernard Wall, © 1957 by Editions du Seuil, Paris, English translation © 1960 by Wm. Collins Sons & Co., Ltd., London and Harper & Row, Publishers, New York; from Pierre Teilhard de Chardin's *Writings in Time of War*, translated by Rene Hague, © 1965 by Editions Bernard Grasset, © 1968 in the English translation by Wm. Collins Sons & Co., Ltd., London and Harper & Row Publishers, New York; from P.B. Clayton's *To Conquer Hate* to the Methodist Printing House; from an article, "Lord's Day" in Volume III of *Hastings' Dictionary of the Bible* by N.J.D. White to Messrs. T. & T. Clark; for G.M. Hopkins' *Felix Randal* and from Louise and Aylmer Maude's translation of Tolstoy's *War and Peace* to Oxford University Press; from *Cyril Forster Garbett* to Charles Smyth and the publishers, Messrs. Hodder and Stoughton; from *Saint Joan* to the Society of Authors on behalf of the Bernard Shaw Estate; from Vita Sackville-West's *The Eagle and the Dove* to Michael Joseph Ltd.; from Leonard Hodgson's *The Doctrine of the Trinity* to James Nisbet & Co., Ltd.; from "Joseph Lister, 1st Baron Lister," *Dictionary of National Biog-*

raphy to the Clarendon Press, Oxford; from Elisabeth Jennings' translation of *The Sonnets of Michelangelo* (published for the members of the Folio Society, 1961) to The Folio Society; to *The Daily Telegraph* for an extract from the edition of May 6, 1968; for Wilfred Owen's "Greater Love" from *Collected Poems*, © Chatto & Windus Ltd., 1946 & 1963, reprinted by permission of New Directions Publishing Corporation, New York; from Constance Garnett's translation, from the Russian, of Fyodor Dostoevsky's *The Brothers Karamazov*, reprinted with permission of Macmillan Publishing Co., Inc., published in the U.S. by Macmillan Publishing Co., Inc.; from A.J. Mason's *Memoir of George Howard Wilkinson* to the Venerable Lancelot Mason; from W.R. Inge's *The Platonic Tradition in English Religious Thought* to Longman Group Ltd.; from *William the Silent* to Dame C.V. Wedgwood and Jonathan Cape Ltd.; from *Collected Poems 1928-1953* to Stephen Spender and Faber and Faber Ltd.; from Hilaire Belloc's *Verses* (1910) to Gerald Duckworth & Co., Ltd.; from Canon Augustine Ambali's *Thirty Years in Nyasaland* to the United Society for the Propagation of the Gospel; from Robert Bridges' *The Testament of Beauty* and for "A Villager," *The Poetical Works of Robert Bridges*, © Oxford University Press 1936, by permission of Oxford University Press, Oxford; from *Letters of William and Dorothy Wordsworth* edited by Ernest de Selincourt, Volume I, *The Early Years 1787-1805* revised by Chester L. Shaver, second edition, and Volume II, *The Middle Years 1806-1811* revised by Mary Moorman, second edition, © Oxford University Press 1967 and 1969 respectively, by permission of Oxford University Press, Oxford; for John Masefield's "The Everlasting Mercy," reprinted with permission of Macmillan Publishing Co., Inc., © 1912 by Macmillan Publishing Co., Inc., renewed 1940 by John Masefield; to the Scout Association for its "Motto"; from *The Old Man and the Sea*, © 1952 Ernest Hemingway, used by permission of Charles Scribner & Sons; for "The Song of a Man Who Has Come Through" from *The Complete Poems of D.H. Lawrence*, edited by Vivian De Sola Pinto and F. Warren Roberts, © 1964, 1971 by Angelo Ravagli and C.M. Weekley, Executors of the estate of Frieda Lawrence Ravagli, reprinted by permission of The Viking Press, Inc., all rights reserved; from the Law Reports to the Incorporated Council of Law

Reporting for England and Wales; from the *New English Bible* (Second Edition, 1970) to the Oxford and Cambridge University Presses; from *The Book of Common Prayer with the Additions and Deviations Proposed in 1928* to the Central Board of Finance of the Church of England; and from *The Calendar and Lessons for the Church's Year* (a Report Submitted by the Church of England Liturgical Commission to the Archbishops of Canterbury and York in November, 1968) to the Society for Promoting Christian Knowledge; from Benedictus de Spinoza's book *Ethics* and *On the Correction of the Understanding*, translated by Andrew Boyle, Everyman's Library Edition, published by E.P. Dutton & Co., Inc. and used with their permission; from Eric Newton & William Neil's *2,000 Years of Christian Art*, © 1966 by Thames and Hudson Ltd., London, reprinted by permission of the publisher.

Extracts from *Hansard*, the Coronation Service, 1953, the Authorized Version of the Bible and the Book of Common Prayer, 1549 and 1662, all of which are Crown Copyright, are reprinted with permission.

Abbreviations

AV	Authorized Version, 1611
RV	Revised Version, 1881
RVmg	Revised Version, 1881 (margin)
RSV	Revised Standard Version, 1946
NEB	New English Bible, 1970
BCP	The Book of Common Prayer, 1662
BCP 1928	The Book of Common Prayer Revised, 1928

1

THE HOUSE OF PRAYER

I

Jesus went into the temple of God, and cast out all them that sold and bought in the temple, and overthrew the tables of the money-changers, and the seats of them that sold doves, and said unto them, It is written, My house shall be called THE HOUSE OF PRAYER, but ye have made it a den of thieves. And the blind and the lame came to him in the temple; and he healed them.

Matthew 21 :12

II

From King Solomon's prayer at the dedication of the Temple
But will God indeed dwell on the earth? behold, the heaven and heaven of heavens cannot contain thee; how much less this house that I have builded? Yet have thou respect unto the prayer of thy servant, and to his supplication, O Lord my God, to hearken unto the cry and to the prayer, which thy servant prayeth before thee to day: that thine eyes may be open toward this house night and day, even toward the place of which thou hast said, My name shall be there: that thou mayest hearken unto the prayer which thy servant shall make toward this place. And hearken thou to the supplication of thy servant, and of thy people Israel, when they shall pray toward this place: and hear thou in heaven thy dwelling place: and when thou hearest, forgive.

1 Kings 8 :27

III

Church Order
First of all, then, I urge that petitions, prayers, intercessions, and thanksgivings be offered for all men; for sovereigns and all in high

office, that we may lead a tranquil and quiet life in full observance of religion and high standards of morality. Such prayer is right, and approved by God our Saviour, whose will it is that all men should find salvation and come to know the truth. For there is one God, and also one mediator between God and men, Christ Jesus, himself man, who sacrificed himself to win freedom for all mankind, so providing, at the fitting time, proof of the divine purpose; of this I was appointed herald and apostle (this is no lie, but the truth), to instruct the nations in the true faith. . . .

I am hoping to come to you before long, but I write this in case I am delayed, to let you know how men ought to conduct themselves in God's household, that is, the church of the living God, the pillar and bulwark of the truth.

1 Timothy 2 :1 ; 3 :14 NEB

IV

WHOSOEVER thou art that enterest this CHURCH, leave it not without one prayer to GOD for thyself, for those who minister, and for those who worship here.

Notice in a Church porch (contemporary)

V

Of the simple ritual which sufficed before the age of church-building began, a valuable notice is preserved in the Apologist Justin [A.D. 150]
'On the day called Sunday,' he writes, 'all those who live in the towns or in the country meet together; and the memoirs of the Apostles and the writings of the Prophets are read, as long as time allows. Then, when the reader has ended, the president addresses words of instruction and exhortation to imitate these good things. Then we all stand up together and offer prayers. And when prayer is ended, bread is brought and wine and water, and the president offers up alike prayers and thanksgivings with all his energy (or ability), and the people give their assent saying the Amen; and the distribution of the elements, over which the thanksgiving has been pronounced, is made so that each partakes; and to those who are absent they are sent by the hands of the deacons. And those who have the means and are so disposed give as much as they will, each

2

Old Church and Steps   L. S. LOWRY 1887–

[*Private Collection, London*]

according to his inclination; and the sum collected is placed in the hands of the president, who himself succours the orphans and widows, and those who through sickness or any other cause are in want, and the prisoners, and the foreigners who are staying in the place, and, in short, he provides for all who are in need.' Justin then goes on to explain why Sunday is selected for these assemblies, as the day at once of the Creation from chaos and of the Resurrection of Christ from the dead.

J. B. LIGHTFOOT (1828–89)
'Christian Life in the Second and Third Centuries' (1872)
in *Historical Essays* (1895)

VI

Once I am sure there's nothing going on
I step inside, letting the door thud shut.
Another church: matting, seats, and stone,
And little books; sprawlings of flowers, cut
For Sunday, brownish now; some brass and stuff
Up at the holy end; the small neat organ;
And a tense, musty, unignorable silence,
Brewed God knows how long. Hatless, I take off
My cycle-clips in awkward reverence,

Move forward, run my hand around the font.
From where I stand, the roof looks almost new—
Cleaned, or restored? Someone would know: I don't.
Mounting the lectern, I peruse a few
Hectoring large-scale verses, and pronounce
'Here endeth' much more loudly than I'd meant.
The echoes snigger briefly. Back at the door
I sign the book, donate an Irish sixpence,
Reflect the place was not worth stopping for.

Yet stop I did: in fact I often do,
And always end much at a loss like this,
Wondering what to look for; wondering, too,
When churches fall completely out of use

What we shall turn them into, if we shall keep
A few cathedrals chronically on show,
Their parchment, plate and pyx in locked cases,
And let the rest rent-free to rain and sheep.
Shall we avoid them as unlucky places?

Or, after dark, will dubious women come
To make their children touch a particular stone;
Pick simples for a cancer; or on some
Advised night see walking a dead one?
Power of some sort or other will go on
In games, in riddles, seemingly at random;
But superstition, like belief, must die,
And what remains when disbelief has gone?
Grass, weedy pavement, brambles, buttress, sky.

A shape less recognisable each week,
A purpose more obscure. I wonder who
Will be the last, the very last, to seek
This place for what it was; one of the crew
That tap and jot and know what rood-lofts were?
Some ruin-bibber, randy for antique,
Or Christmas-addict, counting on a whiff
Of gown-and-bands and organ-pipes and myrrh?
Or will he be my representative,

Bored, uninformed, knowing the ghostly silt
Dispersed, yet tending to this cross of ground
Through suburb scrub because it held unspilt
So long and equably what since is found
Only in separation—marriage, and birth,
And death, and thoughts of these—for whom was built
This special shell? For, though I've no idea
What this accoutred frowsty barn is worth,
It pleases me to stand in silence here;

A serious house on serious earth it is,
In whose blent air all our compulsions meet,

Are recognised, and robed as destinies.
And that much never can be obsolete,
Since someone will forever be surprising
A hunger in himself to be more serious,
And gravitating with it to this ground,
Which, he once heard, was proper to grow wise in,
If only that so many dead lie round.

PHILIP LARKIN (1922–   )
'Church Going' in *The Less Deceived* (1955)

VII

God is everywhere, and therefore we can pray anywhere. But men have always felt the urge to build temples and churches. They wish to meet together for worship, and need a place apart where the world does not intrude. They want to honour God by a beautiful and usually a large work of art. They want to adorn their city, town, village. These mixed motives affect people differently and, of course, involve the influences of taste, means and belief. As a guide, however, we might remember that any place where men meet to worship is only pleasing to God when through it he comes to man.

2

DISTRESS OF NATIONS, WITH PERPLEXITY

I

There shall be signs in the sun, and in the moon, and in the stars; and upon the earth DISTRESS OF NATIONS, WITH PERPLEXITY; the sea and the waves roaring; men's hearts failing them for fear, and for looking after those things which are coming on the earth: for the powers of heaven shall be shaken. And then shall they see the Son of man coming in a cloud with power and great glory. And when these things begin to come to pass, then look up, and lift your heads; for your redemption draweth nigh.

Luke 21 :25

II

Why do the heathen so furiously rage together: and why do the people imagine a vain thing? The kings of the earth stand up, and the rulers take counsel together: against the Lord, and against his Anointed. Let us break their bonds asunder: and cast away their cords from us. He that dwelleth in heaven shall laugh them to scorn: the Lord shall have them in derision.

Psalm 2 :1

III

And Jesus answered and said unto them, Take heed that no man deceive you. For many shall come in my name, saying, I am Christ; and shall deceive many. And ye shall hear of wars and rumours of wars: see that ye be not troubled: for all these things must come to pass, but the end is not yet. For nation shall rise against nation, and kingdom against kingdom: and there shall be famines, and pestilences, and earthquakes, in divers places. All these are the beginning of sorrows.

Matthew 24 :4

IV

All the business of war, and indeed all the business of life, is to endeavour to find out what you don't know by what you do.

ARTHUR WELLESLEY, DUKE OF WELLINGTON (1769–1852)
Croker Papers (1885), iii, 276

V

So that in the nature of man, we find three principall causes of quarrell. First, Competition; Secondly, Diffidence; Thirdly, Glory.

The first, maketh men invade for Gain; the second, for Safety; and the third, for Reputation. The first use Violence, to make themselves Masters of other mens persons, wives, children, and cattell; the second, to defend them; the third, for trifles, as a word, a smile, a different opinion, and any other signe of undervalue, either direct in their Persons, or by reflexion in their Kindred, 'their Friends, their Nation, their Profession, or their Name.

Hereby it is manifest, that during the time men live without a common Power to keep them all in awe, they are in that condition which is called Warre; and such a warre, as is of every man, against every man. For WARRE, consisteth not in Battell onely, or the act of fighting; but in a tract of time, wherein the Will to contend by Battell is sufficiently known: and therefore the notion of *Time*, is to be considered in the nature of Warre; as it is in the nature of Weather. For as the nature of Foule weather, lyeth not in a showre or two of rain; but in an inclination thereto of many dayes together: So the nature of War, consisteth not in actuall fighting; but in the known disposition thereto, during all the time there is no assurance to the contrary. All other time is PEACE.

THOMAS HOBBES (1588–1679)
Leviathan (1651), I, xiii

VI

To-day was a beautiful day, the sky was a brilliant
    Blue for the first time for weeks and weeks
But posters flapping on the railings tell the fluttered

8

Guernica

PABLO PICASSO 1881–1973

[*Museum of Modern Art, New York*]

World that Hitler speaks, that Hitler speaks
And we cannot take it in and we go to our daily
    Jobs to the dull refrain of the caption 'War'
Buzzing around us as from hidden insects
    And we think 'This must be wrong, it has happened before,
Just like this before, we must be dreaming;
    It was long ago these flies
Buzzed like this, so why are they still bombarding
    The ears if not the eyes?'
And we laugh it off and go round town in the evening
    And this, we say, is on me;
Something out of the usual, a Pimm's Number One, a Picon—
    But did you see
The latest? You mean whether Cobb has bust the record
    Or do you mean the Australians have lost their last by ten
Wickets or do you mean that the autumn fashions—
    No, we don't mean anything like that again.
No, what we mean is Hodza, Henlein, Hitler,
    The Maginot Line,
The heavy panic that cramps the lungs and presses
    The collar down the spine.
And when we go out into Piccadilly Circus
    They are selling and buying the late
Special editions snatched and read abruptly
    Beneath the electric signs as crude as Fate.
And the individual, powerless, has to exert the
    Powers of will and choice
And choose between enormous evils, either
    Of which depends on somebody else's voice.
The cylinders are racing in the presses,
    The mines are laid,
The ribbon plumbs the fallen fathoms of Wall Street,
    And you and I are afraid. . . .
And at this hour of the day it is no good saying
    'Take away this cup';
Having helped to fill it ourselves it is only logic
    That now we should drink it up.

Nor can we hide our heads in the sands, the sands have
    Filtered away;
Nothing remains but rock at this hour, this zero
    Hour of the day.

LOUIS MACNEICE (1907–63)
Autumn Journal (1939), V

VII

The Gospels contain a long discourse by Jesus (Mark 13) where a state of things is described very like our own—wars and rumours of wars, earthquakes, floods, famines, 'men's hearts failing them for fear, and for looking after those things which are coming on the earth', 'distress of nations, with perplexity'. But all this is to be followed by the kingdom of God upon earth. Does this not mean that there is here and now a tremendous opportunity for the Christian to confront the world with Christ? For many people, the search for answers to the problems of our age is turning inward, towards a way of life based on spiritual rather than material values. Jesus Christ is now no less than ever that Way, the Truth and the Life, but we each have to find what this means for us.

3

STEWARDS OF THE MYSTERIES OF GOD

I

Let a man so account of us, as of the ministers of Christ, and STEWARDS OF THE MYSTERIES OF GOD. Moreover it is required in stewards, that a man be found faithful.

1 Corinthians 4:1

II

And I came to Jerusalem, and understood of the evil that Eliashib did for Tobiah, in preparing him a chamber in the courts of the house of God. And it grieved me sore: therefore I cast forth all the household stuff of Tobiah out of the chamber. Then I commanded, and they cleansed the chambers: and thither brought I again the vessels of the house of God, with the meat offering and the frankincense. And I perceived that the portions of the Levites had not been given them: for the Levites and the singers, that did the work, were fled every one to his field. Then contended I with the rulers, and said, Why is the house of God forsaken? And I gathered them together, and set them in their place. Then brought all Judah the tithe of the corn and the new wine and the oil unto the treasuries. And I made treasurers over the treasuries, Shelemiah the priest, and Zadok the scribe, and of the Levites, Pedaiah: and next to them was Hanan the son of Zaccur, the son of Mattaniah: for they were counted faithful, and their office was to distribute unto their brethren.

Nehemiah 13:7

III

Blessed are those servants, whom the lord when he cometh shall find watching: verily I say unto you, that he shall gird himself, and make them to sit down to meat, and will come forth and serve them. And if he shall come in the second watch, or come in the

Ordination by the Bishop of Rangoon

[*Society for the Propagation of the Gospel*]

third watch, and find them so, blessed are those servants. And this know, that if the goodman of the house had known what hour the thief would come, he would have watched, and not have suffered his house to be broken through. Be ye therefore ready also: for the Son of man cometh at an hour when ye think not. Then Peter said unto him, Lord, speakest thou this parable unto us, or even to all? And the Lord said, Who then is that faithful and wise steward, whom his lord shall make ruler over his household, to give them their portion of meat in due season? Blessed is that servant, whom his lord when he cometh shall find so doing. Of a truth I say unto you, that he will make him ruler over all that he hath.

Luke 12:37

IV

They left no books,
Memorial to their lonely thought
In grey parishes; rather they wrote
On men's hearts and in the minds
Of young children sublime words
Too soon forgotten. God in his time
Or out of time will correct this.

R. S. THOMAS (1913–   )
'The Country Clergy' in *Poetry for Supper* (1958)

V

You have heard, Brethren, as well in your private examination, as in the exhortation which was now made to you, and in the holy Lessons taken out of the Gospel, and the writings of the Apostles, of what dignity, and of how great importance this Office is, where-unto ye are called. And now again we exhort you, in the Name of our Lord Jesus Christ, that you have in remembrance, into how high a Dignity, and to how weighty an Office and Charge ye are called: that is to say, to be Messengers, Watchmen, and Stewards of the Lord; to teach, and to premonish, to feed and provide for the Lord's family; to seek for Christ's sheep that are dispersed abroad, and for his children who are in the midst of this naughty world, that they may be saved through Christ for ever.

Have always therefore printed in your remembrance, how great a treasure is committed to your charge. For they are the sheep of Christ, which he bought with his death, and for whom he shed his blood. The Church and Congregation whom you must serve, is his Spouse, and his Body. And if it shall happen the same Church, or any Member thereof, to take any hurt or hindrance by reason of your negligence, ye know the greatness of the fault, and also the horrible punishment that will ensue. Wherefore consider with yourselves the end of your Ministry towards the children of God, towards the Spouse and Body of Christ; and see that you never cease your labour, your care and diligence, until you have done all that lieth in you, according to your bounden duty, to bring all such as are or shall be committed to your charge, unto that agreement in the faith and knowledge of God, and to that ripeness and perfectness of age in Christ, that there be no place left among you, either for error in religion, or for viciousness in life.

The Book of Common Prayer:
'The Ordering of Priests' (1549)

VI

When I consider how my light is spent,
 Ere half my days in this dark world and wide,
 And that one Talent which is death to hide,
 Lodg'd with me useless, though my Soul more bent
To serve therewith my Maker, and present
 My true account, least he returning chide,
 Doth God exact day-labour, light deny'd?,
 I fondly ask; But patience to prevent
That murmur, soon replies, God doth not need
 Either man's work or his own gifts, who best
 Bear his milde yoak, they serve him best, his State
Is Kingly. Thousands at his bidding speed
 And post o'er Land and Ocean without rest:
 They also serve who only stand and waite.

JOHN MILTON (1608–74)
On his Blindness (1673)

15

VII

The Steward in a great house would think he was demeaning himself by waiting at table, 'like one of the servants', he would say. This is an attitude which Jesus wanted to get rid of through and through. It is a Christian paradox that those who wait at table are better off than those they serve. The Christian must measure himself by the amount of service he can give. In the society of the Church we are all civil servants; we are citizens and servants where Christ is Head of State.

4

THE RACE THAT IS SET BEFORE US

I

O Lord, raise up (we pray thee) thy power, and come among us, and with great might succour us; that whereas, through our sins and wickedness, we are sore let and hindered in running THE RACE THAT IS SET BEFORE US, thy bountiful grace and mercy may speedily help and deliver us; through the satisfaction of thy Son our Lord, to whom with thee and the Holy Ghost be honour and glory, world without end. Amen.

Collect

II

Whatsoever thy hand findeth to do, do it with thy might; for there is no work, nor device, nor knowledge, nor wisdom, in the grave, whither thou goest. I returned, and saw under the sun, that the race is not to the swift, nor the battle to the strong, neither yet bread to the wise, nor yet riches to men of understanding, nor yet favour to men of skill; but time and chance happeneth to them all.

Ecclesiastes 9:10

III

Know ye not that they which run in a race run all, but one receiveth the prize? So run, that ye may obtain. And every man that striveth for the mastery is temperate in all things. Now they do it to obtain a corruptible crown; but we an incorruptible. I therefore so run, not as uncertainly; so fight I, not as one that beateth the air: but I keep under my body, and bring it into sub- jection: lest that by any means, when I have preached to others, I myself should be a castaway.

1 Corinthians 9:24

IV

Si libenter crucem portas, portabit te.
If you will carry your Cross, it will carry you.

THOMAS A KEMPIS (1380–1471) *Imitatio Christi*, xii, 5

V

I would say to the House, as I said to those who have joined this Government: 'I have nothing to offer but blood, toil, tears and sweat.'

We have before us an ordeal of the most grievous kind. We have before us many, many long months of struggle and of suffering. You ask, What is our policy? I will say: It is to wage war, by sea, land and air, with all our might and with all the strength that God can give us: to wage war against a monstrous tyranny, never surpassed in the dark, lamentable catalogue of human crime. That is our policy. You ask, What is our aim? I can answer in one word: Victory—victory at all costs, victory in spite of all terror, victory, however long and hard the road may be.

WINSTON S. CHURCHILL (1874–1965)
From his first speech to the House of Commons as Prime Minister (13 May 1940)

VI

Days of endeavour have been good: the days
Racing in cutters for the comrades' praise.
The day they led my cutter at the turn
Yet could not keep the lead and dropped astern;
The moment in the spurt when both boats' oars
Dipped in each other's wash and throats grew hoarse
And teeth ground into teeth and both strokes quickened
Lashing the sea, and gasps came, and hearts sickened
And coxswains damned us, dancing, banking stroke,
To put our weights on, though our hearts were broke
And both boats seemed to stick and sea seemed glue,
The tide a mill race we were struggling through

David Hemery   E. D. LACEY

And every quick recover gave us squints
Of them still there, and oar tossed water-glints;
And cheering came, our friends, our foemen cheering,
A long, wild, rallying murmur on the hearing—
'Port Fore!' and 'Starboard Fore!' 'Port Fore!' 'Port Fore!'
'Up with her, Starboard,' and at that each oar
Lightened, though arms were bursting, and eyes shut
And the oak stretchers grunted in the strut
And the curse quickened from the cox, our bows
Crashed, and drove talking water, we made vows,
Chastity vows and temperance; in our pain
We numbered things we'd never eat again
If we could only win; then came the yell
'Starboard,' 'Port Fore,' and then a beaten bell
Rung as for fire to cheer us. 'Now.' Oars bent,
Soul took the looms now body's bolt was spent,
'Damn it, come on now,' 'On now,' 'On now,' 'Starboard.'
'Port Fore.' 'Up with her, Port'; each cutter harboured
Ten eye-shut painsick strugglers, 'Heave, oh heave,'
Catcalls waked echoes like a shrieking sheave.
'Heave,' and I saw a back, then two. 'Port Fore.'
'Starboard.' 'Come on.' I saw the midship oar
And knew we had done them. 'Port Fore.' 'Starboard.' 'Now.'
I saw bright water spurting at their bow,
Their cox' full face an instant. They were done.
The watchers' cheering almost drowned the gun.
We had hardly strength to toss our oars; our cry
Cheering the losing cutter was a sigh.

JOHN MASEFIELD (1878–1967)
'Biography' (*Georgian Poetry*, 1912)

VII

Paul makes the athlete a vivid image of a man striving to do his
duty. But in another passage (Ephesians 6:12) he warns that 'we
wrestle not against flesh and blood, but against principalities,
against powers, against the rulers of the darkness of this world,

against spiritual wickedness in high places'. These are fearful words, however we interpret them. The moral conflict does not take place in the stadium. It is no sport. It requires the determination, energy and enthusiasm of the playing field, but much more also.

5

THE EXPRESS IMAGE OF HIS PERSON

Prelude

Behold the great Creator makes
    Himself a house of clay,
A robe of Virgin flesh he takes
    Which he will wear for ay.

Hark, hark, the wise eternal Word
    Like a weak infant cries!
In form of servant is the Lord,
    And God in cradle lies.

This wonder struck the world amazed,
    It shook the starry frame;
Squadrons of spirits stood and gazed,
    Then down in troops they came.

Glad shepherds ran to view this sight;
    A choir of Angels sings,
And eastern sages with delight
    Adore this King of kings.

Join then, all hearts that are not stone,
    And all our voices prove,
To celebrate this holy One,
    The God of peace and love.

T. PESTEL (*c.* 1584–1659)

I

God, who at sundry times and in divers manners spake in time
past unto the fathers by the prophets, hath in these last days
spoken unto us by his Son, whom he hath appointed heir of all

22

The Holy Family   PETER PAUL RUBENS 1577–1640

[*Wallace Collection, London*]

things, by whom also he made the worlds; who being the bright-ness of his glory, and THE EXPRESS IMAGE OF HIS PERSON, and upholding all things by the word of his power, when he had by himself purged our sins, sat down on the right hand of the Majesty on high; being made so much better than the angels, as he hath by inheritance obtained a more excellent name than they.

Hebrews 1 : 1

II

And God said, Let us make man in our image, after our likeness: and let them have dominion over the fish of the sea, and over the fowl of the air, and over the cattle, and over all the earth, and over every creeping thing that creepeth upon the earth. So God created man in his own image, in the image of God created he him; male and female created he them. And God blessed them, and God said unto them, Be fruitful, and multiply, and replenish the earth, and subdue it: and have dominion over the fish of the sea, and over the fowl of the air, and over every living thing that moveth upon the earth. . . . And God saw every thing that he had made, and, behold, it was very good.

Genesis 1 : 26

III

He rescued us from the domain of darkness and brought us away into the kingdom of his dear Son, in whom our release is secured and our sins forgiven. He is the image of the invisible God; his is the primacy over all created things. In him everything in heaven and on earth was created, not only things visible but also the invisible orders of thrones, sovereignties, authorities, and powers: the whole universe has been created through him and for him. And he exists before everything, and all things are held together in him. He is, moreover, the head of the body, the church. He is its origin, the first to return from the dead, to be in all things alone supreme. For in him the complete being of God, by God's own choice, came to dwell. Through him God chose to reconcile the

24

whole universe to himself, making peace through the shedding of his blood upon the cross—to reconcile all things, whether on earth or in heaven, through him alone.

Colossians 11 :3 NEB

IV

> Youth of delight, come hither,
> And see the opening morn,
> Image of truth new-born.

WILLIAM BLAKE (1757–1827)
'The Voice of the Ancient Bard' in *Songs of Experience*

V

. . . in artistic symbols the spectator is always confronted with something which is less than perfect and, even in the greatest work, with something that is known to be only *primus inter pares*. Whereas, in Christ, the disciples were confronted with something which they knew to be unique: God.

At first sight, this may appear to be a covert form of subjective idealism or Docetism. But for two reasons it is not. First, far from denying the reality and objectivity of Jesus' historical manhood, it asserts the necessity of regarding it as both real and ordinary. For it is only in and through the objective, historical, material event of Jesus that the transcendent God is known. Thus, it no more denies the historical objectivity of the flesh of Jesus than an affirmation of the transcendent truth and value of a painting can be said to deny the objective reality of the material picture. In fact, both affirmations of transcendent value depend for their validity upon the real, material existence of their respective images. Secondly, it says of *Christ* alone that 'he is the image of the invisible God'. It does not go on to say that therefore all men are images of God, let alone that they are mere shadows of the ideal.

A. C. BRIDGE (1914–   )
Images of God (1960), p. 101

25

VI

The windless northern surge, the sea-gull's scream,
And Calvin's kirk crowning the barren brae.
I think of Giotto the Tuscan shepherd's dream,
Christ, man and creature in their inner day.
How could our race betray
The Image, and the Incarnate One unmake
Who chose this form and fashion for our sake?

The Word made flesh is here made word again,
A word made word in flourish and arrogant crook.
See there King Calvin with his iron pen,
And God three angry letters in a book,
And there the logical hook
On which the Mystery is impaled and bent
Into an ideological instrument.

There's better gospel in man's natural tongue,
And truer sight was theirs outside the Law
Who saw the far side of the Cross among
The archaic peoples in their ancient awe,
In ignorant wonder saw
The wooden cross-tree on the bare hillside,
Not knowing that there a God suffered and died.

The fleshless word, growing, will bring us down,
Pagan and Christian man alike will fall,
The auguries say, the white and black and brown,
The merry and sad, theorist, lover, all
Invisibly will fall:
Abstract calamity, save for those who can
Build their cold empire on the abstract man.

A soft breeze stirs and all my thoughts are blown
Far out to sea and lost. Yet I know well
The bloodless word will battle for its own
Invisibly in brain and nerve and cell.
The generations tell

Their personal tale: the One has far to go
Past the mirages and the murdering snow.

EDWIN MUIR (1887–1959)
'The Incarnate One' (1960) in *Collected Poems 1921–1958*

VII

In the birth and infancy of Jesus we have a visible and tangible image of him which is what our weakness and lack of faith so much need. The simple beauty of this Incarnation gives us first the joy and happiness of Christmas, but leads us on to an increasing knowledge of Christ on earth and thence to a greater understanding of the eternal Word.

6

GOD WITH US

I

The angel of the Lord appeared unto Joseph in a dream, saying, Joseph, thou son of David, fear not to take unto thee Mary thy wife: for that which is conceived in her is of the Holy Ghost. And she shall bring forth a son, and thou shalt call his name JESUS: for he shall save his people from their sins. Now all this was done, that it might be fulfilled which was spoken of the Lord by the prophet, saying, Behold, a virgin shall be with child, and shall bring forth a son, and they shall call his name Emmanuel, which being interpreted is, GOD WITH US.

Matthew 1 :20

II

God is our hope and strength: a very present help in trouble. Therefore will we not fear, though the earth be moved: and though the hills be carried into the midst of the sea. Though the waters thereof rage and swell: and though the mountains shake at the tempest of the same. The rivers of the flood thereof shall make glad the city of God: the holy place of the tabernacle of the most Highest. God is in the midst of her, therefore shall she not be removed: God shall help her, and that right early. The heathen make much ado, and the kingdoms are moved: but God hath shewed his voice, and the earth shall melt away. The Lord of hosts is with us: the God of Jacob is our refuge. O come hither, and behold the works of the Lord: what destruction he hath brought upon the earth. He maketh wars to cease in all the world: he breaketh the bow, and knappeth the spear in sunder, and burneth the chariots in the fire. Be still then, and know that I am God: I will be exalted among the heathen, and I will be exalted

Christris Carrying the Cross   STANLEY SPENCER 1891–1959

in the earth. The Lord of hosts is with us: the God of Jacob is our refuge.

Psalm 46:1

III

Let not your heart be troubled: ye believe in God, believe also in me. In my Father's house are many mansions: if it were not so, I would have told you. I go to prepare a place for you. And if I go and prepare a place for you, I will come again, and receive you unto myself; that where I am, there ye may be also. And whither I go ye know, and the way ye know. Thomas saith unto him, Lord, we know not whither thou goest; and how can we know the way? Jesus saith unto him, I am the way, the truth, and the life: no man cometh unto the Father, but by me. If ye had known me, ye should have known my Father also: and from henceforth ye know him, and have seen him.

John 14:1

IV

Tu ne me chercherais pas, si tu ne me possédais: ne t'inquiète donc pas. (You would not be looking for me, if you did not already possess me; so do not disquiet yourself.)

PASCAL (1623–62)
Pensée 555 (1662)

V

[Stanley] Spencer's religious paintings are so single-hearted, so personal and so filled with these fusions of opposites which in the end do not contradict each other, that . . . it is only fair to him to draw up a list of his major religious works with dates and the briefest of comments. The 'Centurion's Servant' (1915) is a translation into terms of the life of Cookham children of the story of healing by prayer (Luke 7), with the sick child tossing with fever on the bed and his friends praying round him. The big 'Resurrection' (a recurrent theme with Spencer) in the Tate Gallery (1923–26) is Spencer's most complete masterpiece. The graves that open in Cookham churchyard to give up their dead are so convincing that one is not even surprised at the scene. Spencer accepts the physical fact of the Resurrection as simply as Blake accepted the singing of the stars in his Job engravings. Christ carries the Cross (1920) through a street in Cookham while the villagers crowd round Him or watch Him from open windows. The Wise Men visit Mary (1940), in bed and exhausted by her travail, in a Cookham bedroom and extend their arms exultantly in gestures of praise. Towards the end of his life Spencer conceived and half completed a series of related pictures on the theme of Christ with His Disciples, preaching from a punt on the Thames during the Cookham Regatta. Something of the crowded and confused complexity of Tintoretto's San Rocco Crucifixion turns the whole series into a kind of village epic, groups of visitors assemble to listen, to report or to partake of a picnic lunch. Each group is united by its own separate urgency yet the sermon firmly links each group to the central dominant theme.

ERIC NEWTON (1893–1965)
in Newton and Neil, *The Christian Faith in Art* (1966), p. 276

VI

It is a beauteous evening, calm and free,
The holy time is quiet as a Nun
Breathless with adoration; the broad sun
Is sinking down in its tranquillity;
The gentleness of heaven broods o'er the Sea:
Listen! the mighty Being is awake,
And doth with his eternal motion make
A sound like thunder—everlastingly.

Dear Child! dear Girl! that walkest with me here,
If thou appear untouched by solemn thought,
Thy nature is not therefore less divine:
Thou liest in Abraham's bosom all the year;
And worshipp'st at the Temple's inner shrine,
God being with thee when we know it not.

WILLIAM WORDSWORTH (1770–1850), *Miscellaneous Sonnets*,
Part I, xxx (1802)

VII

We have a loving Father who is with us at all times, but we do not remember this often enough, and some never remember it at all. But the practice of the presence of God is a well-known religious exercise whereby we can form a habit of realizing more often, more confidently, and more gratefully that he is at our side and on our side for every need.

7

JESUS CHRIST WAS MADE IN
THE LIKENESS OF MEN

I

Grant, we beseech thee, that as thy Son our Lord JESUS CHRIST
WAS MADE IN THE LIKENESS OF MEN, so we may be made partakers of the divine nature.

Collect

II

In the first year of Belshazzar king of Babylon Daniel had a dream
and visions of his head upon his bed: then he wrote the dream,
and told the sum of the matters. Daniel spake and said, I saw . . .
in the night visions, and, behold, one like the Son of man came
with the clouds of heaven, and came to the Ancient of days, and
they brought him near before him. And there was given him
dominion, and glory, and a kingdom, that all people, nations, and
languages, should serve him: his dominion is an everlasting
dominion, which shall not pass away, and his kingdom that
which shall not be destroyed.

Daniel 7:1

III

It became him, for whom are all things, and by whom are all
things, in bringing many sons unto glory, to make the captain of
their salvation perfect through sufferings. For both he that sancti-
fieth and they who are sanctified are all of one: for which cause he
is not ashamed to call them brethren. . . . Forasmuch then as the

33

children are partakers of flesh and blood, he also himself likewise took part of the same; that through death he might destroy him that had the power of death, that is, the devil; and deliver them who through fear of death were all their lifetime subject to bondage. For verily he took not on him the nature of angels; but he took on him the seed of Abraham. Wherefore in all things it behoved him to be made like unto his brethren, that he might be a merciful and faithful high priest in things pertaining to God, to make reconciliation for the sins of the people. For in that he himself hath suffered being tempted, he is able to succour them that are tempted.

Hebrews 2 :10

IV

Ecce homo (Behold the man!)

John 19 :5

V

Pride, a pride which commands our respect, keeps the stoical humanist erect in life's storms. The Christian way, however, puts no such strain on the human self as it actually exists. Its gospel for the sufferer nearing despair is not that he has only to 'pull himself together' to meet every adversity, but rather that, left to himself, he can do nothing of the kind; his only hope is that he can stretch out to the Power, not himself, which can carry him through. The source of strength in the Christian understanding of life is the Redeemer who has known all the griefs of human existence and invites his disciples to cast all their cares on Him. Looking at the cross of Christ the believer sees One who was tortured to death, who was betrayed by a friend, was execrated by his fellow men and cast out, One moreover who endured the experience of being cut off from God. We do not have to explain our agonies to Christ —He shares them.

W. R. MATTHEWS (1880–1973)
'Muted Joy' (*The Daily Telegraph*, 6 July 1968)

Christir with the High Priest   GEORGES ROUAULT 1871–1958

[*Phillips Collection, Washington, D.C.*]

VI

Walking in the Alps, my wife and I
Found a broken cross half buried under
A fall of rock and turf and red scree.

Since it came away, the figure
Of Christ, easily from its rusted
Nail, under a worm-eaten, weather

Worn image of wood we transported
From Italy without permission
We drink our wine now, eat our daily bread.

Since friends who come here often mention
The great skill of an anonymous
Carver of beech-wood, the conversation

Is enriched by this being with us
As at Cana, I'd say, if the bowed head
With any locality or surface

Chatter could be associated.
Leaning forward, as it does, from our wall
To where silence is concentrated

Outside and within the ephemeral
Constellations of energy,
Because it says nothing reasonable

This image explains nothing away
And just by gazing into darkness
Is able to mean more than words can say.

THOMAS BLACKBURN (1916–   )
'A broken image' in *The Fourth Man* (1971)

VII

Knowledge that Jesus Christ, while being the express image of
God's person, is also *one of us* confirms that God made us in his

36

own image, that in each one of us there is something of the divine nature. Experience of life shows that, being made also with free will, we may grow more like God or less. We can increase or diminish our share of divinity.

8

THE GENTILES SHOULD BE FELLOW-HEIRS, AND OF THE SAME BODY

I

He made known unto me the mystery; (as I wrote afore in few words, whereby, when ye read, ye may understand my knowledge in the mystery of Christ) which in other ages was not made known unto the sons of men, as it is now revealed unto his holy apostles and prophets by the Spirit; that THE GENTILES SHOULD BE FELLOW-HEIRS, AND OF THE SAME BODY, and partakers of his promise in Christ by the gospel.

Ephesians 3:3

II

And there shall come forth a rod out of the stem of Jesse, and a Branch shall grow out of his roots: and the spirit of the Lord shall rest upon him, the spirit of wisdom and understanding, the spirit of counsel and might, the spirit of knowledge and of the fear of the Lord; and shall make him of quick understanding in the fear of the Lord: and he shall not judge after the sight of his eyes, neither reprove after the hearing of his ears: but with righteousness shall he judge the poor, and reprove with equity for the meek of the earth: and he shall smite the earth with the rod of his mouth, and with the breath of his lips shall he slay the wicked. And righteousness shall be the girdle of his loins, and faithfulness the girdle of his reins.

The wolf also shall dwell with the lamb, and the leopard shall lie down with the kid; and the calf and the young lion and the fatling together; and a little child shall lead them. And the cow and the bear shall feed; their young ones shall lie down together: and the lion shall eat straw like the ox. And the sucking child shall play on the hole of the asp, and the weaned child shall put his

Adoration of the Kings   ROGIER VAN DER WEYDEN *c.* 1399–1464

[*Alte Pinakothek, Munich*]

hand on the cockatrice' den. They shall not hurt nor destroy in all my holy mountain: for the earth shall be full of the knowledge of the Lord, as the waters cover the sea.

And in that day there shall be a root of Jesse, which shall stand for an ensign of the people; to it shall the Gentiles seek: and his rest shall be glorious.

Isaiah 11:1

III

There were certain Greeks among them that came up to worship at the feast: the same came therefore to Philip, which was of Bethsaida of Galilee, and desired him, saying, Sir, we would see Jesus. Philip cometh and telleth Andrew: and again Andrew and Philip tell Jesus. And Jesus answered them, saying, The hour is come, that the Son of man should be glorified. Verily, verily, I say unto you, Except a corn of wheat fall into the ground and die, it abideth alone: but if it die, it bringeth forth much fruit. He that loveth his life shall lose it; and he that hateth his life in this world shall keep it unto life eternal. If any man serve me, let him follow me; and where I am, there shall also my servant be: if any man serve me, him will my Father honour.

John 12:20

IV

All people that on earth do dwell,
    Sing to the Lord with cheerful voice;
Him serve with fear, His praise forth tell,
    Come ye before Him, and rejoice.

WILLIAM KETHE (*d.* 1608?)
Daye's Psalter (1560)

V

Unity of Man

We have begun to realize that a world society will not come into existence without conscious human effort. That is a new factor in the problem, for until recently, if we have thought about the question at all, most of us have assumed that international society and international law might be left to grow unaided. We have begun to see, however, that though the problem of world community remains essentially a moral problem, it is also in part a problem of statesmanship, and that international society needs institutions through which its members can learn to work together for common social ends. The League of Nations was the first great experiment with that end in view, and we know that it did not succeed. We are making a second attempt now with the United Nations, and hitherto this too has disappointed our hopes. But it is right that we should remember that only one generation has passed since men began to look on the building of a world community as a practical problem, and less than that since most of us began to see that the problem is really urgent.

J. L. BRIERLY (1881–1955)
The Law of Nations, II, §1 (sixth edition, 1963,
edited by Sir Humphrey Waldock)

VI

Unity of God

> What if the foot, ordain'd the dust to tread,
> Or hand to toil, aspir'd to be the head?
> What if the head, the eye, or ear repin'd
> To serve mere engines to the ruling Mind?
> Just as absurd for any part to claim
> To be another, in this gen'ral frame:
> Just as absurd, to mourn the tasks or pains
> The great directing MIND of ALL ordains.
>
> All are but parts of one stupendous whole,
> Whose body Nature is, and God the soul;
> That, chang'd thro' all, and yet in all the same,
> Great in the earth, as in th'æthereal frame,
> Warms in the sun, refreshes in the breeze,
> Glows in the stars, and blossoms in the trees,

Lives thro' all life, extends thro' all extent,
Spreads undivided, operates unspent,
Breathes in our soul, informs our mortal part,
As full, as perfect, in a hair as heart;
As full, as perfect, in vile Man that mourns,
As the rapt Seraph that adores and burns;
To him no high, no low, no great, no small;
He fills, he bounds, connects, and equals all.

ALEXANDER POPE (1688–1744)
The Essay on Man

VII

Consider this situation. A small nation (the Jews), which has hardly ever had a land of its own, is nevertheless so unique that the human race is divided into just two sections, the Jews and the Rest (the Gentiles). A young Jew called Paul sees that a new nation is rising up (the Christians) owing very much to the Jews, yet destined to surpass them. The problem this will create can only be solved by all mankind becoming one people. Some progress is made toward this, but more and quicker progress is vital. This is what the New Testament was about, and still is.

9

SITTING IN THE MIDST OF THE DOCTORS

I

Now his parents went to Jerusalem every year at the feast of the passover. And when he was twelve years old, they went up to Jerusalem after the custom of the feast. And . . . as they returned, the child Jesus tarried behind in Jerusalem. . . . And when they found him not, they turned back again to Jerusalem, seeking him. And it came to pass, that after three days they found him in the temple, SITTING IN THE MIDST OF THE DOCTORS, both hearing them, and asking them questions. And all that heard him were astonished at his understanding and answers. And when they saw him, they were amazed: and his mother said unto him, Son, why hast thou thus dealt with us? behold, thy father and I have sought thee sorrowing. And he said unto them, How is it that ye sought me? wist ye not that I must be about my Father's business? And they understood not the saying which he spake unto them. And he went down with them, and came to Nazareth, and was subject unto them: but his mother kept all these sayings in her heart.

Luke 2:41

Jesus detaches himself from his family and, no longer a child and not yet a man, he begins his ministry, perhaps all unconsciously, by confronting his future opponents in the temple.

II

My son, if thou wilt receive my words, and hide my commandments with thee; so that thou incline thine ear unto wisdom, and apply thine heart to understanding; yea, if thou criest after knowledge, and liftest up thy voice for understanding: if thou seekest her as silver, and searchest for her as for hid treasures; then shalt thou understand the fear of the Lord, and find the knowledge of God. For the Lord giveth wisdom: out of his mouth cometh knowledge and understanding.

Proverbs 2:1

III

Peter began to say unto him, Lo, we have left all, and have followed thee. And Jesus answered and said, Verily I say unto you, There is no man that hath left house, or brethren, or sisters, or father, or mother, or wife, or children, or lands, for my sake, and the gospel's, but he shall receive an hundredfold now in this time, houses, and brethren, and sisters, and mothers, and children, and lands, with persecutions; and in the world to come eternal life.

Mark 10:28

IV

If a child belongs to anyone, he belongs to God.

SIR JOHN WOLFENDEN (1906–   )

V

I believe that during their teens, children need their parents more than they did during their earlier schooldays, but they need them in a different way. Naturally, their growing minds are beginning to widen their interests and to turn to many things outside home. This is right and proper preparation for emotional independence, and yet it can make parents feel that they are not wanted any more.

In fact, you probably will feel ignored and unimportant for much of the time, but your teenager is not yet emotionally independent. He is going through a particularly difficult time and it is vitally important to him to know that you are there and that he can turn to you. This means, of course, that you may spend a lot of the time standing on the side-lines or being used as a spring-board.

JULIA DAWKINS (1932–73)
Teach your child about sex (1964)

Christis among the Doctors   BERNARDINO BUTINONE *c.* 1450–1507

[*The Mound, Edinburgh*]

VI

> For now a trouble came into my mind
> From unknown causes. I was left alone,
> Seeking the visible world, nor knowing why.
> The props of my affections were remov'd,
> And yet the building stood, as if sustain'd
> By its own spirit! All that I beheld
> Was dear to me, and from this cause it came,
> That now to Nature's finer influxes
> My mind lay open, to that more exact
> And intimate communion which our hearts
> Maintain with the minuter properties
> Of objects which already are belov'd,
> And of those only. Many are the joys
> Of youth; but oh! what happiness to live
> When every hour brings palpable access
> Of knowledge, when all knowledge is delight,
> And sorrow is not there.

WILLIAM WORDSWORTH (1770–1850)
Prelude (1850), II, 276–288

VII

We are glad to have this glimpse of Jesus in his adolescence, and of his anxious mother too. But the adolescent must grow up, and it is the adult Jesus who is our teacher and example. St Paul has something to say about this (Ephesians 4:13 NEB): 'So shall we all attain . . . to mature manhood, measured by nothing less than the full stature of Christ. We are no longer to be children . . . No, let us speak the truth in love; so shall we fully grow up with Christ.' We must ask ourselves whether we are grown up in Christ—are we grown-up Christians?

10

WHATSOEVER HE SAITH UNTO YOU, DO IT

I

The third day there was a marriage in Cana of Galilee; and the mother of Jesus was there: and both Jesus was called, and his disciples, to the marriage. And when they wanted wine, the mother of Jesus saith unto him, They have no wine. Jesus saith unto her, Woman, what have I to do with thee? mine hour is not yet come. His mother saith unto the servants, WHATSOEVER HE SAITH UNTO YOU, DO IT.

John 2 :1

II

And it came to pass after these things, that God did tempt Abraham, and said unto him, Abraham: and he said, Behold, here I am. And he said, Take now thy son, thine only son Isaac, whom thou lovest, and get thee into the land of Moriah; and offer him there for a burnt offering upon one of the mountains which I will tell thee of. And Abraham rose up early in the morning, and saddled his ass, and took two of his young men with him, and Isaac his son, and clave the wood for the burnt offering, and rose up, and went unto the place of which God had told him. Then on the third day Abraham lifted up his eyes, and saw the place afar off. And Abraham said unto his young men, Abide ye here with the ass; and I and the lad will go yonder and worship, and come again to you.

And Abraham took the wood of the burnt offering, and laid it upon Isaac his son; and he took the fire in his hand, and a knife; and they went both of them together. And Isaac spake unto Abraham his father, and said, My father: and he said, Here am I, my son. And he said, Behold the fire and the wood: but where is the lamb for a burnt offering? And Abraham said, My son, God

47

will provide himself a lamb for a burnt offering: so they went both of them together. And they came to the place which God had told him of; and Abraham built an altar there, and laid the wood in order, and bound Isaac his son, and laid him on the altar upon the wood. And Abraham stretched forth his hand, and took the knife to slay his son. And the angel of the Lord called unto him out of heaven, and said, Abraham, Abraham: and he said, Here am I. And he said, Lay not thine hand upon the lad, neither do thou any thing unto him: for now I know that thou fearest God, seeing thou hast not withheld thy son, thine only son from me.

And Abraham lifted up his eyes, and looked, and behold behind him a ram caught in a thicket by his horns: and Abraham went and took the ram, and offered him up for a burnt offering in the stead of his son.

Genesis 22 :1

III

Let this mind be in you, which was also in Christ Jesus: who, being in the form of God, did not cling to his equality with God:[1] but made himself of no reputation, and took upon him the form of a servant, and was made in the likeness of men: and being found in fashion as a man, he humbled himself, and became obedient unto death, even the death of the cross. Wherefore God also hath highly exalted him, and given him a name which is above every name: that at the name of Jesus every knee should bow, of things in heaven, and things in earth, and things under the earth; and that every tongue should confess that Jesus Christ is Lord, to the glory of God the Father.

Philippians 2 :5

IV

Remember that you are only an actor in a play, which the manager directs.

EPICTETUS (A.D. *c.* 55–135)

[1] Jerusalem Bible.

La Classe de Danse de M. Perrot   EDGAR DEGAS 1834–1917

[*Musée du Louvre, Paris*]

V

It is one of the most surprising experiences, but at the same time one of the most incontrovertible, that evil—often in a surprisingly short time—proves its own folly and defeats its own object. That does not mean that punishment follows hard on the heels of every evil action; but it does mean that deliberate transgression of the divine law in the supposed interests of worldly self-preservation has exactly the opposite effect. We learn this from our own experience, and we can interpret it in various ways. At least it seems possible to infer with certainty that in social life there are laws more powerful than anything that may claim to dominate them, and that it is therefore not only wrong but unwise to disregard them. . . .

It is true that all historically important action is constantly overstepping the limits set by these laws. But it makes all the difference whether such overstepping of the appointed limits is regarded in principle as the superseding of them, and is therefore given out to be a law of a special kind, or whether the overstepping is deliberately regarded as a fault which is perhaps unavoidable, justified only if the law and the limit are re-established and respected as soon as possible. It is not necessarily hypocrisy if the declared aim of political action is the restoration of the law, and not mere self-preservation. The world *is*, in fact, so ordered that a basic respect for ultimate laws and human life is also the best means of self-preservation, and that these laws may be broken only on the odd occasion in case of brief necessity, whereas anyone who turns necessity into a principle, and in so doing establishes a law of his own alongside them, is inevitably bound, sooner or later, to suffer retribution. The immanent righteousness of history rewards and punishes only men's deeds, but the eternal righteousness of God tries and judges their hearts.

DIETRICH BONHOEFFER (1906–45)
'After ten years' in *Letters and Papers from Prison*

VI
Piping down the valleys wild,
Piping songs of pleasant glee,
On a cloud I saw a child,
And he laughing said to me:

'Pipe a song about a Lamb!'
So I piped with merry chear.
'Piper, pipe that song again;'
So I piped: he wept to hear.

'Drop thy pipe, thy happy pipe;
Sing thy songs of happy chear:'
So I sang the same again,
While he wept with joy to hear.

'Piper, sit thee down and write
In a book, that all may read.'
So he vanish'd from my sight,
And I pluck'd a hollow reed,

And I made a rural pen,
And I stain'd the water clear,
And I wrote my happy songs
Every child may joy to hear.

WILLIAM BLAKE (1757–1827), *Songs of Innocence* (1789)

VII

In the common ways of life, if we do our duty, we are obedient to some rule or law or custom or to some person a hundred times a day. It is the only way to be free from hindrances and vexations for ourselves or others which detract from the purpose and happiness of life. We have, of course, an overriding duty to God, and situations do arise where he can only be served by temporal disobedience, whatever faith and courage this may demand. The need to disobey is sometimes obvious to a Christian, but more often it calls for a most careful scrutiny of motives, lest actions justified on 'principle' or 'grounds of conscience' be in reality 'the easy way out'. In all this we need God's guidance, as we do to an even greater extent when in command.

51

11

STRETCH FORTH THY RIGHT HAND
TO HELP AND DEFEND US

I

Almighty and everlasting God, mercifully look upon our infirmities, and in all our dangers and necessities STRETCH FORTH THY RIGHT HAND TO HELP AND DEFEND US; through Jesus Christ our Lord. Amen.

Collect

II

Thou whom I have taken from the ends of the earth, and called thee from the chief men thereof, and said unto thee, Thou art my servant; I have chosen thee, and not cast thee away. Fear thou not; for I am with thee: be not dismayed; for I am thy God: I will strengthen thee; yea, I will help thee; yea, I will uphold thee with the right hand of my righteousness. Behold, all they that were incensed against thee shall be ashamed and confounded: they shall be as nothing; and they that strive with thee shall perish. Thou shalt seek them, and shalt not find them, even them that contended with thee: they that war against thee shall be as nothing, and as a thing of nought. For I the Lord thy God will hold thy right hand, saying unto thee, Fear not; I will help thee.

Isaiah 41:9

III

Peter therefore was kept in prison; but prayer was made without ceasing of the church unto God for him. And when Herod would have brought him forth, the same night Peter was sleeping between two soldiers, bound with two chains: and the keepers before the door kept the prison. And, behold, the angel of the Lord came upon him, and a light shined in the prison: and he

The Hand of God AUGUSTE RODIN 1840–1917

[*Musée Rodin, Paris*]

smote Peter on the side, and raised him up, saying, Arise up quickly. And his chains fell off from his hands. And the angel said unto him, Gird thyself, and bind on thy sandals. And so he did. And he saith unto him, Cast thy garment about thee, and follow me. And he went out, and followed him; and wist not that it was true which was done by the angel: but thought he saw a vision. When they were past the first and the second ward, they came unto the iron gate that leadeth unto the city; which opened to them of his own accord: and they went out, and passed on through one street; and forthwith the angel departed from him. And when Peter was come to himself, he said, Now I know of a surety, that the Lord hath sent his angel, and hath delivered me out of the hand of Herod, and from all the expectation of the people of the Jews. And when he had considered the thing, he came to the .house of Mary the mother of John, whose surname was Mark; where many were gathered together praying.

Acts 12:5

IV

Everyman, I will go with thee, and be thy guide,
In thy most need to go by thy side.

Everyman (15th century)

V

'How long, how long, will you keep saying "To-morrow"?' 'Why not now?' 'Why not an end to my shame in this very hour?' This was what I was saying, and with bitter contrition in my heart, when suddenly from a house close by I heard the voice of a boy or girl, I don't know which, singing and constantly repeating the words 'Take and read, take and read.' Instantly my look of sadness changed, and I began to consider intently whether there was any kind of game in which children used to repeat a song with words like that in it, and I could not recall having heard them anywhere at all. Stifling my tears I rose, reckoning that this was nothing less than a command from God to open the book and read the

54

first passage I came upon. . . . I went back to where Alypius was sitting, and where I had put down the book of St Paul's Epistles when I got up. I seized it and read in silence the first passage my eyes fell upon: Not in rioting and drunkenness, not in chambering and wantonness, not in strife and envying: but put ye on the Lord Jesus Christ, and make not provision for the flesh, to fulfil the lusts thereof [Romans 13:13]. I had no wish to read further, and there was no need. The moment I came to the end of this sentence, the light of certainty flooded my heart, as it were, and every cloud of hesitation rolled away.

ST AUGUSTINE (354–430)
Confessions (A.D. 386), viii, 12

VI

Came up that cold sea at Cromer like a running grave
    Beside him as he struck
Wildly towards the shore, but the blackcapped wave
    Crossed him and swung him back,
And he saw his son digging in the castled dirt that could save.
    Then the farewell rock
Rose a last time to his eyes. As he cried out
    A pawing gag of the sea
Smothered his cry and he sank in his own shout
    Like a dying airman. Then she
Deep near her son asleep on the hourglass sand
    Was awakened by whom
Save the Fate who knew that this was the wrong time:
    And opened her eyes
On the death of her son's begetter. Up she flies
    Into the hydra-headed
Grave as he closes his life upon her who for
    Life has so richly bedded him.
But she drove through his drowning like Orpheus and tore
    Back by the hair
Her escaping bridegroom. And on the sand their son
    Stood laughing where

He was almost an orphan. Then the three lay down
  On that cold sand,
Each holding the other by a living hand.

GEORGE BARKER (1913–   )
'On a Friend's Escape from Drowning off the
Norfolk Coast' in *Collected Poems 1930–1955* (1957)

VII

What greater comfort could there be than to look back and find
that God has been all the time guiding and protecting me along
the path of life? But this can only be if I have asked to be shown
the way and not chosen for myself. I must let God take me by the
hand.

12

THE FRAILTY OF OUR NATURE

I

O God, who knowest us to be set in the midst of so many and great dangers, that by reason of THE FRAILTY OF OUR NATURE we cannot always stand upright; Grant to us such strength and protection, as may support us in all dangers, and carry us through all temptations; through Jesus Christ our Lord. Amen.

Collect

II

Lord, let me know mine end, and the number of my days: that I may be certified how long I have to live. Behold, thou hast made my days as it were a span long: and mine age is even as nothing in respect of thee; and verily every man living is altogether vanity. For man walketh in a vain shadow, and disquieteth himself in vain: he heapeth up riches, and cannot tell who shall gather them. And now, Lord, what is my hope: truly my hope is even in thee. Deliver me from all mine offences: and make me not a rebuke unto the foolish. . . . Hear my prayer, O Lord, and with thine ears consider my calling: hold not thy peace at my tears. For I am a stranger with thee: and a sojourner, as all my fathers were. O spare me a little, that I may recover my strength: before I go hence, and be no more seen.

Psalm 39:5

III

The same day, when the even was come, he saith unto them, Let us pass over unto the other side. And when they had sent away the multitude, they took him even as he was in the ship. And there were also with him other little ships. And there arose a great

57

storm of wind, and the waves beat into the ship, so that it was now
full. And he was in the hinder part of the ship, asleep on a pillow:
and they awake him, and say unto him, Master, carest thou not
that we perish? And he arose, and rebuked the wind, and said unto
the sea, Peace, be still. And the wind ceased, and there was a
great calm. And he said unto them, Why are ye so fearful? how
is it that ye have no faith? And they feared exceedingly, and said
one to another, What manner of man is this, that even the wind
and the sea obey him.

Mark 4:35

IV

> The Soul's dark Cottage, batter'd and decay'd,
> Lets in new Light thro' chinks that time has made;
> Stronger by weakness, wiser Men become
> As they draw near to their Eternal home.

EDMUND WALLER (1606–87)
On the Foregoing Divine Poems (1686)

V

*Virgil leads Dante to the place to which impenitent sinners are con-
signed, and there Paolo and Francesca accost them and tell how their
love had brought them to their death at the hand of her terrible husband. Dante takes up their story at this point.*

When I heard these stricken souls I bowed my head until at last
the poet [Virgil] said to me, 'What is passing through your mind?'
And I answered, 'Alas, what sweet thoughts, what longing brought
them to this sorry plight!' Then I turned and spoke to them.
'Francesca,' I said, 'your torments make me shed tears of grief and
pity. But tell me; in that time of sighs and sweetness how and by
what means did love first plant in you its hesitant desires?' Then
she said to me, 'There is no greater grief than to recall a happy
hour in times of misery. Your learned guide [Virgil] knows that.
But if you are so strongly moved to learn of the first stirrings of
our love, I will tell you, but it is as when in telling there are tears.
One day for diversion we were reading how Love got the better of

58

The Cry   EDVARD MUNCH 1863–1944

[Lithograph: National Gallery of Art, Washington, D.C. Rosenwald Collection]

Lancelot. We were alone and thought no harm. As we read our eyes often met and our cheeks went now white, now red. But it was at one point that we were overcome. When we read how the great lover kissed the smiling face of his beloved, then he from whom I shall never more be parted kissed me on the lips all trembling. The book and he who wrote it pandered to our love. We read no more that day.' While she told me this, Paolo wept, so that for very pity I fell into a deadly faint, and dropped as a man drops dead.

DANTE (1265–1321)
Divine Comedy (*c.* 1310): *Inferno*, V, 109–142

VI

When I have fears that I may cease to be
    Before my pen has glean'd my teeming brain,
Before high-pilèd books, in charact'ry,
    Hold like rich garners the full-ripen'd grain;
When I behold, upon the night's starr'd face,
    Huge cloudy symbols of a high romance,
And think that I may never live to trace
    Their shadows, with the magic hand of chance;
And when I feel, fair creature of an hour!
    That I shall never look upon thee more,
Never have relish in the faery power
    Of unreflecting love!—then on the shore
Of the wide world I stand alone, and think
Till love and fame to nothingness do sink.

JOHN KEATS (1795–1821)
Sonnet (1818)

VII

We may take comfort in the thought that the frailty of our nature means that we are fragile, for many things that we call fragile are beautiful, though unfortunately only as long as they remain undamaged, as for example a flower or a butterfly or a Chinese vase. We need to ask God to keep us incorrupt, intact, 'unspotted from the world' (James 1:27), for we are in spirit delicate creatures.

13

PSALMS AND HYMNS AND SPIRITUAL SONGS

I

Let the word of Christ dwell in you richly in all wisdom; teaching and admonishing one another in PSALMS AND HYMNS AND SPIRITUAL SONGS, singing with grace in your hearts to the Lord.

Colossians 3 :16

II

The Spirit of the Lord departed from Saul, and an evil spirit from the Lord troubled him. And Saul's servants said unto him, Behold now, an evil spirit from God troubleth thee. Let our lord now command thy servants, which are before thee, to seek out a man, who is a cunning player on an harp: and it shall come to pass, when the evil spirit from God is upon thee, that he shall play with his hand, and thou shalt be well. And Saul said unto his servants, Provide me now a man that can play well, and bring him to me. Then answered one of the servants and said, Behold, I have seen a son of Jesse the Beth-lehemite, that is cunning in playing, and a mighty valiant man, and a man of war, and prudent in matters, and a comely person, and the Lord is with him. . . . And David came to Saul, and stood before him: and he loved him greatly; and he became his armourbearer. And Saul sent to Jesse, saying, Let David, I pray thee, stand before me; for he hath found favour in my sight. And it came to pass, when the evil spirit from God was upon Saul, that David took an harp, and played with his hand: so Saul was refreshed, and was well, and the evil spirit departed from him.

1 Samuel 16 :14

III

As they did eat, Jesus took bread, and blessed, and brake it, and gave to them, and said, Take, eat: this is my body. And he took the cup, and when he had given thanks, he gave it to them: and they all drank of it. And he said unto them, This is my blood of the new testament, which is shed for many. Verily I say unto you, I will drink no more of the fruit of the vine, until that day that I drink it new in the kingdom of God. And when they had sung an hymn, they went out.

Mark 14 :22

IV

An art aims, above all, at producing something *beautiful* which affects not our feelings, but the organ of pure contemplation, our *imagination*.

EDUARD HANSLICK (1825–1904),
The Beautiful in Music (Vom Musikalisch-Schönen,
seventh edition, 1885, trans. Gustav Cohen, 1891)

V

Reasons briefely set downe by th'auctor, to perswade euery one to learne to sing.
First, it is a knowledge easely taught, and quickly learned, where there is a good Master, and an apt Scoller.

2 The exercise of singing is delightfull to Nature, & good to preserve the health of Man.

3 It doth strengthen all parts of the brest, & doth open the pipes.

4 It is a singuler good remedie for a stutting & stamering in the speech.

5 It is the best meanes to procure a perfect pronunciation, & to make a good Orator.

6 It is the onely way to know where Nature hath bestowed the benefit of a good voyce: which guift is so rare, as there is not one among a thousand, that hath it: and in many, that excellent guift is lost, because they want Art to expresse Nature.

7 There is not any Musicke of Instruments whatsoever, comparable to that which is made of the voyces of Men, where the voices are good, and the same well sorted and ordered.

זה דוד המנגן בנבל "

King David playing the Harp

[*A late 13th century miniature in North-French style : British Library, London*]

8   The better the voyce is, the meeter it is to honour and serve
God there-with: and the voyce of man is chiefely to be im-
ployed to that ende.

Omnis spiritus laudet Dominum.

Since singing is so good a thing,
I wish all men would learne to sing.

WILLIAM BYRD (1542–1623)
Psalmes, Sonets, & songs of sadnes and pietie (1588)

VI

How sweet the moonlight sleeps upon this bank!
Here will we sit and let the sounds of music
Creep in our ears; soft stillness and the night
Become the touches of sweet harmony.
Sit, Jessica. Look how the floor of heaven
Is thick inlaid with patines of bright gold;
There's not the smallest orb which thou behold'st
But in his motion like an angel sings,
Still quiring to the young-ey'd cherubins;
Such harmony is in immortal souls,
But whilst this muddy vesture of decay
Doth grossly close it in, we cannot hear it.

WILLIAM SHAKESPEARE (1564–1616)
The Merchant of Venice (1596), V, i, 54

VII

Heaven is naturally thought of as being without sin, and sometimes without the sea (Revelation 21:1), but never, it is to be supposed, without music. For music speaks a universal language, its
medium is the air, and its most characteristic attribute is sweetness. Let us keep it heavenly and, what it always has been, the
handmaid of religion.

14

A GREAT SOUND OF A TRUMPET

I

Then shall appear the sign of the Son of man in heaven: and then shall all the tribes of the earth mourn, and they shall see the Son of man coming in the clouds of heaven with power and great glory. And he shall send his angels with A GREAT SOUND OF A TRUMPET, and they shall gather together his elect from the four winds, from one end of heaven to the other.

Matthew 24:30

II

God has just spoken the Ten Commandments

And all the people saw the thunderings, and the lightnings, and the noise of the trumpet, and the mountain smoking: and when the people saw it, they removed, and stood afar off. And they said unto Moses, Speak thou with us, and we will hear: but let not God speak with us, lest we die. And Moses said unto the people, Fear not: for God is come to prove you, and that his fear may be before your faces, that ye sin not. And the people stood afar off, and Moses drew near unto the thick darkness where God was.

Exodus 20:18

III

Now this I say, brethren, that flesh and blood cannot inherit the kingdom of God; neither doth corruption inherit incorruption. Behold, I shew you a mystery; We shall not all sleep, but we shall all be changed, in a moment, in the twinkling of an eye, at the last trump: for the trumpet shall sound, and the dead shall be raised incorruptible, and we shall be changed. For this corruptible must

65

put on incorruption, and this mortal must put on immortality. So when this corruptible shall have put on incorruption, and this mortal shall have put on immortality, then shall be brought to pass the saying that is written, Death is swallowed up in victory. O death, where is thy sting? O grave, where is thy victory? The sting of death is sin; and the strength of sin is the law. But thanks be to God, which giveth us the victory through our Lord Jesus Christ.

1 Corinthians 15 :50

IV

Blow out, you bugles, over the rich Dead!
There's none of these so lonely and poor of old,
But, dying, has made us rarer gifts than gold.

RUPERT BROOKE (1887–1915)
The Dead (1914)

V

After this, it was noised abroad, that Mr *Valiant-for-truth* was taken with a Summons by the same *Post* as the other; and had this for a Token that the Summons was true, *That his Pitcher was broken at the Fountain* [Ecclesiastes 12:6]. When he understood it, he called for his Friends, and told them of it. Then said he, I am going to my Fathers, and tho' with great Difficulty I am got hither, yet now I do not repent me of all the Trouble I have been at to arrive where I am. *My Sword*, I give to him that shall Succeed me in my Pilgrimage; and my *Courage* and *Skill*, to him that can get it. My *Marks* and *Scars* I carry with me, to be a Witness for me, that I have fought his Battle, who now will be my Rewarder. When the Day that he must go hence, was come, many accompanied him to the River-side, into which as he went, he said, *Death, where is thy Sting?* And as he went down deeper, he said, *Grave, where is thy Victory?* So he passed over, and all the Trumpets sounded for him on the other side.

JOHN BUNYAN (1628–88)
Pilgrim's Progress (1678)

Organ Case, King's College Chapel, Cambridge

VI

At the round earths imagin'd corners, blow
Your trumpets, Angells, and arise, arise
From death, you numberlesse infinities
Of soules, and to your scattred bodies goe,
All whom the flood did, and fire shall o'erthrow,
All whom warre, death, age, agues, tyrannies,
Despaire, law, chance, hath slaine, and you whose eyes,
Shall behold God, and never tast deaths woe,
But let them sleepe, Lord, and mee mourne a space,
For, if above all these, my sinnes abound,
'Tis late to aske abundance of thy grace,
When wee are there; here on this lowly ground,
Teach mee how to repent; for that's as good
As if thou'hadst seal'd my pardon, with thy blood.

JOHN DONNE (1571?–1631)
Holy Sonnets (1633)

VII

The trumpet is a noble instrument, and in the form of a bugle it has military associations from Reveille to a Royal Salute. That will be a great Reveille when the trumpet shall sound and the dead shall be raised incorruptible. And that will be a right Royal Salute, when the Lord himself shall descend from heaven with a shout, the voice of an archangel and the trump of God (1 Thessalonians 4:16). The coming of Christ is indeed a Royal Visit.

15

HE HAD AGREED WITH THE LABOURERS
FOR A PENNY A DAY

I

The kingdom of heaven is like unto a man that is an householder, which went out early in the morning to hire labourers into his vineyard. And when HE HAD AGREED WITH THE LABOURERS FOR A PENNY A DAY, he sent them into his vineyard.

Matthew 20 :1

II

In the sweat of thy face shalt thou eat bread, till thou return unto the ground; for out of it wast thou taken: for dust thou art, and unto dust shalt thou return.

Genesis 3 :19

Thou shalt not defraud thy neighbour, neither rob him: the wages of him that is hired shall not abide with thee all night until the morning.

Leviticus 19 :13

I will come near to you to judgment; and I will be a swift witness against the sorcerers, and against the adulterers, and against false swearers, and against those that oppress the hireling in his wages, the widow and the fatherless, and that turn aside the stranger from his right, and fear not me, saith the Lord of hosts. For I am the Lord, I change not.

Malachi 3 :5

They gave money also unto the masons, and to the carpenters; and meat, and drink, and oil, unto them of Zidon, and to them of Tyre, to bring cedar trees from Lebanon to the sea of Joppa, according to the grant that they had of Cyrus king of Persia.

Ezra 3 :7

Woe unto him that buildeth his house by unrighteousness, and his chambers by wrong; that useth his neighbour's service without wages, and giveth him not for his work.

Jeremiah 22 :13

III

Come unto me, all ye that labour and are heavy laden, and I will give you rest.

Matthew 11 :28

He that reapeth receiveth wages, and gathereth fruit unto life eternal: that both he that soweth and he that reapeth may rejoice together.

John 4 :36

The harvest truly is plenteous, but the labourers are few; pray ye therefore the Lord of the harvest, that he will send forth labourers into his harvest.

Matthew 9 :37

We give thanks to God always for you all, making mention of you in our prayers; remembering without ceasing your work of faith, and labour of love, and patience of hope in our Lord Jesus Christ.

1 Thessalonians 1 :2

The wages of sin is death; but the gift of God is eternal life through Jesus Christ our Lord.

Romans 6 :23

IV

We shall rest, and, faith, we shall need it—lie down for an æon or two,

Work

FORD MADOX BROWN 1821–93

[*City Art Gallery, Manchester*]

Till the Master of All Good Workmen shall put us to work anew!

RUDYARD KIPLING (1865–1936)
'L'Envoi' in *Verses 1889–1896* (1897)

V

We shall find the best and simplest illustration of the relations of master and operative in the position of domestic servants. . . . It may indeed happen, and does happen often, that if the master is a man of sense and energy, a large quantity of material work may be done under mechanical pressure, enforced by strong will and guided by wise method; also it may happen, and does happen often, that if the master is indolent and weak (however good-natured), a very small quantity of work, and that bad, may be produced by the servant's undirected strength, and contemptuous gratitude. But the universal law of the matter is that, assuming any given quantity of energy and sense in master and servant, the greatest material result obtainable by them will be, not through antagonism to each other, but through affection for each other; and that if the master, instead of endeavouring to get as much work as possible from the servant, seeks rather to render his appointed and necessary work beneficial to him, and to forward his interests in all just and wholesome ways, the real amount of work ultimately done, or of good rendered, by the person so cared for, will indeed be the greatest possible.

JOHN RUSKIN (1819–1900)
Unto this Last (First Lecture, 1860)

VI

'Work—work—work
Till the brain begins to swim;
Work—work—work
Till the eyes are heavy and dim!
Seam, and gusset, and band,
Band, and gusset, and seam,

72

Till over the buttons I fall asleep,
　　And sew them on in a dream!

'O! Men with Sisters dear!
　　O! Men! with Mothers and Wives!
It is not linen you're wearing out,
　　But human creatures' lives!
　　　　Stitch—stitch—stitch,
　　In poverty, hunger, and dirt,
Sewing at once, with a double thread,
　　A Shroud as well as a Shirt. . . .

'Oh but for one short hour!
　　A respite however brief!
No blessed leisure for Love or Hope,
　　But only time for Grief!
A little weeping would ease my heart,
　　But in their briny bed
My tears must stop, for every drop
　　Hinders needle and thread!'

With fingers weary and worn,
　　With eyelids heavy and red,
A Woman sate in unwomanly rags,
　　Plying her needle and thread—
　　　　Stitch! stitch! stitch!
　　In poverty, hunger, and dirt,
And still with a voice of dolorous pitch,—
Would that its tone could reach the Rich!—
　　She sang this 'Song of the Shirt!'

THOMAS HOOD (1799–1845)
'The Song of the Shirt' (1843)

VII

In the Bible there is a great deal of teaching about work and many
varying attitudes. The Law prescribes alleviations for the worker; the Prophets rage against oppression by the employer; the Sermon

73

on the Mount tells us not to worry. But when these various attitudes are translated into action they all seem to fail. Does the present age promise greater success? Or is it that any improvements only end in impoverishing human life? What ought we to think? What has God in mind?

16

THE MYSTERIES OF THE KINGDOM OF GOD

I

When he had said these things, he cried, He that hath ears to hear, let him hear. And his disciples asked him, saying, What might this parable be? And he said, Unto you it is given to know THE MYSTERIES OF THE KINGDOM OF GOD: but to others in parables; that seeing they might not see, and hearing they might not understand.

Luke 8:8

II

Vision

Abram believed in the Lord; and he counted it to him for righteousness. And he said unto him, I am the Lord that brought thee out of Ur of the Chaldees, to give thee this land to inherit it. And he said, Lord God, whereby shall I know that I shall inherit it? And he said unto him, Take me an heifer of three years old, and a she goat of three years old, and a ram of three years old, and a turtledove, and a young pigeon. And he took unto him all these, and divided them in the midst, and laid each piece one against another: but the birds divided he not. . . . And when the sun was going down, a deep sleep fell upon Abram; and, lo, an horror of great darkness fell upon him. . . . And it came to pass, that, when the sun went down, and it was dark, behold a smoking furnace, and a burning lamp that passed between those pieces. In the same day the Lord made a covenant with Abram, saying, Unto thy seed have I given this land, from the river of Egypt unto the great river, the river Euphrates.

Genesis 15:6

III

Sacrament

Husbands, love your wives, even as Christ also loved the church,

75

and gave himself for it; that he might sanctify and cleanse it with the washing of water by the word, that he might present it to himself a glorious church, not having spot, or wrinkle, or any such thing; but that it should be holy and without blemish. So ought men to love their wives as their own bodies. He that loveth his wife loveth himself. For no man ever yet hated his own flesh; but nourisheth and cherisheth it, even as the Lord the church: for we are members of his body, of his flesh, and of his bones. For this cause shall a man leave his father and mother, and shall be joined unto his wife, and they two shall be one flesh. This is a great mystery: but I speak concerning Christ and the church.

Ephesians 5 :25

IV

. . . mans estate:
Where is deciphered to true iudgements eye
A deep, conceal'd, and precious misterie.

BEN JONSON (1573 ?–1637)
Every Man in his Humor (1598), II, ii

V

The religious sense

I have carefully browsed through Trevelyan's *Life and Letters of Macaulay*, and Francis Darwin's 1 vol. Life of his Father. Macaulay is certainly a most lovable character,—full of tenderest domestic affection, but a profoundly uninteresting mind; or rather the mind becomes interesting to one as a vivid exemplification of what is, after all, a very common form of human mind: a form, surely, mysterious to anyone who believes in the omnipresent operation of God's Spirit. For it is, this mind, as entirely un-mystical, as free too from any even vague sense of any incompleteness of its own, as if the great Source and Crown of all mysticism were not in the world and pressing upon each soul within it. Darwin is a deeply attractive mind and heart: humble, self-diffident, with the grand, semi-dumb objectivity of the instruments of God in the world; without a touch of 'cleverness', ever

The Story of Lazarus: Martha and Mary kneeling before Christ

[*A 12th century carving from Chichester Cathedral, Edwin Smith*]

effecting more than he knows or can at all master himself. And if his loss of the religious sense is mysterious: yet *here*, there was, at first, this sense: and when it went, D., up to the very end, was quite evidently haunted by a sense that he himself was, certainly in *other* respects, by now, a stunted being, and that very possibly he had become such, in this matter also.

BARON FRIEDRICH VON HÜGEL (1852-1925)
(*Selected Letters:* '12th June, 1905')

VI

O world that is within us, yet must still
Out of the eternal mystery be wooed
Ere it be ours and, breathing in the blood,
Live in its beauty, as the miracle
Of the divine colour of flowers in night
Was not, and is not of themselves alone
Nor of the dawn-beam, but of both made one,—
A marriage-mystery of earth and light!
O undiscovered world that all about us lies
When spirit to Spirit surrenders, and like young Love sees
Heaven with human eyes!
World of radiant morning! Joy's untravelled region!
Why lies it solitary? and O why tarry we?
Why daily wander out from Paradise?

LAURENCE BINYON (1869-1943)
The Sirens: an Ode (1925), III, 3

VII

Despite the achievements of science, there is much in heaven and earth that remains a mystery. Still less advanced is our under-standing of the relationship between matter and spirit; indeed, in this respect we seem to have fallen back. The need is to heighten the sensitivity of soul, and thus, like the Disciples, to progress from parable to reality, from imagery to vision, from symbol to truth.

17

NOW WE SEE THROUGH A GLASS, DARKLY

I

NOW WE SEE THROUGH A GLASS, DARKLY; but then face to face:
now I know in part; but then shall I know even as also I am known.

1 Corinthians 13:12

II

What man is he that can know the counsel of God? or who can
think what the will of the Lord is? For the thoughts of mortal men
are miserable, and our devices are but uncertain. For the corruptible body presseth down the soul, and the earthy tabernacle
weigheth down the mind that museth upon many things. And
hardly do we guess aright at things that are upon earth, and with
labour do we find the things that are before us: but the things that
are in heaven who hath searched out? And thy counsel who hath
known, except thou give wisdom, and send thy Holy Spirit from
above?

Wisdom 9:13

III

The angel of the Lord spake unto Philip, saying, Arise, and go
toward the south unto the way that goeth down from Jerusalem
unto Gaza, which is desert. And he arose and went: and, behold,
a man of Ethiopia, an eunuch of great authority under Candace
queen of the Ethiopians, who had the charge of all her treasure,
and had come to Jerusalem for to worship, was returning, and
sitting in his chariot read Isaiah the prophet. Then the Spirit said
unto Philip, Go near, and join thyself to this chariot. And Philip
ran thither to him, and heard him read the prophet Isaiah, and
said, Understandest thou what thou readest? And he said, How

79

can I, except some man should guide me? And he desired Philip that he would come up and sit with him. The place of the scripture which he read was this, He was led as a sheep to the slaughter; and like a lamb dumb before his shearer, so opened he not his mouth: in his humiliation his judgment was taken away: and who shall declare his generation? for his life is taken from the earth. And the eunuch answered Philip, and said, I pray thee, of whom speaketh the prophet this? of himself, or of some other man? Then Philip opened his mouth, and began at the same scripture, and preached unto him Jesus.

Acts 8:26

IV

If we knew everything we should at once ask why that was all.

W. R. LETHABY (1855–1931)
From a collection of his sayings printed in
The Times Literary Supplement (17 April 1953)

V

Probable Evidence, in its very nature, affords but an imperfect kind of Information; and is to be considered as relative only to Beings of limited Capacities. For nothing which is the possible object of Knowledge, whether past, present, or future, can be probable to an infinite Intelligence; since it cannot but be discerned absolutely as it is in itself, certainly true, or certainly false: But to us, probability is the very Guide of Life.

From these things it follows, that in Questions of Difficulty or such as are thought so, where more satisfactory Evidence cannot be had, or is not seen; if the result of Examination be, that there appears upon the whole, any the lowest Presumption on One side, and none on the Other, or a greater Presumption on One side, though in the lowest Degree greater; this determines the Question, even in matters of Speculation; and in matters of Practice, will lay us under an absolute and formal Obligation, in point of Prudence and of Interest, to act upon that Presumption or low Probability, though it be so low as to leave the mind in very great Doubt which

The Slanted Light (engraved glass)

LAURENCE WHISTLER 1912–

is the Truth. For surely a Man is as really bound in Prudence, to do what upon the whole appears, according to the best of his Judgment, to be for his Happiness, as what he certainly knows to be so.

BISHOP JOSEPH BUTLER (1692–1752)
The Analogy of Religion (1736), Introduction

VI

Strong Son of God, immortal Love,
   Whom we, that have not seen thy face,
   By faith, and faith alone, embrace,
Believing where we cannot prove; . . .

We have but faith: we cannot know;
   For knowledge is of things we see;
   And yet we trust it comes from thee,
A beam in darkness: let it grow.

Let knowledge grow from more to more,
   But more of reverence in us dwell;
   That mind and soul, according well,
May make one music as before,

But vaster. We are fools and slight;
   We mock thee when we do not fear;
   But help thy foolish ones to bear;
Help thy vain worlds to bear thy light.

ALFRED, LORD TENNYSON (1809–92)
In Memoriam (1849), I

VII

Life, for all its dark tracts of ignorance and grief, brings countless intimations of perfect and eternal joy; and though as yet I journey on bewildered, others have blazed the path before me, and if I tread it manfully, I shall see God face to face in his good time. The light shineth in darkness.

18

ACKNOWLEDGING OUR WRETCHEDNESS

I

Almighty and everlasting God, who hatest nothing that thou hast made, and dost forgive the sins of all them that are penitent; Create and make in us new and contrite hearts, that we worthily lamenting our sins, and ACKNOWLEDGING OUR WRETCHEDNESS, may obtain of thee, the God of all mercy, perfect remission and forgiveness; through Jesus Christ our Lord. Amen.

Collect

II

Therefore thou shalt say this word unto them; Let mine eyes run down with tears night and day, and let them not cease: for the virgin daughter of my people is broken with a great breach, with a very grievous blow. If I go forth into the field, then behold the slain with the sword! and if I enter into the city, then behold them that are sick with famine! yea, both the prophet and the priest go about into a land that they know not. Hast thou utterly rejected Judah? hath thy soul lothed Zion? why hast thou smitten us, and there is no healing for us? we looked for peace, and there is no good; and for the time of healing, and behold trouble! We acknowledge, O Lord, our wickedness, and the iniquity of our fathers: for we have sinned against thee. Do not abhor us, for thy name's sake, do not disgrace the throne of thy glory.

Jeremiah 14:17

III

I know that in me (that is, in my flesh,) dwelleth no good thing: for to will is present with me; but how to perform that which is good I find not. For the good that I would I do not: but the evil which I would not, that I do. Now if I do that I would not, it is no more I that do it, but sin that dwelleth in me. I find then a law, that, when I would do good, evil is present with me. For I delight in the law of God after the inward man: but I see another law in my members, warring against the law of my mind, and bringing me into captivity to the law of sin which is in my members. O wretched man that I am! who shall deliver me from the body of this death? I thank God through Jesus Christ our Lord.

Romans 7 :18

IV

Man. I am *now* a Man of Despair, and am shut up in it, as in this Iron Cage. I cannot get out; O *now* I cannot.

JOHN BUNYAN (1628–88)
Pilgrim's Progress (1678)

V

The people of Calais in peril, 4 August 1347
The king said he would none otherwise but that they should yield them up simply to his pleasure. Then sir Gaultier said: 'Sir, saving your displeasure, in this ye may be in the wrong, . . .' Then the king said: . . . 'Sir Gaultier of Manny, ye shall go and say to the captain that all the grace that he shall find now in me is that they let six of the chief burgesses of the town come out bare-headed, bare-footed, and bare-legged, and in their shirts, with halters about their necks, with the keys of the town and castle in their hands, and let them six yield themselves purely to my will, and the residue I will take to mercy.' . . . At last the most rich burgess of all the town, called Eustace of Saint-Pierre, rose up and said openly: 'Sirs, great and small, great mischief it should be to suffer to die such people as be in this town, other by famine or otherwise, when there is a mean to save them. I think he or they should have great merit of our Lord God that might keep them from such mis-

84

The Burghers of Calais   AUGUSTE RODIN 1840–1917

[*Musée Rodin, Paris* © *S.P.A.D.E.M. Paris, 1973*]

chief. As for my part, I have so good trust in our Lord God, that if I die in the quarrel to save the residue, that God would pardon me: wherefore to save them I will be the first to put my life in jeopardy.' . . . Then another honest burgess rose and said: 'I will keep company with my gossip Eustace.' He was called John d'Aire. Then rose up Jaques of Wissant, who was rich in goods and heritage; he said also that he would hold company with his two cousins. In like wise so did Peter of Wissant his brother; and then rose two other; they said they would do the same. Then they went and apparelled them as the king desired. . . .

When sir Gaultier presented these burgesses to the king, . . . the king looked felly on them, for greatly he hated the people of Calais for the great damages and displeasures they had done him on the sea before. Then he commanded their heads to be stricken off: then every man required the king for mercy, but he would hear no man in that behalf: then sir Gaultier of Manny said: 'Ah, noble king, for God's sake refrain your courage: ye have the name of sovereign nobless; therefore now do not a thing that should blemish your renown, . . . Then the king wryed away from him and commanded to send for the hangman, . . . Then the queen, being great with child, kneeled down and sore weeping said: 'Ah, gentle sir, sith I passed the sea in great peril, I have desired nothing of you; therefore I now humbly require you in the honour of the Son of the Virgin Mary and for the love of me that ye will take mercy of these six burgesses.' The king beheld the queen and stood still in a study of a space, and then said: 'Ah, dame, I would ye had been as now in some other place; ye make such request to me that I cannot deny you. Wherefore I give them to you, to do your pleasure with them.' Then the queen caused them to be brought into her chamber, and made the halters to be taken from their necks, and caused them to be new clothed, and gave them their dinner at their leisure: and then she gave each of them six nobles and made them to be brought out of the host in safe-guard and set at their liberty.

The Chronicles of Froissart
(*c.* 1400, trans. by John Bourchier, Lord Berners, 1525;
edited by G. C. Macaulay, 1895), ch. 146

VI

King Lear : Poor naked wretches, whereso'er you are,
That bide the pelting of this pitiless storm,
' How shall your houseless heads and unfed sides,
Your loop'd and window'd raggedness, defend you
From seasons such as these? O, I have ta'en
Too little care of this! Take physic, pomp;
Expose thyself to feel what wretches feel,
That thou mayst shake the superflux to them,
And show the heavens more just.

WILLIAM SHAKESPEARE (1564–1616)
King Lear (1608), III, iv, 28

VII

There was a common saying among the ancient Greeks—*pathos mathos*—suffering is learning; to suffer is to learn; suffering teaches. We must try to learn something each time we suffer. Certainly we may try to forget our sufferings, but only after we have reflected upon them and learnt their lesson. And this, of course, is truer still of sin.

19

HAVING NOTHING, AND YET
POSSESSING ALL THINGS

I

We then, as workers together with him, beseech you also that ye receive not the grace of God in vain. (For he saith, I have heard thee in a time accepted, and in the day of salvation have I succoured thee: behold, now is the accepted time; behold, now is the day of salvation.) Giving no offence in any thing, that the ministry be not blamed: but in all things approving ourselves as the ministers of God, in much patience, in afflictions, in necessities, in distresses, in stripes, in imprisonments, in tumults, in labours, in watchings, in fastings; by pureness, by knowledge, by long-suffering, by kindness, by the Holy Ghost, by love unfeigned, by the word of truth, by the power of God, by the armour of righteousness on the right hand and on the left, by honour and dishonour, by evil report and good report: as deceivers, and yet true; as unknown, and yet well known; as dying, and, behold, we live; as chastened, and not killed; as sorrowful, yet alway rejoicing; as poor, yet making many rich; as HAVING NOTHING, AND YET POSSESSING ALL THINGS.

2 Corinthians 6 : 1

II

Having all things, but possessing nothing

God hath delivered my soul from the place of hell: for he shall receive me. Be not thou afraid, though one be made rich: or if the glory of his house be increased; for he shall carry nothing away with him when he dieth: neither shall his pomp follow him. For while he lived, he counted himself an happy man: and so long as thou doest well unto thyself, men will speak good of thee. He shall

St Francis discards his secular clothing   GIOTTO 1266–1337

[*The Upper Church, Assisi : Mansell*]

follow the generation of his fathers: and shall never see light. Man being in honour hath no understanding: but is compared unto the beasts that perish.

Psalm 49:15

III

Possessing all things, but not having the One Thing

Behold, one came and said unto him, Good Master, what good thing shall I do, that I may have eternal life? And he said unto him, Why callest thou me good? there is none good but one, that is, God: but if thou wilt enter into life, keep the commandments. He saith unto him, Which? Jesus said, Thou shalt do no murder, Thou shalt not commit adultery, Thou shalt not steal, Thou shalt not bear false witness, Honour thy father and thy mother: and, Thou shalt love thy neighbour as thyself. The young man saith unto him, All these things have I kept from my youth up: what lack I yet? Jesus saith unto him, If thou wilt be perfect, go and sell that thou hast, and give to the poor, and thou shalt have treasure in heaven: and come and follow me. But when the young man heard that saying, he went away sorrowful: for he had great possessions.

Matthew 19:16

IV

This man is freed from servile bands
Of hope to rise, or fear to fall:
Lord of himself, though not of lands,
And having nothing, yet hath all.

SIR HENRY WOTTON (1568–1639)
'The Character of a Happy Life' (1672)

V

Having nothing, but possessing the One Thing

Above all others, let this vice be extirpated in the monastery. No one, without leave of the abbot, shall presume to give, or receive, or keep as his own, anything whatever: neither book, nor tablets, nor pen: nothing at all. For monks are men who can claim no dominion even over their own bodies or wills. All that is necessary, however, they may hope from the Father of the monastery; but they shall keep nothing which the abbot has not given or allowed. All things are to be common to all, as it is written, *Neither did any one say or think that aught was his own* [Acts 4:32]. Hence if any one shall be found given to this most wicked vice let him be admonished once or twice, and if he do not amend let him be subjected to correction.

The Rule of Saint Benedict (A.D. 572),
ch. 33 (trans. Abbot Gasquet)

VI

Having nothing, yet possessing all things

Afoot and light-hearted I take to the open road,
Healthy, free, the world before me,
The long brown path before me leading wherever I choose.

Henceforth I ask not good-fortune, I myself am good-fortune,
Henceforth I whimper no more, postpone no more, need nothing,
Done with indoor complaints, libraries, querulous criticisms,
Strong and content I travel the open road.

The earth, that is sufficient,
I do not want the constellations any nearer,
I know they are very well where they are,
I know they suffice for those who belong to them. . . .

You road I enter upon and look around, I believe you are not
all that is here,
I believe that much unseen is also here.

WALT WHITMAN (1819–92)
'Song of the Open Road' in *Leaves of Grass* (1856)

VII

For 'having nothing, and yet possessing all things', NEB has 'penniless, we own the world', a fine gesture of independence with a touch of contempt. Although the claims of this world prevent it from ever being literally true, it represents an heroic attitude we can valuably assume, and an ideal virtually unattainable but nevertheless inspiring, as so many ideals are. We can certainly aim at wanting very little that money can buy, and having our treasure and our heart in heaven.

20

EVIL THOUGHTS WHICH MAY
ASSAULT AND HURT THE SOUL

I

Almighty God, who seest that we have no power of ourselves to help ourselves; Keep us both outwardly in our bodies, and inwardly in our souls; that we may be defended from all adversities which may happen to the body, and from all EVIL THOUGHTS WHICH MAY ASSAULT AND HURT THE SOUL; through Jesus Christ our Lord. Amen.

Collect

II,

David has committed adultery with Uriah's wife, while Uriah is at the front, and she is pregnant. Uriah is now on leave.

And David said to Uriah, Tarry here to day also, and to morrow I will let thee depart. So Uriah abode in Jerusalem that day, and the morrow. And when David had called him, he did eat and drink before him; and he made him drunk: and at even he went out to lie on his bed with the servants of his lord, but went not down to his house. And it came to pass in the morning, that David wrote a letter to Joab, and sent it by the hand of Uriah. And he wrote in the letter, saying, Set ye Uriah in the forefront of the hottest battle, and retire ye from him, that he may be smitten and die. And it came to pass, when Joab observed the city, that he assigned Uriah unto a place where he knew that valiant men were. And the men of the city went out, and fought with Joab: and there fell some of the people of the servants of David; and Uriah the Hittite died also. Then Joab sent and told David all the things concerning the war; and charged the messenger, saying, When thou hast made an end of telling the matters of the war unto the king, . . . then say thou, Thy servant Uriah the Hittite is dead also. . . . Then David said unto the messenger, Thus shalt thou say unto Joab, Let not this thing displease thee, for the sword devoureth one as well as another: make thy battle more strong against the city, and over-throw it: and encourage thou him. . . . But the thing that David had done displeased the Lord.

2 Samuel 11 :12

III

Jesus was troubled in spirit, and testified and said, Verily, verily, I say unto you, that one of you shall betray me. Then the disciples looked one on another, doubting of whom he spake. Now there was leaning on Jesus' bosom one of his disciples, whom Jesus loved. Simon Peter therefore beckoned to him, that he should ask who it should be of whom he spake. He then lying on Jesus' breast saith unto him, Lord, who is it? Jesus answered, He it is, to whom I shall give a sop, when I have dipped it. And when he had dipped the sop, he gave it to Judas Iscariot, the son of Simon. And after the sop Satan entered into him. Then said Jesus unto him, That thou doest, do quickly. . . . He then having received the sop went immediately out: and it was night.

John 13 :21

IV

Brethren, whatsoever things are true, whatsoever things are honest, whatsoever things are just, whatsoever things are pure, whatsoever things are lovely, whatsoever things are of good report; if there be any virtue, and if there be any praise, think on these things.

Philippians 4 :8

V

Mrs Darling first heard of Peter when she was tidying up her children's minds. It is the nightly custom of every good mother after her children are asleep to rummage in their minds and put things straight for next morning, repacking into their proper places

94

ruth beset by dark Spirits FRANCISCO GOYA 1746–1828

[Sepia wash drawing: Metropolitan Museum, New York]

the many articles that have wandered during the day. If you could keep awake (but of course you can't) you would see your own mother doing this, and you would find it very interesting to watch her. It is quite like tidying up drawers. You would see her on her knees, I expect, lingering humorously over some of your contents, wondering where on earth you had picked this thing up, making discoveries sweet and not so sweet, pressing this to her cheek as if it were as nice as a kitten, and hurriedly stowing that out of sight. When you wake in the morning, the naughtinesses and evil passions with which you went to bed have been folded up small and placed at the bottom of your mind; and on the top, beautifully aired, are spread out your prettier thoughts, ready for you to put on.

J. M. BARRIE (1860–1937)
Peter Pan (1911)

VI

Vertue could see to doe what vertue would
By her owne radiant light, though sun and moon
Were in the flat sea sunck. And Wisdoms selfe
Oft seeks to sweet retired Solitude
Where with her best nurse Contemplation
She plumes her feathers, and lets grow her wings
That in the various bustle of resort
Were all to ruffl'd, and sometimes impair'd.
He that has light within his owne cleare brest
May sit i'th center and enjoy bright day,
But he that hides a darke soule and foule thoughts
Benighted walks under the mid-day Sun,
Himselfe is his own dungeon.

JOHN MILTON (1608–74)
Comus (1624), 373

VII

Bad language may be used without bad thoughts, though it is

96

always in danger of falling on ears that it offends. By contrast, evil thoughts may not only assault and hurt the thinker of them, but without a word said they seem capable of creating an evil atmosphere, as we call it. Is this an example of the superiority of mind over matter? or the relics of some animal instinct for distinguishing friend from foe? or a mere fancy? or what?

21

AWAKE, THOU THAT SLEEPEST

I

But all things that are reproved are made manifest by the light: for whatever doth make manifest is light. Wherefore he saith, AWAKE, THOU THAT SLEEPEST, and arise from the dead, and Christ shall give thee light.

Ephesians 5 :13

II

My heart is fixed, O God, my heart is fixed: I will sing, and give praise. Awake up, my glory; awake, lute and harp: I myself will awake right early. I will give thanks unto thee, O Lord, among the people: and I will sing unto thee among the nations. For the greatness of thy mercy reacheth unto the heavens: and thy truth unto the clouds. Set up thyself, O God, above the heavens: and thy glory above all the earth.

Psalm 57 :8

III

And they came to a place which was named Gethsemane: and he saith to his disciples, Sit ye here, while I shall pray. And he taketh with him Peter and James and John, and began to be sore amazed, and to be very heavy; and saith unto them, My soul is exceeding sorrowful unto death: tarry ye here, and watch. . . . And he cometh, and findeth them sleeping, and saith unto Peter, Simon, sleepest thou? couldest not thou watch one hour? Watch ye and pray, lest ye enter into temptation. The spirit truly is ready, but the flesh is weak. And again he went away, and prayed, and spake the same words. And when he returned, he found them asleep again, (for their eyes were heavy,) neither wist they what to

The Agony in the Garden

GIOVANNI BELLINI 1430–1516

[*National Gallery, London*]

answer him. And he cometh the third time, and saith unto them, Sleep on now, and take your rest: it is enough, the hour is come; behold, the Son of man is betrayed into the hands of sinners.

Mark 14:32

IV

Some people read books primarily to find confirmation of what they already believe. They are not open to the thoughts and experiences of the author, and they do not find what a particular book has to offer. Instead, they spend their time seeing what is not there, and bewailing what they do not see.

MICHEL QUOIST (1918–   )
Christ is Alive! Foreword (trans. J. F. Bernard)

V

On my first movement towards the anticipation of getting up, I find that such parts of the sheets and bolster, as are exposed to the air of the room, are stone cold. On opening my eyes, the first thing that meets them is my own breath rolling forth, as if in the open air, like smoke out of a cottage-chimney. Think of this symptom. Then I turn my eyes sideways and see the window all frozen over. Think of that. Then the servant comes in. 'It is very cold this morning, is it not?'—'Very cold, Sir.'—'Very cold indeed, isn't it?'—'Very cold indeed, Sir.'—'More than usually so, isn't it, even for this weather?' (Here the servant's wit and good nature are put to a considerable test, and the inquirer lies on thorns for the answer.) 'Why, sir – – – I think it *is*.' (Good creature! There is not a better, or more truth-telling servant going.) 'I must rise however —Get me some warm water.'—Here comes a fine interval between the departure of the servant and the arrival of the hot water; during which, of course, it is of 'no use' to get up. The hot water comes. 'Is it quite hot?'—'Yes, Sir.'—'Perhaps too hot for shaving: I must wait a little?'—'No, Sir; it will just do.' (There is an over-nice propriety sometimes, an officious zeal of virtue, a little troublesome.) 'Oh—the shirt—you must air my clean shirt:— linen gets very damp this weather.'—'Yes, Sir.' Here another delicious five minutes. A knock at the door. 'Oh, the shirt—very well. My stockings—I think the stockings had better be aired too.' —'Very well, Sir.'—Here another interval. At length every thing is ready, except myself.

J. H. LEIGH HUNT (1784–1859)
'*Getting up on cold mornings*'
(*The Indicator*, No. xv, 19 January 1820)

VI

Why hath the rose faded and fallen, yet these eyes have not seen?
Why hath the bird sung shrill in the tree—and this mind deaf
    and cold?
Why have the rains of summer veiled her flowers with their sheen
    And this black heart untold?

Here is calm Autumn now, the woodlands quake,
And, where this splendour of death lies under the tread,
The spectre of frost will stalk, and a silence make,
    And snow's white shroud be spread.

O self! O self! Wake from thy common sleep!
Fling off the destroyer's net. He hath blinded and bound thee.
In nakedness sit; pierce thy stagnation, and weep;
    Or corrupt in thy grave—all Heaven around thee.

WALTER DE LA MARE (1873–1956)
'Awake!' (*Collected Poems*)

VII

By day we do not see a quarter of this world round about us, because in half our waking hours we are half asleep, while by night we may get too little sleep or too much. Could we form a habit of always being either wide awake or fast asleep? It may be that we could, and most of us would be all the better for it, both in body and in spirit.

22

JERUSALEM WHICH NOW IS—
JERUSALEM WHICH IS ABOVE

I

Tell me, ye that desire to be under the law, do ye not hear the law?
For it is written, that Abraham had two sons, the one by a bond-
maid, the other by a freewoman. But he who was of the bond-
woman was born after the flesh; but he of the freewoman was by
promise. Which things are an allegory: for these are the two
covenants; the one from the mount Sinai, which gendereth to
bondage, which is Agar. For this Agar is mount Sinai in Arabia,
and answereth to JERUSALEM WHICH NOW IS, and is in bondage
with her children. But JERUSALEM WHICH IS ABOVE is free, which
is the mother of us all.

Galatians 4:21

II

By the waters of Babylon we sat down and wept: when we
remembered thee, O Sion. As for our harps, we hanged them up:
upon the trees that are therein. For they that led us away captive
required of us then a song, and melody, in our heaviness: Sing us
one of the songs of Sion. How shall we sing the Lord's song: in a
strange land? If I forget thee, O Jerusalem: let my right hand
forget her cunning. If I do not remember thee, let my tongue
cleave to the roof of my mouth: yea, if I prefer not Jerusalem in
my mirth.

Psalm 137:1

III

And I saw a new heaven and a new earth: for the first heaven and

View of Jerusalem, 1858

EDWARD LEAR 1812–88

[*Tate Gallery, London*]

the first earth were passed away; and there was no more sea. And I John saw the holy city, new Jerusalem, coming down from God out of heaven, prepared as a bride adorned for her husband. And I heard a great voice out of heaven saying, Behold, the tabernacle of God is with men, and he will dwell with them, and they shall be his people, and God himself shall be with them, and be their God. And God shall wipe away all tears from their eyes; and there shall be no more death, neither sorrow, nor crying, neither shall there be any more pain: for the former things are passed away. And he that sat upon the throne said, Behold, I make all things new.

Revelation 21 :1

IV

Not throned above the skies,
    Nor golden-walled afar,
But where Christ's two or three
    In his name gathered are,
Be in the midst of them,
God's own Jerusalem.

F. T. PALGRAVE (1824–97)
English Hymnal, No. 464

V

I know of no other Christianity and of no other Gospel than the liberty both of body & mind to exercise the Divine Arts of Imagination—Imagination the real & eternal World of which this Vegetable Universe is but a faint shadow & in which we shall live in our Eternal or Imaginative Bodies, when these Vegetable Mortal Bodies are no more. The Apostles knew of no other Gospel. What were all their spiritual gifts? What is the Divine Spirit? is the Holy Ghost any other than an Intellectual Fountain? What is the Harvest of the Gospel & its Labours? What is that Talent which it is a curse to hide? What are the Treasures of Heaven which we are to lay up for ourselves, are they any other than Mental Studies & performances? What are all the Gifts of the Gospel, are they not all Mental Gifts? Is God a Spirit who must be worshipped in Spirit & in Truth and are not the Gifts of the Spirit Every-thing to Man? O ye Religious discountenance every one among you who shall pretend to despise Art & Science! I call upon you in the Name of Jesus! What is the Life of Man but Art & Science? is it Meat & Drink? is not the Body more than Raiment? What is Mortality but the things relating to the Body, which Dies? What is Immortality but the things relating to the Spirit, which Lives Eternally? What is the Joy of Heaven but Improvement in the things of the Spirit? What are the Pains of Hell but Ignorance, Bodily Lust, Idleness & devastation of the things of the Spirit? Answer this to yourselves, & expel from among you those who pretend to despise the labours of Art & Science, which alone are the labours of the Gospel: Is not this plain & manifest to the thought? Can you think at all, & not pronounce heartily! That to Labour in Knowledge is to Build up Jerusalem: and to Despise Knowledge is to Despise Jerusalem & her Builders. And remember: He who despises & mocks a Mental Gift in another; calling it pride & selfishness & sin: mocks Jesus the giver of every Mental Gift, which always appear to the ignorance-loving Hypocrite as Sins, but that which is a Sin in the sight of cruel Man, is not so in the sight of our kind God. Let every Christian as much as in him lies engage himself openly & publicly before all the World in some Mental pursuit for the Building up of Jerusalem.

WILLIAM BLAKE (1757–1827)
Jerusalem (1804), f.77

VI

The 'Jerusalem' referred to in the following passage is Jerusalem Chamber at Westminster Abbey

King Henry: Doth any name particular belong
                Unto the lodging where I first did swoon?
Warwick: 'Tis call'd Jerusalem, my noble lord.
King Henry: Laud be to God! Even there my life must end.
                It hath been prophesied to me many years,
                I should not die but in Jerusalem;

Which vainly I suppos'd the Holy Land.
But bear me to that chamber; there I'll lie;
In that Jerusalem shall Harry die.

WILLIAM SHAKESPEARE (1564–1616)
Henry IV, Part II (1597), IV, v, 233

VII

Each of us must build his own Jerusalem above, a spiritual home, to which he can always resort and there find God. The mystic will build nowhere, but in his mind. For others, it may be Durham, or Florence, or some other great cathedral city that is pictured in this context; it may be Jerusalem that now is; or, for those of a different temperament, it is perhaps their own church, or an old home, school or university. Yet, whatever our personal approach, the picture must not distort the truth: Jerusalem which is above is free, free from entrance charges, free from the expense and discomforts of travel, free from the world's distractions for mind and body, and—unlike Jerusalem of old—able to recognize and welcome its Lord and Saviour.

23

GOOD THINGS TO COME

I

Christ being come an high priest of GOOD THINGS TO COME, by a greater and more perfect tabernacle, not made with hands, that is to say, not of this building; neither by the blood of goats and calves, but by his own blood he entered in once into the holy place, having obtained eternal redemption for us.

Hebrews 9:11

II

Thou shalt keep the commandments of the Lord thy God, to walk in his ways, and to fear him. For the Lord thy God bringeth thee into a good land, a land of brooks of water, of fountains and depths that spring out of valleys and hills; a land of wheat, and barley, and vines, and fig trees, and pomegranates; a land of oil olive, and honey; a land wherein thou shalt eat bread without scarceness, thou shalt not lack any thing in it; a land whose stones are iron, and out of whose hills thou mayest dig brass. When thou hast eaten and art full, then thou shalt bless the Lord thy God for the good land which he hath given thee.

Deuteronomy 8:6

III

And his father Zacharias was filled with the Holy Ghost, and prophesied, saying, Blessed be the Lord God of Israel; for he hath visited and redeemed his people, and hath raised up an horn of salvation for us in the house of his servant David; as he spake by the mouth of his holy prophets, which have been since the world began: that we should be saved from our enemies, and from the hand of all that hate us; to perform the mercy promised to our fathers, and to remember his holy covenant; the oath which he sware to our father Abraham, that he would grant unto us, that we being delivered out of the hands of our enemies might serve him without fear, in holiness and righteousness before him, all the days of our life. And thou, child, shalt be called the prophet of the Highest: for thou shalt go before the face of the Lord to prepare his ways; to give knowledge of salvation unto his people by the remission of their sins, through the tender mercy of our God; whereby the dayspring from on high hath visited us, to give light to them that sit in darkness and in the shadow of death, to guide our feet into the way of peace. And the child grew, and waxed strong in spirit, and was in the deserts till the day of his shewing unto Israel.

Luke 1 :67

IV

These things shall be! A loftier race
Than e'er the world hath known shall rise,
With flame of freedom in their souls,
And light of knowledge in their eyes.

JOHN ADDINGTON SYMONDS (1840–93)
Hymn (c. 1880)

V

Warren Hastings

With all his faults,—and they were neither few nor small,—only one cemetery was worthy to contain his remains. In that temple of silence and reconciliation where the enmities of twenty generations lie buried, in the Great Abbey which has during many ages afforded a quiet resting-place to those whose minds and bodies have been shattered by the contentions of the Great Hall, the dust of the illustrious accused should have mingled with the dust of the illustrious accusers. This was not to be. Yet the place of interment was not ill chosen. Behind the chancel of the parish church of

Firs in Coed y Brenin Forest

[*Forestry Commission*]

Daylesford, in earth which already held the bones of many chiefs of the house of Hastings, was laid the coffin of the greatest man who has ever borne that ancient and widely extended name. On that very spot probably, fourscore years before, the little Warren, meanly clad and scantily fed, had played with the children of ploughmen. Even then his young mind had revolved plans which might be called romantic. Yet, however romantic, it is not likely that they had been so strange as the truth. Not only had the poor orphan retrieved the fallen fortunes of his line. Not only had he repurchased the old lands, and rebuilt the old dwelling. He had preserved and extended an empire. He had founded a polity. He had administered government and war with more than the capacity of Richelieu. He had patronised learning with the judicious liberality of Cosmo. He had been attacked by the most formidable combination of enemies that ever sought the destruction of a single victim; and over that combination, after a struggle of ten years, he had triumphed. He had at length gone down to his grave in the fulness of age, in peace, after so many troubles, in honour, after so much obloquy.

LORD MACAULAY (1800–59)
Warren Hastings (1841)

VI

In this world (the *Isle of Dreames*)
While we sit by sorrowes streames,
Teares and terrors are our theames
    Reciting:

But when once from hence we flie,
More and more approaching nigh
Unto young Eternitie
    Uniting:

In that *whiter Island*, where
Things are evermore sincere;
Candour here, and lustre there
    Delighting:...

There in calm and cooling sleep
We our eyes shall never steep;
But eternall watch shall keep,
                    Attending

Pleasures, such as shall pursue
Me immortaliz'd, and you;
And fresh joyes, as never too
                    Have ending.
                    ROBERT HERRICK (1591–1674)
                    'The white Island'

VII

Wishful thinking about good things to come is quite admissible if the things are worth having, and more so if wishing turns to hope and hope to expectation. But the fulfilment, if it comes, often brings disappointment with it. The remedy is not to expect too much of life, and then to find that we have had much more out of it than we deserved. Whatever the outcome, we may reflect that, even at its best, this life is but a pale shadow of that to which we can look forward.

24

THE EXAMPLE OF HIS PATIENCE

I

Almighty and everlasting God, who, of thy tender love towards mankind, hast sent thy Son, our Saviour Jesus Christ, to take upon him our flesh, and to suffer death upon the cross, that all mankind should follow the example of his great humility; Mercifully grant, that we may both follow THE EXAMPLE OF HIS PATIENCE, and also be made partakers of his resurrection; through the same Jesus Christ our Lord. Amen.

Collect

II

The Lord said unto Satan, Hast thou considered my servant Job, that there is none like him in the earth, a perfect and an upright man, one that feareth God, and escheweth evil? and still he holdeth fast his integrity, although thou movedst me against him, to destroy him without cause. And Satan answered the Lord, and said, Skin for skin, yea, all that a man hath will he give for his life. But put forth thine hand now, and touch his bone and his flesh, and he will curse thee to thy face. And the Lord said unto Satan, Behold, he is in thine hand; but save his life. So went Satan forth from the presence of the Lord, and smote Job with sore boils from the sole of his foot unto his crown. And he took him a potsherd to scrape himself withal; and he sat down among the ashes. Then said his wife unto him, Doth thou still retain thine integrity? curse God, and die. But he said unto her, Thou speakest as one of the foolish women speaketh. What? shall we receive good at the hand of God, and shall we not receive evil? In all this did not Job sin with his lips.

Job 2 :3

El Espolio   EL GRECO 1541–1614

[*Museo San Vincente, Toledo*]

III

Be patient therefore, brethren, unto the coming of the Lord. Behold, the husbandman waiteth for the precious fruit of the earth, and hath long patience for it, until he receive the early and latter rain. Be ye also patient; stablish your hearts: for the coming of the Lord draweth nigh. . . . Take, my brethren, the prophets, who have spoken in the name of the Lord, for an example of suffering affliction, and of patience. Behold, we count them happy which endure. Ye have heard of the patience of Job, and have seen the end of the Lord; that the Lord is very pitiful, and of tender mercy.

James 5 :7

IV

You have to perform a task which will need your courage, your energy, your patience.

LORD KITCHENER (1850–1916)
*A Message to the soldiers of the British
Expeditionary Force, 1914, to be kept by
each soldier in his active service pay book*
(Sir G. Arthur's *Life of Kitchener*, iii, 27)

V

Amongst other things he ever affirmed that the preaching of the gospel would cost him his life, to the which thing he did most cheerfully arm and prepare himself, . . . Therefore not long after Queen Mary was proclaimed, a pursuivant was sent down into the country for to call him up. . . . He said unto him, 'My friend, you be a welcome messenger to me, and be it known unto you and to the whole world, that I go as willingly to London at this present, being called by my prince to render a reckoning of my doctrine, as ever I was to any place in the world, and I do not doubt, but that God, as he hath made me worthy to preach his word before two excellent princes, so he will able me to witness the same unto the third, either to her comfort, or discomfort eternally. . . .' How patiently he took his imprisonment, and how boldly and willingly he in the end adventured his life in the defence of the glorious gospel of Jesus Christ; because these things be at large described in the book of the martyrs by that most godly, learned, and excellent instrument of God, Master John Foxe, I will not spend the time now to rehearse the same saving one thing, the which I would wish all godly bishops and faithful preachers to note, the which is this: that he being in prison comfortless, and destitute of all worldly help, most of all did rejoice in this, that God had given him grace, to apply his office of preaching, and assisted him without fear or flattery to tell unto the wicked their faults, and admonish them of their wickedness; neither allowing, nor consenting to any thing, that might be prejudicial or hurtful unto the gospel of Christ, although the refusal thereof did cast him in danger of his life. God grant that all those that be in that office may follow his footsteps.

AUGUSTINE BERNHER (*floruit* 1554)
Dedication of certain sermons made by
Master Doctor Latimer (1562)

VI

Love, from its awful throne of patient power
In the wise heart, from the last giddy hour
    Of dead endurance, from the slippery, steep
And narrow verge of crag-like agony, springs
And folds over the world its healing wings.

Gentleness, Virtue, Wisdom, and Endurance,
These are the seals of that most firm assurance
    Which bars the pit over Destruction's strength;
And if, with infirm hand, Eternity,
Mother of many acts and hours, should free
    The serpent that would clasp her with his length;
These are the spells by which to re-assume
An empire o'er the disentangled doom.

To suffer woes which Hope thinks infinite;
To forgive wrongs darker than death or night;
   To defy Power, which seems omnipotent;
To love, and bear; to hope till Hope creates
From its own wreck the thing it contemplates;
   Neither to change, nor falter, nor repent;
This, like thy glory, Titan, is to be
Good, great and joyous, beautiful and free;
This is alone Life, Joy, Empire and Victory.

P. B. SHELLEY (1792–1822)
Prometheus Unbound (1820) (the end)

VII

Patience is a negative virtue, but none the less heroic. It implies being passive rather than active, having something done to you rather than doing something, like the patient in hospital. It implies suffering, of which the overwhelming example is the Passion of Christ. A great philosopher wrote of 'an energy of non-motion'. Patience often requires a great deal of energy, impatience often none at all.

25

HE SAID, IT IS FINISHED

I

After this, Jesus knowing that all things were now accomplished, that the scripture might be fulfilled, saith, I thirst. Now there was set a vessel full of vinegar: and they filled a spunge with vinegar, and put it upon hyssop, and put it to his mouth. When Jesus therefore had received the vinegar, HE SAID, IT IS FINISHED: and he bowed his head, and gave up the ghost.

John 19:28

II

So Saul died, and his three sons, and his armourbearer, and all his men, that same day together. . . . And it came to pass on the morrow, when the Philistines came to strip the slain, that they found Saul and his three sons fallen in mount Gilboa. And they cut off his head, and stripped off his armour, and sent into the land of the Philistines round about, to publish it in the house of their idols, and among the people. And they put his armour in the house of Ashtaroth: and they fastened his body to the wall of Beth-shan. And when the inhabitants of Jabesh-gilead heard of that which the Philistines had done to Saul; all the valiant men arose, and went all night, and took the body of Saul and the bodies of his sons from the wall of Beth-shan, and came to Jabesh, and burnt them there. And they took their bones, and buried them under a tree at Jabesh, and fasted seven days.

1 Samuel 31:6

III

Stephen before the religious authorities in Jerusalem
When they heard these things, they were cut to the heart, and they

117

gnashed on him with their teeth. But he, being full of the Holy Ghost, looked up steadfastly into heaven, and saw the glory of God. . . . Then they cried out with a loud voice, and stopped their ears, and ran upon him with one accord, and cast him out of the city, and stoned him: and the witnesses laid down their clothes at a young man's feet, whose name was Saul. And they stoned Stephen, calling upon God, and saying, Lord Jesus, receive my spirit. And he kneeled down, and cried with a loud voice, Lord, lay not this sin to their charge. And when he had said this, he fell asleep.

Acts 7 :54

IV

The righteous man will be scourged, racked, imprisoned, and have his eyes burnt out, and finally, having suffered every ill, he will be crucified.

PLATO (*c.* 429–347 B.C.)
Republic (388 B.C.), II, 361 E

V

The Cross has always been a symbol of conflict, and a principle of selection, among men. The Faith tells us that it is by the willed attraction or repulsion exercised upon souls by the Cross that the sorting of the good seed from the bad, the separation of the chosen elements from the unutilisable ones, is accomplished at the heart of mankind. Wherever the Cross appears, unrest and antagonisms are inevitable. But there is no reason why these conflicts should be needlessly exacerbated by preaching the doctrine of Christ crucified in a discordant or provocative manner. Far too often the Cross is presented for our adoration, not so much as a sublime end to be attained by our transcending ourselves, but as a symbol of sadness, of limitation and repression.

This way of preaching the Passion is, in many cases, merely the result of the clumsy use of pious vocabulary in which the most solemn words (sacrifice, immolation, expiation), emptied of their meaning by routine, are used, quite unconsciously, in a light and

Christ on the Cross   PETER PAUL RUBENS 1577–1640

[*Wallace Collection, London*]

frivolous way. They become formulas to be juggled with. But this manner of speech ends by conveying the impression that the kingdom of God can only be established in mourning, and by thwarting and going against the current of man's aspirations and energies. In spite of the verbal fidelity displayed by the use of this kind of language, a picture is presented that is utterly unchristian. . . .

In its highest and most general sense, the doctrine of the Cross is that to which all men adhere who believe that the vast movement and agitation of human life opens on to a road which leads somewhere, and that that road *climbs upward*. Life has a term: therefore it imposes a particular direction, orientated, in fact, towards the highest possible spiritualisation by means of the greatest possible effort. To admit that group of fundamental principles is already to range oneself among the disciples—distant, perhaps, and implicit, but nevertheless real—of Christ crucified.

PIERRE TEILHARD DE CHARDIN (1881–1955)
Le Milieu Divin (1957), 'The Meaning of the Cross'

VI

PILATE MUSES

In another and far more splendid Upper Room, on the first Good Friday night, Pilate, having sent for the Centurion, is seated alone, musing thus:

'A King upon a cross—the jest was shrewd.
Quod scripsi, scripsi—ah! I had them there:
They'll learn the stuff Rome's made of! Yet, I vow
The Teacher stood in triumph, of a truth.
Triumph of Truth? Those were his very words.
I pass'd them off and wash'd my hands of him.
Yet crosses are outrageous instruments:
No cultur'd man could ever handle them
Without disgust, disdain, and deep despair
That men can be so cruel and so crude;
Civilisation should abolish them.
They taint the air, these vermin on a cross!

No gentleman, until the world runs down,
Will ever sleep where crosses cast their shade.'

(*The Centurion knocks and enters*)

'Centurion, good evening! Your report?
I sent for you to learn from your own lips
Your recent duty, how it was despatched.
There is a Jew—a well-considered man—
Waiting my pleasure whether he may take
The body on his followers' behalf
And give it private burial—no fuss,
Nothing demonstrative, to cause a clash.
But is he dead already?'

'Aye, he's dead,
Your Excellency, Aye, my God, he's dead.'

P. B. CLAYTON (1885–1972)
To Conquer Hate (1963)

VII

We must never forget that ours is a religion of the Cross, distinguished by an acceptance of defeat which ever turns to glory and by victory which never stoops to conquest. The truth is that victory and defeat as we ordinarily think of them have no place in Christian religion. Its victories are unmistakable, and its defeats indistinguishable from victory.

26

GOD, WHO THROUGH JESUS CHRIST HAST OVERCOME DEATH

Prelude

Most glorious Lord of lyfe that on this day
  Didst make thy triumph over death and sin:
  and having harrowd hell didst bring away,
  captivity thence captive, us to win.
This ioyous day, deare Lord, with ioy begin,
  and grant that we for whom thou diddest dye,
  being with thy deare blood clene washt from sin,
  may live for ever in felicity.
And that thy love we weighing worthily,
  may likewise love thee for the same againe:
  and for thy sake that all lyke deare didst buy,
  with love may one another entertayne.
So let us love, deare love, lyke as we ought,
  love is the lesson which the Lord us taught.

EDMUND SPENSER (1552?-99)
Amoretti (1595), Sonnet 68

I

Almighty GOD, WHO THROUGH thine only-begotten Son JESUS CHRIST HAST OVERCOME DEATH, and opened unto us the gate of everlasting life; We humbly beseech thee, that, as by thy special grace preventing us thou dost put into our minds good desires, so by thy continual help we may bring the same to good effect; through Jesus Christ our Lord, who liveth and reigneth with thee and the Holy Ghost, ever one God, world without end. Amen.

Collect

The Resurrection   FRA ANGELICO 1387?–1455

[*Museo di S. Marco, Florence : Mansell*]

II

For God created man to be immortal, and made him to be an image of his own eternity. Nevertheless through envy of the devil came death into the world: and they that do hold of his side do find it. But the souls of the righteous are in the hand of God, and there shall no torment touch them. In the sight of the unwise they seemed to die: and their departure is taken for misery, and their going from us to be utter destruction: but they are in peace. For though they be punished in the sight of men, yet is their hope full of immortality. And having been a little chastened, they shall be greatly rewarded: for God proved them, and found them worthy of himself.

Wisdom 2 :23

III

Be not thou . . . ashamed of the testimony of our Lord, nor of me his prisoner: but be thou partaker of the afflictions of the gospel according to the power of God; who hath saved us, and called us with an holy calling, not according to our works, but according to his own purpose and grace, which was given us in Christ Jesus before the world began, but is now made manifest by the appearing of our Saviour Jesus Christ, who hath abolished death, and hath brought life and immortality to light through the gospel.

2 Timothy 1 :8

IV

Why fear death? It is the most beautiful adventure in life.

CHARLES FROHMAN (1860–1915)
His last words before going down in the
Lusitania (7 May 1915)

V

A good and simple, yet somewhat dry and conventional Roman Catholic priest, a worker for many years among souls, told me one

124

day, in a South of England town, of the sudden revelation of heights and depths of holiness that had just enveloped and enlarged his head and heart. He had been called, a few nights before, to a small pot-house in the outskirts of this largely fashionable town. And there, in a dreary little garret, lay, stricken down with sudden double pneumonia, an Irish young woman, twenty-eight years of age, doomed to die within an hour or two. A large fringe covered her forehead, and all the other externals were those of an average barmaid who had, at a public bar, served half-tipsy, coarsely-joking men, for some ten years or more. And she was still full of physical energy—of the physical craving for physical existence. Yet, as soon as she began to pour out her last and general confession, my informant felt, so he told me, a lively impulse to arise and to cast himself on the ground before her. For there, in her intention, lay one of the simple, strong, sweet saints of God at his feet. She told how deeply she desired to become as pure as possible for this grand grace, this glorious privilege, so full of peace, of now abandoning her still young, vividly pulsing life, of placing it utterly within the hands of the God, of the Christ whom she loved so much, and who loved her so much more; that this great gift, she humbly felt, would bring the grace of its full acceptance with it, and might help her to aid, with God and Christ, the souls she loved so truly, the souls He loved so far more deeply than ever she herself could love them. And she died soon after in a perfect rapture of joy—in a joy overflowing, utterly sweetening all the mighty bitter floods of her pain. Now *that* is Supernatural.

BARON FRIEDRICH VON HÜGEL (1852–1925)
Essays & Addresses on the Philosophy
of Religion, I (1921), 223

VI

Fear death?—to feel the fog in my throat,
    The mist in my face,
When the snows begin, and the blasts denote
    I am nearing the place,
The power of the night, the press of the storm,

The post of the foe;
Where he stands, the Arch Fear in a visible form,
    Yet the strong man must go:
For the journey is done and the summit attained,
    And the barriers fall,
Though a battle's to fight ere the guerdon be gained,
    The reward of it all.
I was ever a fighter, so—one fight more,
    The best and the last!
I would hate that death bandaged my eyes and forbore,
    And bade me creep past.
No! let me taste the whole of it, fare like my peers
    The heroes of old,
Bear the brunt, in a minute pay glad life's arrears
    Of pain, darkness and cold.
For sudden the worst turns the best to the brave,
    The black minute's at end,
And the elements' rage, the fiend-voices that rave,
    Shall dwindle, shall blend,
Shall change, shall become first a peace out of pain,
    Then a light, then thy breast,
O thou soul of my soul! I shall clasp thee again,
    And with God be the rest!

ROBERT BROWNING (1812–89)
Prospice

VII

The word that went round among the Apostles on the first Easter
morning was: 'The Lord is risen indeed and hath appeared to
Simon [Peter]' (Luke 24:34). They did not trouble themselves
about the empty tomb or how the Resurrection happened. But
seven weeks later Peter, addressing a great gathering, said: 'It was
not possible that he should be holden of death' (Acts 2:24). The
power of resurrection in nature and in human history is irresis-
tible. The tree *will* put on its leaves. Man *will* be free. And Jesus
Christ *must* rise from the dead.

27

THE FIRST DAY OF THE WEEK

I

The same day at evening, being THE FIRST DAY OF THE WEEK, when the doors were shut where the disciples were assembled for fear of the Jews, came Jesus and stood in the midst, and saith unto them, Peace be unto you.

John 20 :19

II

In the beginning God created the heaven and the earth. And the earth was without form, and void; and darkness was upon the face of the deep. And the Spirit of God moved upon the face of the waters. And God said, Let there be light: and there was light. And God saw the light, that it was good: and God divided the light from the darkness. And God called the light Day, and the darkness he called Night. And the evening and the morning were the first day.

Genesis 1 :1

III

I John, who also am your brother, and companion in tribulation, and in the kingdom and patience of Jesus Christ, was in the isle that is called Patmos, for the word of God, and for the testimony of Jesus Christ. I was in the Spirit on the Lord's day, and heard behind me a great voice, as of a trumpet, saying, I am Alpha and Omega, the first and the last: and, What thou seest, write in a book, and send it unto the seven churches which are in Asia; unto Ephesus, and unto Smyrna, and unto Pergamos, and unto Thyatira, and unto Sardis, and unto Philadelphia, and unto Laodicea.

And I turned to see the voice that spake with me. And being turned, I saw seven golden candlesticks; and in the midst of the seven candlesticks one like unto the Son of man, clothed with a garment down to the foot, and girt about the paps with a golden girdle. His head and his hairs were white like wool, as white as snow; and his eyes were as a flame of fire; and his feet like unto fine brass, as if they burned in a furnace; and his voice as the sound of many waters. And he had in his right hand seven stars: and out of his mouth went a sharp twoedged sword: and his countenance was as the sun shineth in his strength. And when I saw him, I fell at his feet as dead. And he laid his right hand upon me, saying unto me, Fear not; I am the first and the last; I am he that liveth, and was dead; and behold, I am alive for evermore, Amen; and have the keys of hell and of death.

Revelation 1 :9

IV

The Lord's Day is, and is not, the Sabbath, much as John the Baptist was, and was not, Elijah.

N. J. D. WHITE (1860–1936)
Hastings' Dictionary of the Bible (1900)
under 'Lord's Day'

V

The Vicar's first Sunday in a new Living. He has recently suffered financial reverses

When Sunday came, it was indeed a day of finery, which all my sumptuary edicts could not restrain. . . . The first Sunday in particular their behaviour served to mortify me: I had desired my girls the preceding night to be drest early the next day; for I always loved to be at church a good while before the rest of the congregation. They punctually obeyed my directions; but when we were to assemble in the morning at breakfast, down came my wife and daughters, drest out in all their former splendour: their hair plasterred up with pomatum, their faces patch'd to taste, their trains bundled up into an heap behind, and rustling at every

Coming from Evening Church   SAMUEL PALMER 1805–81

motion. I could not help smiling at their vanity, particularly that of my wife, from whom I expected more discretion. In this exigence, therefore, my only resource was to order my son, with an important air, to call our coach. The girls were amazed at the command; but I repeated it with more solemnity than before.— 'Surely, my dear; you jest,' cried my wife, 'we can walk it perfectly well: we want no coach to carry us now.' 'You mistake, child,' returned I, 'we do want a coach; for if we walk to church in this trim, the very children in the parish will hoot after us for a show.' 'Indeed,' replied my wife, 'I always imagined that my Charles was fond of seeing his children neat and handsome about him.' 'You may be as neat as you please,' interrupted I, 'and I shall love you the better for it; but all this is not neatness, but frippery. These rufflings, and pinkings, and patchings, will only make us hated by all the wives of all our neighbours. No, my children,' continued I, more gravely, 'those gowns may be altered into something of a plainer cut. . . . I don't know whether such flouncing and shredding is becoming even in the rich, if we consider, upon a moderate calculation, that the nakedness of the indigent world may be cloathed from the trimmings of the vain.'

This remonstrance had the proper effect; they went with great composure, that very instant, to change their dress; and the next day I had the satisfaction of finding my daughters, at their own request, employed in cutting up their trains into Sunday waistcoats for Dick and Bill, the two little ones; and, what was still more satisfactory, the gowns seemed improved by being thus curtailed.

OLIVER GOLDSMITH (1728–74)
The Vicar of Wakefield (1766), I, ch. 4

VI

Mysterious night, when the first man but knew
Thee by report, unseen, and heard thy name,
Did he not tremble for this lovely frame,
This glorious canopy of light and blue?
Yet 'neath a curtain of translucent dew

Bathed in the rays of the great setting flame,
Hesperus, with the host of heaven, came,
And lo! creation widened on his view!
   Who could have thought what darkness lay concealed
Within thy beams, oh Sun? Or who could find,
    Whilst fly, and leaf, and insect stood revealed,
That to such endless orbs thou mad'st us blind?
Weak man! Why to shun death, this anxious strife?
If *light* can thus deceive, wherefore not *life*?

JOSEPH BLANCO WHITE (1775–1841)
'Night and Death' in *The Bijou* (1828)

VII

Sunday has become a problem for the Christian. It may be best to start by simply regarding it as 'a day off', and then seeing how the conflicting claims of rest, recreation, week-ending and worship can best be reconciled. It is not an occasion for being dogmatically sabbatarian. It is a situation where each of us must consult his conscience and exercise his common sense. Perhaps the basic consideration is the very old one that we must earn our day off by labouring and doing all that we have to do on the working days. We may then find worship what it should be, a spiritual recreation.

28

THE SHEPHERD AND BISHOP OF YOUR SOULS

I

Ye were as sheep going astray; but are now returned unto THE
SHEPHERD AND BISHOP OF YOUR SOULS.

1 Peter 2:25

II

Thus saith the Lord God; Behold I, even I, will both search my
sheep, and seek them out. As a shepherd seeketh out his flock in
the day that he is among his sheep that are scattered; so will I seek
out my sheep, and will deliver them out of all places where they
have been scattered in the cloudy and dark day. And I will bring
them out from the people, and gather them from the countries,
and will bring them to their own land, and feed them upon the
mountains of Israel by the rivers, and in all the inhabited places
of the country. I will feed them in a good pasture, and upon the
high mountains of Israel shall their fold be: there shall they lie in a
good fold, and in a fat pasture shall they feed upon the mountains
of Israel. I will feed my flock, and I will cause them to lie down,
saith the Lord God. I will seek that which was lost, and bring
again that which was driven away, and will bind up that which was
broken, and will strengthen that which was sick.

Ezekiel 34:11

III

The Pharisees and scribes murmured, saying, This man receiveth
sinners, and eateth with them. And he spake this parable unto
them, saying, What man of you, having an hundred sheep, if he
lose one of them, doth not leave the ninety and nine in the wilder-

Il buon Pastore

[A mid 5th century mosaic, Mausoleum of Galla Placidia, Ravenna : Mansell]

ness, and go after that which is lost, until he find it? And when he
hath found it, he layeth it on his shoulders, rejoicing. And when he
cometh home, he calleth together his friends and neighbours, saying unto them, Rejoice with me; for I have found my sheep which
was lost. I say unto you, that likewise joy shall be in heaven over
one sinner that repenteth, more than over ninety and nine just
persons, which need no repentance.

Luke 15 :2

*It seems rather unfair on 'the ninety and nine just persons, which need
no repentance', but in fact there are no such persons.*

IV

I cannot ope mine eyes,
But thou art ready there to catch
My morning-soul and sacrifice: . . .

GEORGE HERBERT (1593–1633)
'Mattens' (1633)

V

The bishop's works must surpass other men's works as much as
the shepherd's life is superior to that of the flock. It behoves him to
think and carefully consider how very necessary it is for him to be
bound to righteousness with the rope of understanding through
whose dignity the people is called flock; it befits the shepherd to be
lofty in works, profitable in words, and discreet in silence; he
must grieve for the troubles of others as if he suffered equally with
them; he must care and provide for all; through humility he must
be the equal of all well-doers; he must be stern with sinners, and
through righteousness he must feel indignation at their ill deeds;
and yet in his care of them he is not to neglect the obedient; nor
also in his love of the latter is he to neglect the disobedient.

POPE GREGORY THE GREAT (540–604)
Regula Pastoralis (*c*. 590, trans. into
Anglo-Saxon by King Alfred, *c*. 890, and
thence into English by Henry Sweet, 1871)

VI

I be the Shepherd o' the farm:
    An' be so proud a-roven round
Wi' my long crook a-thirt my yarm,
    As ef I wer a king a-crown'd.

An' I da bide al day among
    The bleäten sheep, an' pitch ther vuold;
An' when the evemen shiades be long
    Da zee 'em al a-penn'd an' tuold.

An' I da zee the frisken lam's,
    Wi' swingen tails and woolly lags,
A-playen roun' ther veeden dams,
    An' pullen o' ther milky bags.

An' I, bezide a hawtharn tree,
    Da zit upon the zunny down,
While shiades o' zummer clouds da vlee
    Wi' silent flight along the groun'.

An' there, among the many cries
    O' sheep an' lam's, my dog da pass
A zultry hour wi' blinken eyes,
    An' nose a-stratch'd upon the grass.

But in a twinklen, at my word,
    The shaggy rogue is up an' gone
Out roun' the sheep lik' any bird,
    To do what he's a-zent upon. . . .

An' I da goo to washen pool,
    A-sousen auver head an' ears
The shaggy sheep, to cleän ther wool,
    An' miake 'em ready var the sheärs.

An' when the shearen time da come,
    I be at barn vrom dawn till dark,
Wher zome da catch the sheep, and zome
    Da mark ther zides wi' miaster's mark.

An' when the shearen's al a-done,
　　Then we da eat, an' drink, an' zing
In miaster's kitchen, till the tun[1]
　　Wi' merry sounds da shiake an' ring.

I be the Shepherd o' the farm:
　　An' be so proud a-roven round
Wi' my long crook a–thirt my yarm,
　　As ef I wer a king a-crown'd.

WILLIAM BARNES (1801–86)
Poems of Rural Life (1844)

VII

We are glad to claim the Lord as our shepherd, but in so doing we must accept that 'his sheep' is an image of ourselves. There are certainly some pleasing traits in our image of sheep, but we should not forget the other side of the picture. To be called 'sheepish' is scant praise. The sheep is generally a follower of others, it panics easily, it will rush about aimlessly and needs to be rounded up. Do we and should we have these characteristics?

[1] chimney pot.

29

YOUR JOY NO MAN TAKETH FROM YOU

I

Ye shall weep and lament, but the world shall rejoice: and ye shall be sorrowful, but your sorrow shall be turned into joy. A woman when she is in travail hath sorrow, because her hour is come: but as soon as she is delivered of the child, she remembereth no more the anguish, for joy that a man is born into the world. And ye now therefore have sorrow: but I will see you again, and your heart shall rejoice, and YOUR JOY NO MAN TAKETH FROM YOU.

John 16:20

II

I will magnify thee, O Lord, for thou hast set me up: and not made my foes to triumph over me. O Lord my God, I cried unto thee: and thou hast healed me. Thou, Lord, hast brought my soul out of hell: thou hast kept my life from them that go down to the pit. Sing praises unto the Lord, O ye saints of his: and give thanks unto him for a remembrance of his holiness. For his wrath endureth but the twinkling of an eye, and in his pleasure is life: heaviness may endure for a night, but joy cometh in the morning. And in my prosperity I said, I shall never be removed: thou, Lord, of thy goodness hast made my hill so strong. Thou didst turn thy face from me: and I was troubled. Then cried I unto thee, O Lord: and gat me to my Lord right humbly. What profit is there in my blood: when I go down to the pit? Shall the dust give thanks unto thee: or shall it declare thy truth? Hear, O Lord, and have mercy upon me: Lord, be thou my helper. Thou hast turned my heaviness into joy: thou hast put off my sackcloth, and girded me with gladness. Therefore shall every good man sing of thy praise without ceasing: O my God, I will give thanks unto thee for ever.

Psalm 30:1

This is a Psalm of vicissitude, but joy is victor in the end.

III

Blessed be the God and Father of our Lord Jesus Christ, which according to his abundant mercy hath begotten us again unto a lively hope by the resurrection of Jesus Christ from the dead, to an inheritance incorruptible, and undefiled, and that fadeth not away, reserved in heaven for you, who are kept by the power of God through faith unto salvation ready to be revealed in the last time. Wherein ye greatly rejoice, though now for a season, if need be, ye are in heaviness through manifold temptations; that the trial of your faith, being much more precious than of gold that perisheth, though it be tried with fire, might be found unto praise and honour and glory at the appearing of Jesus Christ: whom having not seen, ye love; in whom, though now ye see him not, yet believing, ye rejoice with joy unspeakable and full of glory.

1 Peter 1:3

IV

> Joy & Woe are woven fine,
> A Clothing for the soul divine.
> Under every grief & pine
> Runs a joy with silken twine.

WILLIAM BLAKE (1757–1827)
Auguries of Innocence (1803)

V

And at last his eyes seemed to open to some new ways. He found that he could look back upon the brass and bombast of his earlier gospels and see them truly. He was gleeful when he discovered that he now despised them.

He was emerged from his struggles, with a large sympathy for

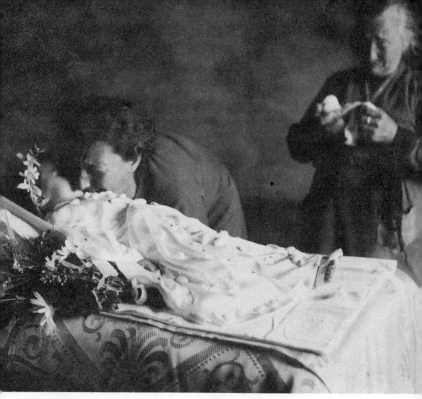

In the Abruzzi   FRANK MONACO 1917–

the machinery of the universe. With his new eyes, he could see that the secret and open blows which were being dealt about the world with such heavenly lavishness were in truth blessings. It was a deity laying about him with the bludgeon of correction.

His loud mouth against these things had been lost as the storm ceased. He would no more stand upon places high and false, and denounce the distant planets. He beheld that he was tiny but not inconsequent to the sun. In the space-wide whirl of events no grain like him would be lost.

With this conviction came a store of assurance. He felt a quiet manhood, nonassertive but of sturdy and strong blood. He knew that he would no more quail before his guides wherever they should point. He had been to touch the great death, and found that, after all, it was but the great death and was for others. He was a man.

So it came to pass that as he trudged from the place of blood and wrath his soul changed. He came from hot plowshares to prospects of clover tranquilly, and it was as if hot plowshares were not. Scars faded as flowers.

It rained. The procession of weary soldiers became a bedraggled train, despondent and muttering, marching with churning effort in a trough of liquid brown mud under a low, wretched sky. Yet the youth smiled, for he saw that the world was a world for him, though many discovered it to be made of oaths and walking sticks. He had rid himself of the red sickness of battle. The sultry nightmare was in the past. He had been an animal blistered and sweating in the heat and pain of war. He turned now with a lover's thirst to images of tranquil skies, fresh meadows, cool brooks—an existence of soft and eternal peace.

Over the river a golden ray of sun came through the hosts of leaden rain clouds.

STEPHEN CRANE (1871–1900)
The Red Badge of Courage (1895), The Conclusion

VI

> When in disgrace with Fortune and men's eyes,
> I all alone beweep my outcast state,

And trouble deaf heaven with my bootless cries,
And look upon myself, and curse my fate,
Wishing me like to one more rich in hope,
Featur'd like him, like him with friends possess'd,
Desiring this man's art, and that man's scope,
With what I most enjoy contented least;
Yet in these thoughts myself almost despising,
Haply I think on thee, and then my state,
Like to the lark at break of day arising
From sullen earth, sings hymns at heaven's gate;
For thy sweet love rememb'red such wealth brings
That then I scorn to change my state with kings.

WILLIAM SHAKESPEARE (1564-1616)
Sonnet xxix (1609)

VII

The following thought takes us through and beyond the joy of the Resurrection:
This lasting joy which no power on earth can take from the disciples is not confined to the passing appearances. The risen Christ is the object of the joy, the appearances mark the beginning of it. What guarantees its perpetual continuance is the actual possession of the glorified Christ through the agency of the Spirit, to which will be added the direct vision in the eternal Kingdom.

ALFRED LOISY (1859-1940)
Le Quatrième Evangile (1903)

30

THE SUNDRY AND MANIFOLD
CHANGES OF THE WORLD

I

O Almighty God, who alone canst order the unruly wills and affections of sinful men; Grant unto thy people, that they may love the thing which thou commandest, and desire that which thou dost promise; that so, among THE SUNDRY AND MANIFOLD CHANGES OF THE WORLD, our hearts may surely there be fixed, where true joys are to be found; through Jesus Christ our Lord. Amen.

Collect

II

To every thing there is a season, and a time to every purpose under the heaven: a time to be born, and a time to die; a time to plant, and a time to pluck up that which is planted; a time to kill, and a time to heal; a time to break down, and a time to build up; a time to weep, and a time to laugh; a time to mourn, and a time to dance; a time to cast away stones, and a time to gather stones together; a time to embrace, and a time to refrain from embracing; a time to get, and a time to lose; a time to keep, and a time to cast away; a time to rend, and a time to sew; a time to keep silence, and a time to speak; a time to love, and a time to hate; a time of war, and a time of peace.

Ecclesiastes 3:1

III

Of the Jews five times received I forty stripes save one. Thrice was I beaten with rods, once was I stoned, thrice I suffered shipwreck, a night and a day I have been in the deep; in journeyings

142

The Raft of the Medusa

THÉODORE GÉRICAULT 1791–1824

[Musée du Louvre, Paris]

often, in perils of waters, in perils of robbers, in perils by mine own countrymen, in perils by the heathen, in perils in the city, in perils in the wilderness, in perils in the sea, in perils among false brethren; in weariness and painfulness, in watchings often, in hunger and thirst, in fastings often, in cold and nakedness. . . . In Damascus the governor under Aretas the king kept the city of the Damascenes with a garrison, desirous to apprehend me: and through a window in a basket was I let down by the wall, and escaped his hands.

2 Corinthians 11 :24

IV

I N. take thee N. . . . to have and to hold from this day forward, for better for worse, for richer for poorer, in sickness and in health, to love and to cherish, till death us do part.

Book of Common Prayer:
'Solemnization of Matrimony' (1662)

V

For, indeed, a change was coming upon the world, the meaning and direction of which even still is hidden from us, the change from era to era. The paths trodden by the footsteps of ages were broken up; old things were passing away, and the faith and the life of ten centuries were dissolving like a dream. Chivalry was dying; the abbey and the castle were soon together to crumble into ruins; and all the forms, desires, beliefs, convictions of the old world were passing away, never to return. A new continent had risen up beyond the western sea. The floor of heaven, inlaid with stars, had sunk back into an infinite abyss of immeasurable space: and the firm earth itself, unfixed from its foundations, was seen to be but a small atom in the awful vastness of the universe. In the fabric of habit in which they had so laboriously built for themselves, mankind were to remain no longer. And now it is all gone— like an unsubstantial pageant faded; and between us and the old English there lies a gulf of mystery which the prose of the historian will never adequately bridge. They cannot come to us, and our imagination can but feebly penetrate to them.

J. A. FROUDE (1818–94)
The History of England (1856), Ch. 1

VI

Felix Randal the farrier, O he is dead then? my duty all ended,
Who have watched his mould of man, big-boned and hardy-handsome
Pining, pining, till time when reason rambled in it and some
Fatal four disorders, fleshed there, all contended?

Sickness broke him. Impatient he cursed at first, but mended
Being anointed and all; though a heavenlier heart began some
Months earlier, since I had our sweet reprieve and ransom
Tendered to him. Ah well, God rest him all road ever he offended!

This seeing the sick endears them to us, us too it endears.
My tongue had taught thee comfort, touch had quenched thy tears,
Thy tears that touched my heart, child, Felix, poor Felix Randal;

How far from then forethought of, all thy more boisterous years,
When thou at the random grim forge, powerful amidst peers,
Didst fettle for the great grey drayhorse his bright and battering sandal!

GERARD MANLEY HOPKINS (1844–89)
'Felix Randal'

VII

It is a commonplace that life has its ups and downs, and it is good that this should be so, for from it springs the humour, the eager love, the stubbornness even, which makes us glad to be alive. Life is no dead-calm sea; we love it for its waves, and the rough conditions of setback or suffering have their aftermath and their reward.

31

THY MERCIFUL GUIDING

I

O Lord, from whom all good things do come; Grant to us thy humble servants, that by thy holy inspiration we may think those things that be good, and by THY MERCIFUL GUIDING may perform the same; through our Lord Jesus Christ. Amen.

Collect

II

And Joseph said unto his brethren, I am Joseph; doth my father yet live? And his brethren could not answer him; for they were troubled at his presence. And Joseph said unto his brethren, Come near to me, I pray you. And they came near. And he said, I am Joseph your brother, whom ye sold into Egypt. Now therefore be not grieved, nor angry with yourselves, that ye sold me hither: for God did send me before you to preserve life. For these two years hath the famine been in the land: and yet there are five years, in the which there shall neither be earing nor harvest. And God sent me before you to preserve you a posterity in the earth, and to save your lives by a great deliverance. So now it was not you that sent me hither, but God: and he hath made me a father to Pharaoh, and lord of all his house, and a ruler throughout all the land of Egypt. Haste ye, and go up to my father, and say unto him, Thus saith thy son Joseph, God hath made me lord of all Egypt: come down unto me, tarry not.

Genesis 45:3

III

After the shipwreck

The centurion, willing to save Paul, . . . commanded that they which could swim should cast themselves first into the sea, and

146

St Matthew and the Angel   MICHELANGELO MERISI
DA CARAVAGGIO 1569–1609

[*San Luigi dei Francesi, Rome : Mansell*]

get to land: and the rest, some on boards, and some on broken pieces of the ship. And so it came to pass, that they escaped all safe to land. And when they were escaped, then they knew that the island was called Melita [Malta]. And the barbarous people shewed us no little kindness: for they kindled a fire, and received us every one, because of the present rain, and because of the cold. And when Paul had gathered a bundle of sticks, and laid them on the fire, there came a viper out of the heat, and fastened on his hand. And when the barbarians saw the venomous beast hang on his hand, they said among themselves, No doubt this man is a murderer, whom, though he hath escaped the sea, yet vengeance suffereth not to live. And he shook off the beast into the fire, and felt no harm. Howbeit they looked when he should have swollen, or fallen down dead suddenly: but after they had looked a great while, and saw no harm come to him, they changed their minds, and said that he was a god.

Acts 27 :43

IV

When in the slipp'ry Paths of Youth
　　With heedless Steps I ran,
Thine Arm unseen convey'd me safe,
　　And led me up to Man.

JOSEPH ADDISON (1672–1719)
The Spectator, No. CCCCLIII (9 August 1712)

V

It is a commonplace of religious experience that when a Christian looks back over his own individual life—his secular career as well as his spiritual development—it becomes apparent to him that there has been a mysterious pattern running through it all, and that, not by his own initiative, and not always by his own volition, his life has been brought into conformity with that pattern by the hand of God. No hypothesis but that of an overruling Providence is sufficient to account for what has happened. Character is shaped by destiny as truly as destiny is shaped by character: and as the Christian reviews in retrospect the events by which his progress

148

has been determined and controlled, the opportunities that have been granted to him, and all the other blessings of this life, he cannot fail to recognise, not with complacency or spiritual pride, but rather with humility and penitence and thankfulness and trust, the hand of God patiently moulding him in accordance with His eternal purpose for that one individual soul. A man can see this most clearly in his own life, for obvious reasons: but it is often strikingly apparent to him in the lives of others, as if all the resources of the omniscience and loving providence of God had been concentrated upon this single object, of fashioning that one soul precisely for the specific end for which it was created, and of making that particular individual all that God intended him to be. The evidence for this doctrine of particular Providence in human lives is far too strong to be neglected or ignored.

CHARLES SMYTH (1903–   )
Cyril Forster Garbett (1959), Ch. 17

VI

Does the road wind up-hill all the way?
   Yes, to the very end.
Will the day's journey take the whole long day?
   From morn to night, my friend.

But is there for the night a resting-place?
   A roof for when the slow dark hours begin.
May not the darkness hide it from my face?
   You cannot miss that inn.

Shall I meet other wayfarers at night?
   Those who have gone before.
Then must I knock, or call when just in sight?
   They will not keep you standing at that door.

Shall I find comfort, travel-sore and weak?
   Of labour you shall find the sum.
Will there be beds for me and all who seek?
   Yea, beds for all who come.

CHRISTINA ROSSETTI (1830–94)
'Up-Hill'

VII

We often feel we are deciding for ourselves. A man may think the most important decision he ever made was in the choice of a wife. Yet in many cases, long before he seemed to decide, circumstances (including his own temperament) had made the choice inevitable. Again, a man may apply for a job, but fail to get it. Years after, he may see that his failure was most fortunate. Perhaps, if we had sufficient faith and patience, we should more often wait for God to make the decisions. The Gospel seems to say so.

32

HE WAS RECEIVED UP

I

So then after the Lord had spoken unto them [the Eleven], HE WAS RECEIVED UP into heaven, and sat on the right hand of God. And they went forth, and preached every where, the Lord working with them, and confirming the word with signs following. Amen.

Mark 16:19

II

Moses went up from the plains of Moab unto the mountain of Nebo, to the top of Pisgah, that is over against Jericho. And the Lord shewed him all the land of Gilead, unto Dan, and all Naphtali, and the land of Ephraim, and Manasseh, and all the land of Judah, unto the utmost sea, and the south, and the plain of the valley of Jericho, the city of palm trees, unto Zoar. And the Lord said unto him, This is the land which I sware unto Abraham, unto Isaac, and unto Jacob, saying, I will give it unto thy seed: I have caused thee to see it with thine eyes, but thou shalt not go over thither. So Moses the servant of the Lord died there in the land of Moab, according to the word of the Lord. And he buried him in a valley in the land of Moab, over against Beth-peor: but no man knoweth of his sepulchre unto this day.

Deuteronomy 34:1

III

The majestic ending of the Gospel
Then the eleven disciples went away into Galilee, into a mountain where Jesus had appointed them. And when they saw him, they

worshipped him: but some doubted. And Jesus came and spake unto them, saying, All power is given unto me in heaven and in earth. Go ye therefore, and teach all nations, baptizing them in the name of the Father, and of the Son, and of the Holy Ghost: teaching them to observe all things whatsoever I have commanded you: and, lo, I am with you alway, even unto the end of the world. Amen.

Matthew 28 :16

IV

He that descended, He it is that also ascended above all heavens, that He might fill all things (Eph. 4:10)

From its depths to its heights He has compassed the universe. He has left nothing unvisited by His presence.

ARMITAGE ROBINSON (1858–1933)
St Paul's Epistle to the Ephesians (1903), p. 96

V

Oedipus is blind

God called him over and over again: Oedipus, Oedipus, why do we hesitate to go? Too long you make delay. And when he perceived that he was being called of God, he asked that Theseus, the king of the land, should come to him. And when he came he said, Pledge the faith of your right hand to my children;—and, children, pledge yours to him:—and promise never of free will to desert them, but wish them well, and do what seems best for them. And he, like the noble man he was, promised with an oath and with no reservation to do it.

And on that Oedipus, feeling with dim hands for his daughters, said: My children, you must be of good courage and leave this place, and claim neither to see what it is not right to see, nor to hear speech which it is not right to hear. But go as quickly as may be; let only lord Theseus stay and learn what befalls me. So he spoke, and we all heard and followed the maidens in floods of tears. But looking back shortly after, we saw that he was no longer there;

The Ascension   [*A 13th century window, Jerusalem Chamber, Westminster Abbey Crown copyright*]

but the prince himself we saw holding his hand to his face to shade his eyes as though from some dread, intolerable sight. Then after no long interval we saw him make obeisance to the Earth and to Olympus, the abode of the gods, in one united act of prayer.

But how Oedipus met his doom no mortal man could tell save Theseus. It was no flashing thunderbolt of God that made an end of him in that hour, nor sudden storm stirred up at sea; but some escort sent from the gods, or kindly pit gaping in the nether world, took him away. Without a sigh, without a pang, he passed hence painlessly, and in heroic fashion, if ever man did.

SOPHOCLES (495–406 B.C.)
Oedipus Coloneus, 1626–1665

VI

My Soul, there is a Countrie
    Far beyond the stars,
Where stands a winged Centrie
    All skilfull in the wars,
There above noise, and danger
    Sweet peace sits crown'd with smiles,
And one born in a Manger
    Commands the Beauteous files,
He is thy gracious friend,
    And (O my Soul awake!)
Did in pure love descend
    To die here for thy sake,
If thou canst get but thither,
    There growes the flowre of peace,
The Rose that cannot wither,
    Thy fortresse, and thy ease;
Leave then thy foolish ranges;
    For none can thee secure,
But one, who never changes,
    Thy God, thy life, thy Cure.

HENRY VAUGHAN (1622–95)
'Peace', in *Silex Scintillans* (1650)

VII

At first the Apostles only knew that their Lord had left them. That he had gone up is first asserted in Acts 1:10 (Mark 16:9 and Luke 24:51 are later insertions in the Gospels). Yet the idea was implicit in his departure, for going up is a type of all achievement. Gravity not only affects our bodies but colours our thought. Going up is hard; going down often only too easy. Upper and lower often indicate better and worse. A boy goes up the school. A good man goes up in reputation. The notion of ascending enters in everywhere, and the Ascension of Christ is the master thought and inspiration.

33

THESE THINGS HAVE I SPOKEN UNTO YOU

I

When the Comforter is come, whom I will send unto you from the Father, even the Spirit of truth, which proceedeth from the Father, he shall testify of me: and ye also shall bear witness, because ye have been with me from the beginning. THESE THINGS HAVE I SPOKEN UNTO YOU, that ye should not be offended.

John 15 :26

II

God spake all these words, saying, I am the Lord thy God, which have brought thee out of the land of Egypt, out of the house of bondage. Thou shalt have no other gods before me.

Thou shalt not make unto thee any graven image, or any likeness of any thing that is in heaven above, or that is in the earth beneath, or that is in the water under the earth: thou shalt not bow down thyself to them, nor serve them: for I the Lord thy God am a jealous God, visiting the iniquity of the fathers upon the children unto the third and fourth generation of them that hate me; and shewing mercy unto thousands of them that love me, and keep my commandments.

Thou shalt not take the name of the Lord thy God in vain; for the Lord will not hold him guiltless that taketh his name in vain.

Remember the sabbath day, to keep it holy. Six days shalt thou labour, and do all thy work: but the seventh day is the sabbath of the Lord thy God: in it thou shalt not do any work, thou, nor thy son, nor thy daughter, thy manservant, nor thy maidservant, nor thy cattle, nor thy stranger that is within thy gates: for in six days the Lord made heaven and earth, the sea, and all that in them

The Child Samuel   SIR JOSHUA REYNOLDS 1723–92

[Tate Gallery, London]

is, and rested the seventh day: wherefore the Lord blessed the sabbath day, and hallowed it.

Honour thy father and thy mother: that thy days may be long upon the land which the Lord thy God giveth thee.

Thou shalt not kill. Thou shalt not commit adultery. Thou shalt not steal. Thou shalt not bear false witness against thy neighbour. Thou shalt not covet thy neighbour's house, thou shalt not covet thy neighbour's wife, nor his manservant, nor his maidservant, nor his ox, nor his ass, nor any thing that is thy neighbour's.

Exodus 20 :1

III

Jesus went up into a mountain: and when he was set, his disciples came unto him: and he opened his mouth, and taught them, saying, Blessed are the poor in spirit: for their's is the kingdom of heaven.

Blessed are they that mourn: for they shall be comforted.

Blessed are the meek: for they shall inherit the earth.

Blessed are they which do hunger and thirst after righteousness: for they shall be filled.

Blessed are the merciful: for they shall obtain mercy.

Blessed are the pure in heart: for they shall see God.

Blessed are the peacemakers: for they shall be called the children of God.

Blessed are they which are persecuted for righteousness' sake: for their's is the kingdom of heaven.

Blessed are ye, when men shall revile you, and persecute you, and shall say all manner of evil against you falsely, for my sake.

Rejoice, and be exceeding glad: for great is your reward in heaven.

Matthew 5 :1

IV

Where more is meant than meets the ear.

JOHN MILTON (1608–74)
Il Penseroso (1645), l. 120

V

Robert What did you mean when you said that St Catherine and St Margaret talked to you every day?

Joan [*of Arc*] They do.

Robert What are they like?

Joan (*suddenly obstinate*) I will tell you nothing about that: they have not given me leave.

Robert But you actually see them; and they talk to you just as I am talking to you?

Joan No: it is quite different. I cannot tell you: you must not talk to me about my voices.

Robert How do you mean? voices?

Joan I hear voices telling me what to do. They come from God.

Robert They come from your imagination.

Joan Of course. That is how the messages of God come to us.

BERNARD SHAW (1856–1950)
Saint Joan (1924), Sc. 1

VI

Behold my love, and give me thine again,
   Behold I died thy ransom for to pay;
See how my heart is open broad and plain,
   Thy ghostly enemies only to affray:
An harder battle no man might essay,
   Of all triumphs the greatest high emprise;
Wherefore, O man, no longer thee dismay,
   I gave my blood for thee in sacrifice.

Turn home again: thy sin do thou forsake,
   Behold and see if aught be left behind,
How I to mercy am ready thee to take.
   Give me thy heart, and be no more unkind;
My love and thine, together do them bind,
   And let them never parte in no wise.
When thou wert lost, thy soul again to find
   My blood I offered for thee in sacrifice. . . .

Tarry no longer; toward thine heritage
   Haste on thy way, and be of right good cheer.
Go each day onward on thy pilgrimage,
   Think how short time thou shalt abiden here.
Thy place is bigg'd[1] above the starres clear,
   None earthly palace wrought in so stately wise.
Come on, my friend, my brother most entire,
   For thee I offered my blood in sacrifice.

JOHN LYDGATE (1370?-1451?)
The Testament of Dan (1445), Stanzas 115, 116, 118

VII

God speaks to man in a hundred different ways; the commonest way is by what we read. But reading is nothing but words unless it raises images all the time. Sometimes what we read suddenly captures the imagination and chains it inseparably to the words for ever—God has spoken. The effect is vivid. It may issue in immediate action. It may be simply a fortifying treasure in the soul.

[1] built

34

YE IN ME, AND I IN YOU

Prelude

Love bade me welcome: yet my soul drew back,
    Guiltie of dust and sinne.
But quick-ey'd Love, observing me grow slack
    From my first entrance in,
Drew nearer to me, sweetly questioning,
    If I lack'd any thing.

A guest, I answer'd, worthy to be here:
    Love said, You shall be he.
I the unkinde, ungratefull? Ah my deare,
    I cannot look on thee.
Love took my hand, and smiling did reply,
    Who made the eyes but I?

Truth Lord, but I have marr'd them: let my shame
    Go where it doth deserve.
And know you not, sayes Love, who bore the blame?
    My deare, then I will serve.
You must sit down, sayes Love, and taste my meat:
    So I did sit and eat.

GEORGE HERBERT (1593–1633)
The Temple (1633)

I

I will not leave you comfortless: I will come to you. Yet a little while, and the world seeth me no more; but ye see me: because I live, ye shall live also. At that day ye shall know that I am in my Father, and YE IN ME, AND I IN YOU.

John 14:18

II

> Wear me as a seal upon your heart,
>   as a seal upon your arm;
> for love is strong as death,
> passion cruel as the grave;
>   it blazes up like blazing fire,
>   fiercer than any flame.
> Many waters cannot quench love,
>   no flood can sweep it away;
> if a man were to offer for love
>   the whole wealth of his house,
>   it would be utterly scorned.

The Song of Songs 8 :6 NEB

III

Again I heard what sounded like a vast crowd, like the noise of rushing water and deep roars of thunder, and they cried:
'Alleluia! The Lord our God, sovereign over all, has entered on his reign! Exult and shout for joy and do him homage, for the wedding-day of the Lamb has come! His bride has made herself ready, and for her dress she has been given fine linen, clean and shining.'
(Now the fine linen signifies the righteous deeds of God's people.) Then the angel said to me, 'Write this: "Happy are those who are invited to the wedding-supper of the Lamb!" ' And he added, 'These are the very words of God.' At this I fell at his feet to worship him. But he said to me, 'No, not that! I am but a fellow-servant with you and your brothers who bear their testimony to Jesus. It is God you must worship. Those who bear testimony to Jesus are inspired like the prophets.'

Revelation 19 :6 NEB

IV

Somewhere *there must be a standpoint* from which Christ and the earth can be so situated in relation to one another that it is impossible for me to possess the one without embracing the other, to be

162

Buttermere

J. M. W. TURNER 1775–1851

[Tate Gallery, London]

in communion with the one without being absorbed into the other, to be absolutely Christian without being desperately human.

PIERRE TEILHARD DE CHARDIN (1881–1955)
Writings in Time of War (1968)

V

For a person of her age—she was now ten—Thérèse had already lived through some considerable mental experiences. . . . But all this was as nothing compared with the emotion aroused in her by her first communion. It was a moment to which all else had been a preparation, and with the rapture of first love she received it. 'Ah, how sweet was the first kiss of Jesus to my soul! Yes, it was a kiss of love! I felt that I was loved, and I said also, "I love you, I give myself to you for ever." Jesus asked nothing of me, He required no sacrifice. He and the little Thérèse had long since looked at one another and had understood. That day, our meeting could no longer be called a simple look, but a *fusion*. We were no longer two.'

This revealing passage, with sentiments reproduced a hundred times throughout the pages of Thérèse's autobiography, conveys very exactly and convincingly the absolute abandonment of self into the keeping of another; the absolute submergence in union; the entire surrender, the fusion as Thérèse, with her final cry in her search for the right word, calls and italicises it. She may or may not have known that it was the recognised word appropriate to the experience. The language is the language of human love; it is amorous; it is passionate; it is the bride finding herself for the first time in the arms of her lover.

VITA SACKVILLE-WEST (1892–1962)
'St Thérèse of Lisieux' (*The Eagle and the Dove*, 1943)

VI

> '*In no Strange Land*'
> O world invisible, we view thee,
> O world intangible, we touch thee,
> O world unknowable, we know thee,
> Inapprehensible, we clutch thee!

Does the fish soar to find the ocean,
The eagle plunge to find the air—
That we ask of the stars in motion
If they have rumour of thee there?

Not where the wheeling systems darken,
And our benumbed conceiving soars!—
The drift of pinions, would we hearken,
Beats at our own clay-shuttered doors.

The angels keep their ancient places;—
Turn but a stone, and start a wing!
'Tis ye, 'tis your estrangèd faces,
That miss the many-splendoured thing.

But (when so sad thou canst not sadder)
Cry;—and upon thy so sore loss
Shall shine the traffic of Jacob's ladder
Pitched betwixt Heaven and Charing Cross.

Yea, in the night, my Soul, my daughter,
Cry,—clinging Heaven by the hems;
And lo, Christ walking on the water
Not of Gennesareth, but Thames!

FRANCIS THOMPSON (1859–1907)
'The Kingdom of God'

VII

Spirit is equally at home in heaven and on earth. We may go further
and say that there is no spirit which has not some link with matter,
and no matter that has not some spiritual life. We may think that
even sticks and stones have a life of their own, some capacity for
change, some striving to be other than they are. But matter,
though it is marvellous, imposes limitations, while spirit has no
purpose but to liberate.

35

A DOOR WAS OPENED IN HEAVEN

I

After this I looked, and, behold, A DOOR WAS OPENED IN HEAVEN:
and the first voice which I heard was as it were of a trumpet talking
with me; which said, Come up hither, and I will shew thee things
which must be hereafter. And immediately I was in the spirit.

Revelation 4:1

II

Jacob went out from Beer-sheba, and went toward Haran. And he
lighted upon a certain place, and tarried there all night, because
the sun was set; and he took of the stones of that place, and put
them for his pillows, and lay down in that place to sleep. And he
dreamed, and behold a ladder set up on the earth, and the top of it
reached to heaven: and behold the angels of God ascending and
descending on it. And, behold, the Lord stood above it, and said,
I am the Lord God of Abraham thy father, and the God of Isaac:
the land whereon thou liest, to thee will I give it, and to thy seed;
and thy seed shall be as the dust of the earth, and thou shalt spread
abroad to the west, and to the east, and to the north, and to the
south: and in thee and in thy seed shall all the families of the earth
be blessed. And, behold, I am with thee, and will keep thee in all
places whither thou goest, and will bring thee again into this land;
for I will not leave thee, until I have done that which I have spoken
to thee of. And Jacob awaked out of his sleep, and he said, Surely
the Lord is in this place; and I knew it not. And he was afraid, and
said, How dreadful is this place! this is none other but the house of
God, and this is the gate of heaven.

Genesis 28:10

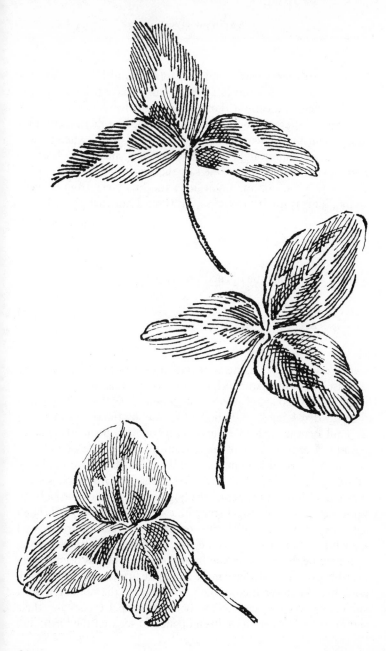

Clover   ENID LEVETUS

III

Then cometh Jesus from Galilee to Jordan unto John, to be baptized of him. But John forbad him, saying, I have need to be baptized of thee, and comest thou to me? And Jesus answering said unto him, Suffer it to be so now: for thus it becometh us to fulfil all righteousness. Then he suffered him. And Jesus, when he was baptized, went up straightway out of the water: and, lo, the heavens were opened unto him, and he saw the Spirit of God descending like a dove, and lighting upon him: and lo a voice from heaven, saying, This is my beloved Son, in whom I am well pleased.

Matthew 3:13

IV

Knock, and it shall be opened unto you.

The Sermon on the Mount
(Matthew 7:7)

V

Let us now try to imagine ourselves in the position of a man who is conscious of being the recipient of divine revelation. I am not, to begin with, thinking of Amos as he followed his flock, of Isaiah in the year that King Uzziah died, of Ezekiel by the river Chebar, of St Paul on the road to Damascus or of St John in the Isle of Patmos. I am thinking of some quite ordinary man of today to whom the word of God in the gospel of Jesus Christ comes home in a way which grips him and takes hold upon his whole self. It may come through the actual reading of the Bible, or through the presentation of the gospel story in a sermon or book, or through some experience by which the gospel story which is already well known to him is made to 'come alive' as it has never done before, or it may be that on reflection he realises what he has been imperceptibly growing to believe more and more firmly as the years have gone by. Whatever the occasion, the result is the same. He has a subjective certainty concerning both the gospel events and their significance. His eyes have been opened to see that the birth, life, death and resurrection of Jesus Christ were God in action rescuing His world from evil and bringing a message of forgiveness and hope to penitent sinners. This inner, subjective certainty may extend beyond the events of the gospel story, to include the whole of the Bible, the content of creeds or confessions of faith, or such things as miracles in the lives of the saints, but for the moment this is irrelevant.

LEONARD HODGSON (1889–1969)
The Doctrine of the Trinity (1943)

VI

        that blessed mood,
 In which the burthen of the mystery,
 In which the heavy and the weary weight
 Of all this unintelligible world,
 Is lightened:—that serene and blessed mood,
 In which the affections gently lead us on,—
 Until, the breath of this corporeal frame
 And even the motion of our human blood
 Almost suspended, we are laid asleep
 In body, and become a living soul:
 While with an eye made quiet by the power
 Of harmony, and the deep power of joy,
 We see into the life of things.

WILLIAM WORDSWORTH (1770–1850)
'Lines composed a few miles above Tintern Abbey'
(13 July 1798)

VII

We must be content with intimations and glimpses of spiritual truths, but that is enough. These intimations and glimpses, just because they are spiritual, can often bring absolute certainty, either with a flash of new knowledge, or with the perfect assurance of what before was only conjecture or no more than hope. Thus the Holy Trinity at work is a vision that can come alive.

36

THE SAVIOUR OF THE WORLD

I

Herein is love, not that we loved God, but that he loved us, and sent his Son to be the propitiation for our sins. Beloved, if God so loved us, we ought also to love one another. No man hath seen God at any time. If we love one another, God dwelleth in us, and his love is perfected in us. Hereby know we that we dwell in him, and he in us, because he hath given us of his Spirit. And we have seen and do testify that the Father sent the Son to be THE SAVIOUR OF THE WORLD.

1 John 4:10

II

I will mention the lovingkindnesses of the Lord, and the praises of the Lord, according to all that the Lord hath bestowed on us, and the great goodness toward the house of Israel, which he hath bestowed on them according to his mercies, and according to the multitude of his lovingkindnesses. For he said, Surely they are my people, children that will not lie: so he was their Saviour. In all their affliction he was afflicted, and the angel of his presence saved them: in his love and in his pity he redeemed them; and he bare them, and carried them all the days of old.

Isaiah 63:7

III

Peter has healed a lame man

It came to pass on the morrow, that their rulers, and elders, and scribes, and Annas the high priest, and Caiaphas, and John, and Alexander, and as many as were of the kindred of the high priest, were gathered together at Jerusalem. And when they had set them

St Peter healing the sick   MASACCIO 1401–28

[*Chiesa del Carmine, Florence : Mansell*]

in the midst, they asked, By what power, or by what name, have ye done this? Then Peter, filled with the Holy Ghost, said unto them, Ye rulers of the people, and elders of Israel, if we this day be examined of the good deed done to the impotent man, by what means he is made whole;[1] be it known unto you all, and to all the people of Israel, that by the name of Jesus Christ of Nazareth, whom ye crucified, whom God raised from the dead, even by him doth this man stand here before you whole. This is the stone which was set at nought of you builders, which is become the head of the corner. Neither is there salvation[1] in any other: for there is none other name under heaven given among men, whereby we must be saved.[1] Now when they saw the boldness of Peter and John, and perceived that they were unlearned and ignorant men, they marvelled; and they took knowledge of them, that they had been with Jesus. And beholding the man which was healed standing with them, they could say nothing against it.

Acts 4:5

IV

Safe and sound (*salvus et sanus*)

V

Joseph Lister, 1st Baron Lister, 1827–1912

As a result of his main discoveries, all made in the course of a very few years, the practice of surgery underwent a complete revolution. In Lister's wards septic diseases did not occur, post-operative pyaemia, hospital gangrene, and tetanus disappeared, and erysipelas was rare, unless introduced. Occasionally wounds did not heal without suppuration, but even this was exceptional, and whenever it occurred, all the factors in the case were carefully investigated to ascertain the cause of the failure. Very soon his methods were applied to all kinds of surgical operations. The vanishing of septic diseases enlarged enormously the field of

---

[1] In Greek the same verb is used here for 'made whole' and 'be saved'; and the corresponding noun is the word for 'salvation' and also for 'good health'.

surgery, since operations formerly dreaded, owing to this risk, could now be carried out in safety. Lister himself introduced many new operations for the treatment of diseases and disabilities, that would have been quite impracticable without the assurance that the operation wound would heal with no septic complications. The modern development of surgery in relation to disease and injury of deep-seated organs in the chest, abdomen, &c., was only possible as the result of his discoveries, and it is probable that no man's work has had a greater influence on the progress of surgery; the saving of human life and suffering that he effected is incalculable.

The Dictionary of National Biography, 1912–1921

VI

From heaven he came, in mortal clothing, when
All that was worst and best had been observed.
Living, he came to view the God he served
To give us the entire, true light again.

For that bright star which with its vivid rays
Picked out the humble place where I was born—
For this, the world would be a prize to scorn;
None but its Maker can return its praise.

I speak of Dante, he whose work was spurned
By the ungrateful crowd, those who can give
Praise only to the worthless. I would live

Happy were I but he, by such men scorned,
If, with his torments, I could also share
His greatness, both his joy and exile bear.

MICHELANGELO (1475–1564)
'On Dante Alighieri' (trans. by
Elizabeth Jennings, 1961)

VII

The Gospels and Acts are largely the record of a ministry directed jointly to the body and the soul, and we are following in the steps of the Apostles when we pray for the sick *and* send for the doctor. Latterly, medical science has concentrated almost entirely on the body, and no wonder, when it effects such cures and performs such miracles of surgery. But, thanks particularly to psychology and the related sciences, it is becoming increasingly clear—as it certainly was clear to the Apostles and many of their contemporaries—that body and soul cannot be separated in this manner. They both need and indeed they both contribute to the healing art and Christians have much to say as well as to learn about this.

37

HE LAID DOWN HIS LIFE FOR US

I

Hereby perceive we the love of God, because HE LAID DOWN HIS LIFE FOR US: and we ought to lay down our lives for the brethren.

1 John 3 :16

II

Three of the thirty chief went down, and came to David in the harvest time unto the cave of Adullam: and the troop of the Philistines pitched in the valley of Rephaim. And David was then in an hold, and the garrison of the Philistines was then in Beth-lehem. And David longed, and said, Oh that one would give me drink of the water of the well of Beth-lehem, which is by the gate! And the three mighty men brake through the host of the Philistines, and drew water out of the well of Beth-lehem, that was by the gate, and took it, and brought it to David: nevertheless he would not drink thereof, but poured it out unto the Lord. And he said, Be it far from me, O Lord, that I should do this: is not this the blood of the men that went in jeopardy of their lives? therefore he would not drink it. These things did these three mighty men.

2 Samuel 23 :13

III

Jesus cried with a loud voice, and gave up the ghost. And the veil of the temple was rent in twain from the top to the bottom. And when the centurion, which stood over against him, saw that he so cried out, and gave up the ghost, he said, Truly this man was the Son of God. . . . And now when the even was come, because it was the preparation, that is, the day before the sabbath, Joseph of Arimathaea, an honourable counsellor, which also waited for the kingdom of God, came, and went in boldly unto Pilate, and craved the body of Jesus. And Pilate marvelled if he were already dead: and calling unto him the centurion, he asked him whether he had been any while dead. And when he knew it of the centurion, he gave the body to Joseph. And he bought fine linen, and took him down, and wrapped him in the linen, and laid him in a sepulchre which was hewn out of a rock, and rolled a stone unto the door of the sepulchre.

Mark 15 :37

IV

As David went, thus he said, O my son Absalom, my son, my son Absalom! would God I had died for thee, O Absalom, my son, my son!

2 Samuel 18 :33

V

Police are keeping a 'discreet' guard on Christine Black, 12, of Gateshead, the only person who can identify the killer of her friend, Carol Scullion, also 12 and of Gateshead. The murderer is believed to be a youth aged about 20. Detectives said Carol died defending Christine. They were ambushed on Saturday afternoon while walking along a woodland path in Dunston-on-Tyne, Co. Durham. The man first attacked them with a brick. While Christine lay injured on the ground Carol started hitting him with a basket. The man then pulled a knife from his belt and stabbed her several times.

Daily Telegraph (6 May 1968)

VI

Red lips are not so red
  As the stained stones kissed by the English dead.
Kindness of wooed and wooer
Seems shame to their love pure.

Death in Action

ROBERT CAPA   d. 1954

[*Magnum Photos*]

O Love, your eyes lose lure
    When I behold eyes blinded in my stead!

Your slender attitude
    Trembles not exquisite like limbs knife-skewed,
Rolling and rolling there
Where God seems not to care;
Till the fierce Love they bear
    Cramps them in death's extreme decrepitude.

Your voice sings not so soft,—
    Though even as wind murmuring through raftered loft,—
Your dear voice is not dear,
Gentle, and evening clear,
As theirs whom none now hear,
    Now earth has stopped their piteous mouths that coughed.

Heart, you were never hot,
    Nor large, nor full like hearts made great with shot;
And though your hand be pale,
Paler are all which trail
Your cross through flame and hail:
    Weep, you may weep, for you may touch them not.

WILFRED OWEN (1893–1918)
'Greater Love'

VII

Without derogating from the unique sacrifice made by Christ upon the Cross, I can say of everyone who has died since Adam that he has laid down his life for me. My present situation results from the past having been a continuous conflict between good and evil, in which good in the end has had the victories. Good, gentle as it is, has proved to be of sterner stuff than evil, so evil by having a share in this has by a paradox done some good. If I look down on a gravestone, whether the life it records is good or bad, it says to me, 'I have laid down my life for you.'

38

AN HEARTY DESIRE TO PRAY

I

O Lord, we beseech thee mercifully to hear us; and grant that we, to whom thou hast given AN HEARTY DESIRE TO PRAY, may by thy mighty aid be defended and comforted in all dangers and adversities; through Jesus Christ our Lord. Amen.

Collect

II

In those days was Hezekiah sick unto death. And the prophet Isaiah the son of Amoz came to him, and said unto him, Thus saith the Lord, Set thine house in order; for thou shalt die, and not live. Then he turned his face to the wall, and prayed unto the Lord, saying, I beseech thee, O Lord, remember now how I have walked before thee in truth and with a perfect heart, and have done that which is good in thy sight. And Hezekiah wept sore. And it came to pass, afore Isaiah was gone out into the middle court, that the word of the Lord came to him, saying, Turn again, and tell Hezekiah the captain of my people, Thus saith the Lord, the God of David thy father, I have heard thy prayer, I have seen thy tears: behold, I will heal thee: on the third day thou shalt go up unto the house of the Lord. And I will add unto thy days fifteen years; and I will deliver thee and this city out of the hand of the king of Assyria; and I will defend this city for mine own sake, and for my servant David's sake. And Isaiah said, Take a lump of figs. And they took and laid it on the boil, and he recovered.

2 Kings 20 :1

It will be noticed that in this case prayer and medical treatment go together. This is also true in the following case.

III

Is any among you afflicted? let him pray. Is any merry? let him sing psalms. Is any sick among you? let him call for the elders of the church; and let them pray over him, anointing him with oil in the name of the Lord: and the prayer of faith shall save the sick, and the Lord shall raise him up; and if he have committed sins, they shall be forgiven him. Confess your faults one to another, and pray one for another, that ye may be healed. The effectual fervent prayer of a righteous man availeth much.

James 5:13

IV

Every time you pray, if your prayer is sincere, there will be new feeling and new meaning in it, which will give you fresh courage, and you will understand that prayer is an education.

FËDOR DOSTOEVSKY (1821–81)
The Brothers Karamazov, bk. VI, ch. 3
(1880, trans. Constance Garnett)

V

Willenhall was chiefly inhabited by a population of miners, lock-smiths, and iron-workers. Wilkinson only preached twice, and took part in the prayer meetings after the sermons, but he made and received a deep impression. After the first of these sermons, which was on Ahab (a favourite subject of his), he found himself guided to a man at the bottom of the church. Wilkinson told him to pray. 'But,' the man answered, 'I never prayed in my life, and I do not know how to do it.' 'Then kneel down', he said, 'and tell God that you do not know how to pray, and ask Him to show you how.' The man did so, and before long Wilkinson had to come back from dealing with some other souls and ask him to restrain himself, as the man was confessing all his sins in a loud voice and in deadly earnest.

A. J. MASON (1851–1928)
Memoir of George Howard Wilkinson (1909),
3rd Period, ch. 8

Prodigal Son   ALBRECHT DÜRER 1471–1528

[*Etching : British Library, London*]

VI

Macbeth	I have done the deed. Didst thou not hear a noise?
Lady Macbeth	I heard the owl scream and the crickets cry.
	Did not you speak?
Macbeth	When?
Lady Macbeth	Now.
Macbeth	As I descended?
Lady Macbeth	Ay.
Macbeth	Hark!
	Who lies i' th' second chamber?
Lady Macbeth	Donalbain.
Macbeth	(*Looking on his hands*) This is a sorry sight.
Lady Macbeth	A foolish thought to say a sorry sight.
Macbeth	There's one did laugh in's sleep, and one cried 'Murder!'
	That they did wake each other. I stood and heard them;
	But they did say their prayers, and address'd them
	Again to sleep.
Lady Macbeth	There are two lodg'd together.
Macbeth	One cried 'God bless us', and 'Amen' the other,
	As they had seen me with these hangman's hands.
	List'ning their fear, I could not say 'Amen'
	When they did say 'God bless us!'
Lady Macbeth	Consider it not so deeply.
Macbeth	But wherefore could not I pronounce 'Amen'?
	I had most need of blessing, and 'Amen'
	Stuck in my throat.
Lady Macbeth	These deeds must not be thought
	After these ways: so, it will make us mad.

WILLIAM SHAKESPEARE (1564–1616)
Macbeth (1606?), II, ii, 14

VII

The Collect tells us that God has given us an hearty desire to pray, but, if so, many of us need to stir up the gift of God which is in us (2 Timothy 1:6). The hearty desire is there, but too often allows itself to be damped down by wandering thoughts, or by want of time, or by want of faith in what we are about, or by no sense of urgency, or by not knowing what we ought to pray for (Romans 8:26). Praying is an art which needs to be learned and the practice of it needs to be organized.

39

THINGS TEMPORAL—THE THINGS ETERNAL

I

O God, the protector of all that trust in thee, without whom nothing is strong, nothing is holy; Increase and multiply upon us thy mercy; that, thou being our ruler and guide, we may so pass through THINGS TEMPORAL, that we finally lose not THE THINGS ETERNAL: Grant this, O heavenly Father, for Jesus Christ's sake our Lord. Amen.

Collect

II

He hath looked down from his sanctuary: out of the heaven did the Lord behold the earth;

That he might hear the mournings of such as are in captivity: and deliver the children appointed unto death;

That they may declare the Name of the Lord in Sion: and his worship at Jerusalem;

When the people are gathered together: and the kingdoms also, to serve the Lord.

He brought down my strength in my journey: and shortened my days.

But I said, O my God, take me not away in the midst of mine age: as for thy years, they endure throughout all generations.

Thou, Lord, in the beginning hast laid the foundation of the earth: and the heavens are the work of thy hands.

They shall perish, but thou shalt endure: they all shall wax old as doth a garment;

And as a vesture shalt thou change them, and they shall be changed: but thou art the same, and thy years shall not fail.

Psalm 102 :19

Separation of Light and Darkness   MICHELANGELO 1475–1564

[*Cappella Sistina, Rome : Mansell*]

III

It is written, I believed, and therefore have I spoken; we also believe, and therefore speak; knowing that he which raised up the Lord Jesus shall raise up us also by Jesus, and shall present us with you. For all things are for your sakes, that the abundant grace might through the thanksgiving of many redound to the glory of God. For which cause we faint not; but though our outward man perish, yet the inward man is renewed day by day. For our light affliction, which is but for a moment, worketh for us a far more exceeding and eternal weight of glory; while we look not at the things which are seen, but at the things which are not seen: for the things which are seen are temporal; but the things which are not seen are eternal. For we know that if our earthly house of this tabernacle were dissolved, we have a building of God, an house not made with hands, eternal in the heavens.

2 Corinthians 4:13

'*The tabernacle*', *i.e. tent, means the human body; the word was so used by Greek philosophers.*

IV

In the *Incarnation* of Christ, we understand *God* in conjunction with humane Nature: and this strengthens our Faith, that humane Nature may be conjoined to God eternally.

BENJAMIN WHICHCOTE (1609–83)
Aphorisms (1703), no. 306

V

To see things under the form of eternity is to see them in their historic and moral truth, not as they seemed as they passed, but as they remain when they are over. When a man's life is over, it remains true that he has lived; it remains true that he has been one sort of man, and not another. In the infinite mosaic of history that bit has its unfading colour and its perpetual function and effect. A man who understands himself under the form of eternity knows the quality that eternally belongs to him, and knows that he cannot wholly die, even if he would; for when the movement of his life is over, the truth of his life remains. The fact of him is a part for ever of the infinite context of facts. This sort of immortality belongs passively to everything; but to the intellectual part of man it belongs actively also, because, in so far as it knows the eternity of truth, and is absorbed in it, the mind *lives* in that eternity. In caring only for the eternal, it has ceased to care for that part of itself which can die.

GEORGE SANTAYANA (1863–1952)
Spinoza's Ethics (1910), Introduction

VI

> When I bethinke me on that speech whyleare,
> Of *Mutability*, and well it way:
> Me seemes, that though she all unworthy were
> Of the Heav'ns Rule; yet very sooth to say,
> In all things else she beares the greatest sway.
> Which makes me loath this state of life so tickle,[1]
> And love of things so vaine to cast away;
> Whose flowring pride, so fading and so fickle,
> Short *Time* shall soon cut down with his consuming sickle.
>
> Then gin I thinke on that which Nature sayd,
> Of that same time when no more *Change* shall be,
> But stadfast rest of all things firmely stayd
> Upon the pillours of Eternity,
> That is contrayr to *Mutabilitie*:
> For all that moveth doth in *Change* delight:
> But thenceforth all shall rest eternally
> With Him that is the God of Sabbaoth[2] hight:
> O that great Sabbaoth God, graunt me that Sabaoths sight.

EDMUND SPENSER (1552?–99)
The Faerie Queene (1609), Bk. VII, canto 8

[1] uncertain
[2] God of Hosts: but Spenser confuses 'Sabbaoth' with 'Sabbath' ('rest').

VII

Time goes back, we know, millions of years, yet we cannot imagine it beginning, nor how it could end. We have an idea of eternity, but can form no image or conception of it. Might we think it just more than fancy to suppose that the vast ages (and the vast spaces of which we know), awesome and yet absurd, are preparing us to inherit eternal life, which otherwise may confuse and astound us?

40

LAUNCH OUT INTO THE DEEP

I

Jesus saw two ships standing by the lake: but the fishermen were gone out of them, and were washing their nets. And he entered into one of the ships, which was Simon's, and prayed him that he would thrust out a little from the land. And he sat down, and taught the people out of the ship. Now when he had left speaking, he said unto Simon, LAUNCH OUT INTO THE DEEP, and let down your nets for a draught. And Simon answering said unto him, Master, we have toiled all the night, and have taken nothing: nevertheless at thy word I will let down the net. And when they had this done, they inclosed a great multitude of fishes.

Luke 5 :2

II

Emigration

Terah took Abram his son, and Lot the son of Haran his son's son, and Sarai his daughter in law, his son Abram's wife; and they went forth with them from Ur of the Chaldees, to go into the land of Canaan; and they came unto Haran, and dwelt there. And the days of Terah were two hundred and five years: and Terah died in Haran. Now the Lord had said unto Abram, Get thee out of thy country, and from thy kindred, and from thy father's house, unto a land that I will shew thee: and I will make of thee a great nation, and I will bless thee, and make thy name great; and thou shalt be a blessing: and I will bless them that bless thee, and curse him that curseth thee: and in thee shall all families of the earth be blessed. So Abram departed, as the Lord had spoken unto him; and Lot went with him: and Abram was seventy and five years old when he departed out of Haran. And Abram took Sarai his wife, and Lot his brother's son, and all their substance that they had gathered, and the souls that they had gotten in Haran; and they went forth to go into the land of Canaan; and into the land of Canaan they came.

Genesis 11 :31

III

Mission

Jesus called his twelve disciples together, and gave them power and authority over all devils, and to cure diseases. And he sent them to preach the kingdom of God, and to heal the sick. And he said unto them, Take nothing for your journey, neither staves, nor scrip, neither bread, neither money; neither have two coats apiece. And whatsoever house ye enter into, there abide, and thence depart. And whosoever will not receive you, when ye go out of that city, shake off the very dust from your feet for a testimony against them. And they departed, and went through the towns, preaching the gospel, and healing every where.

Luke 9 :1

IV

> He either fears his fate too much,
>   Or his deserts are small,
> That puts it not unto the touch
>   To win or lose it all.

JAMES, MARQUESS OF MONTROSE (1612–50)
'My dear and only love' (*c.* 1640)

V

Expedition

On Friday, the 23rd of April, the weather cleared so that the work could be begun. In fine weather in Mudros a haze of beauty comes upon the hills and water till their loveliness is unearthly, it is so rare. Then the bay is like a blue jewel, and the hills lose their savagery, and glow, and are gentle, and the sun comes up from

La Première Sortie   PIERRE AUGUSTE RENOIR 1841–1919

[National Gallery, London]

Troy, and the peaks of Samothrace change colour, and all the marvellous ships in the harbour are transfigured. The land of Lemnos was beautiful with flowers at that season, in the brief Ægean spring, and to seawards always, in the bay, were the ships, more ships, perhaps than any port of modern times has known; they seemed like half the ships of the world. In this crowd of shipping strange beautiful Greek vessels passed, under rigs of old time, with sheep and goats and fish for sale, and tugs of the Thames and Mersey met again the ships they had towed of old, bearing a new freight, of human courage. The transports (all painted black) lay in tiers, well within the harbour, the men-of-war nearer Mudros and the entrance. Now in all that city of ships, so busy with passing picket-boats, and noisy with the labour of men, the getting of the anchors began. Ship after ship, crammed with soldiers, moved slowly out of harbour in the lovely day, and felt again the heave of the sea. No such gathering of fine ships has ever been seen upon this earth, and the beauty and the exultation of the youth upon them made them like sacred things as they moved away. All the thousands of men aboard them gathered on deck to see, till each rail was thronged. These men had come from all parts of the British world, from Africa, Australia, Canada, India, the Mother Country, New Zealand, and remote islands in the sea. They had said good-bye to home that they might offer their lives in the cause we stand for.

*   *   *

They left the harbour very, very slowly; this tumult of cheering lasted a long time; no one who heard it will ever forget it, or think of it unshaken. It broke the hearts of all there with pity and pride: it went beyond the guard of the English heart. Presently all were out, and the fleet stood across for Tenedos, and the sun went down with marvellous colour, lighting island after island and the Asian peaks, and those left behind in Mudros trimmed their lamps knowing that they had been for a little brought near to the heart of things.

JOHN MASEFIELD (1878–1967)
Gallipoli

VI

There lies the port; the vessel puffs her sail:
There gloom the dark broad seas. My mariners,
Souls that have toiled, and wrought, and thought with me—
That ever with a frolic welcome took
The thunder and the sunshine, and opposed
Free hearts, free foreheads—you and I are old;
Old age hath yet his honour and his toil;
Death closes all: but something ere the end,
Some work of noble note, may yet be done,
Not unbecoming men that strove with Gods.
The lights begin to twinkle from the rocks:
The long day wanes: the slow moon climbs: the deep
Moans round with many voices. Come, my friends,
'Tis not too late to seek a newer world.
Push off, and sitting well in order smite
The sounding furrows; for my purpose holds
To sail beyond the sunset, and the baths
Of all the western stars, until I die.

ALFRED, LORD TENNYSON (1809–92)
'Ulysses' (1842)

VII

The words, 'Launch out into the deep', have supplied us with a
well-known metaphor. We say, for example, that our prosperous
neighbours are 'launching out' into this or that (a car, a country
cottage). But for the Christian, the words 'into the deep' are much
more significant. In his adventure—and Christianity is an adventure—he will be concerned with the deep things of life, he will be
in deep waters, he will sometimes be out of his depth. At the end
of it all, 'That which drew from out the boundless deep Turns
again home'. 'Launch out' is a good motto, but 'Into the deep' a
better one.

41

THE LIKENESS OF HIS RESURRECTION

I

Know ye not, that so many of us as were baptized into Jesus Christ were baptized into his death? Therefore we are buried with him by baptism into death: that like as Christ was raised up from the dead by the glory of the Father, even so we also should walk in newness of life. For if we have been planted together in the likeness of his death, we shall be also in THE LIKENESS OF HIS RESURRECTION.

Romans 6 :3
For 'have been planted together', BCP 1928 puts, less close to the Greek but more intelligibly, 'have become united with him'.

II

I charge you, O ye daughters of Jerusalem, by the roes, and by the hinds of the field, that ye stir not up, nor awake my love, till he please.

The voice of my beloved! behold, he cometh leaping upon the mountains, skipping upon the hills. My beloved is like a roe or a young hart: behold, he standeth behind our wall, he looketh forth at the windows, shewing himself through the lattice. My beloved spake, and said unto me, Rise up, my love, my fair one, and come away. For, lo, the winter is past, the rain is over and gone; the flowers appear on the earth; the time of the singing of birds is come, and the voice of the turtle is heard in our land; the fig tree putteth forth her green figs, and the vines with the tender grape give a good smell. Arise, my love, my fair one, and come away.

Song of Songs 2 :7
This passage has by long tradition been read as a Lesson at Eastertide, and in the synagogue at Passover.

The Resurrection of Christ PIERO DELLA FRANCESCA *c.* 1420–92

[*Galleria Comunale, San Sepolcro : Mansell*]

III

Now a certain man was sick, named Lazarus, of Bethany, the town of Mary and her sister Martha. (It was that Mary which anointed the Lord with ointment, and wiped his feet with her hair, whose brother Lazarus was sick.) Therefore his sisters sent unto him, saying, Lord, behold, he whom thou lovest is sick. . . . Now Jesus loved Martha, and her sister, and Lazarus. . . . When Jesus came, he found that he had lain in the grave four days already. . . . Martha, as soon as she heard that Jesus was coming, went and met him. . . . Then said Martha unto Jesus, Lord, if thou hadst been here, my brother had not died. But I know, that even now, whatsoever thou wilt ask of God, God will give it thee. Jesus saith unto her, Thy brother shall rise again. Martha saith unto him, I know that he shall rise again in the resurrection at the last day. Jesus said unto her, I am the resurrection, and the life: he that believeth in me, though he were dead, yet shall he live: and whosoever liveth and believeth in me shall never die. Believest thou this? She saith unto him, Yea, Lord: I believe that thou art the Christ, the Son of God, which should come into the world. . . . Jesus cometh to the grave. It was a cave, and a stone lay upon it. Jesus said, Take ye away the stone. . . . Then they took away the stone from the place where the dead was laid. And Jesus lifted up his eyes, and said, Father, I thank thee that thou hast heard me. And I knew that thou hearest me always: but because of the people which stand by I said it, that they may believe that thou hast sent me. And when he thus had spoken, he cried with a loud voice, Lazarus, come forth. And he that was dead came forth, bound hand and foot with graveclothes: and his face was bound about with a napkin. Jesus saith unto them, Loose him, and let him go.

John 11:1

IV

> And many more, whose names on Earth are dark
>   But whose transmitted effluence cannot die
> So long as fire outlives the parent spark,
>   Rose, robed in dazzling immortality. . . .

P. B. SHELLEY (1792–1822)
'Adonais'

V

On a joyful Easter-day the Servitor was once in very blithesome mood, and as he sat for a short time, according to his custom, in the repose of contemplation, he desired earnestly to hear from God what meed of delights they shall receive from Him in this life who have borne manifold sufferings for His sake. Whereupon, being rapt in ecstasy, a light shone into his soul from God to this effect: Let all who suffer with detachment rejoice, for their patience shall be gloriously rewarded; and as they have been here below an object of pity to many, even so shall many rejoice eternally at the deserved praise and everlasting honour which shall be theirs. They have died with Me, and they shall also rise again with Me in gladness. . . .

These glad tidings filled the Servitor with joy; and when he came to himself again, he sprang up, and began to laugh so heartily that the chapel in which he was reechoed to the sound, and he said within himself joyously: Let him who has suffered come forward and complain. God knows, I can declare that as to myself, methinks I have never had any thing at all to suffer. I know not what suffering is; but I know well what joy and bliss are. Power to wish and to obtain is given me; a thing which many erring hearts must be without. What want I more?

The Life of the Blessed Henry Suso
(1300–65) *by Himself* (1360, trans. from the
German by T. F. Knox, 1865), ch. 34

The Servitor, Henry Suso, had in fact inflicted terrible austerities on himself in earlier life: he had certainly known what suffering is, but it was all gone.

VI

Rise, O my soul, with thy desires to Heaven,
    And with divinest contemplation use
Thy time where time's eternity is given,
    And let vain thoughts no more thy thoughts abuse;
        But down in darkness let them lie:
        So live thy better, let thy worse thoughts die.

197

And thou, my soul, inspired with holy flame,
  View and review with most regardful eye
That holy cross, whence thy salvation came,
  On which thy Saviour and thy sin did die;
    For in that sacred object is much pleasure,
    And in that Saviour is my life, my treasure.

To Thee, O Jesu, I direct mine eye,
  To Thee my hands, to Thee my humble knees;
To Thee my heart shall offer sacrifice,
  To Thee my thoughts, who my thoughts only sees,
    To Thee my self, my self and all I give;
    To Thee I die, to Thee I only live.

ANON. *A Hymn*

VII

Each year almost every one of us sees some bare tree burst into its hundred thousand leaves. We seldom think how or why it happens, but we know it has happened with astonishing vigour, and it makes us glad. This is the likeness of Christ's resurrection. We do not know how it happened, nor did the Apostles. They just knew that Christ was risen. It happened then in Jerusalem, and has been happening ever since in the Church.

42

INCREASE IN US TRUE RELIGION

I

Lord of all power and might, who art the author and giver of all good things; Graft in our hearts the love of thy Name, INCREASE IN US TRUE RELIGION, nourish us with all goodness, and of thy great mercy keep us in the same; through Jesus Christ our Lord. Amen.

Collect

II

Behold, the days come, saith the Lord, that I will make a new covenant with the house of Israel, and with the house of Judah: not according to the covenant that I made with their fathers in the day that I took them by the hand to bring them out of the land of Egypt; which my covenant they brake, although I was an husband unto them, saith the Lord: but this shall be the covenant that I will make with the house of Israel; After those days, saith the Lord, I will put my law in their inward parts, and write it in their hearts; and will be their God, and they shall be my people. And they shall teach no more every man his neighbour, and every man his brother, saying, Know the Lord: for they shall all know me, from the least of them unto the greatest of them, saith the Lord: for I will forgive their iniquity, and I will remember their sin no more.

Jeremiah 31 :31

III

Grace and peace be multiplied unto you through the knowledge of God, and of Jesus our Lord, according as his divine power hath given unto us all things that pertain unto life and godliness, through the knowledge of him that hath called us to glory and virtue: whereby are given unto us exceeding great and precious promises: that by these ye might be partakers of the divine nature, having escaped the corruption that is in the world through lust. And beside this, giving all diligence, add to your faith virtue; and to virtue knowledge; and to knowledge temperance; and to temperance patience; and to patience godliness; and to godliness brotherly kindness; and to brotherly kindness charity. For if these things be in you, and abound, they make you that ye shall neither be barren nor unfruitful in the knowledge of our Lord Jesus Christ.

2 Peter 1 :2

IV

Man without religion is the creature of circumstances: Religion is above circumstance.

JULIUS CHARLES HARE (1795–1855) &
AUGUSTUS WILLIAM HARE (1792–1834)
Guesses at Truth, Series I

V

My contention is that besides the combative Catholic and Protestant elements in the Churches, there has always been a third element, with very honourable traditions, which came to life again at the Renaissance, but really reaches back to the Greek Fathers, to St Paul and St John, and further back still. The characteristics of this type of Christianity are—a spiritual religion, based on a firm belief in absolute and eternal values as the most real things in the universe—a confidence that these things are knowable by man —a belief that they can nevertheless be known only by whole-hearted consecration of the intellect, will, and affections to the great quest—an entirely open mind towards the discoveries of science—a reverent and receptive attitude to the beauty, sublimity, and wisdom of the creation, as a revelation of the mind and character of the Creator—a complete indifference to the current valuations of the worldling.

W. R. INGE (1860–1954)
*The Platonic Tradition in English
Religious Thought* (1926), Lecture 1

The Sunday School

ROBERT MCINNES 1801–86

[*Leger Gallery, London*]

VI

The first line is derived from Habakkuk 2:2

> There is a book, who runs may read,
>   Which heavenly truth imparts,
> And all the lore its scholars need,
>   Pure eyes and Christian hearts.
>
> The works of God above, below,
>   Within us and around,
> Are pages in that book, to shew
>   How God himself is found. . . .
>
> Two worlds are ours: 'tis only Sin
>   Forbids us to descry
> The mystic heaven and earth within,
>   Plain as the sea and sky.
>
> Thou, who hast given me eyes to see
>   And love this sight so fair,
> Give me a heart to find out Thee,
>   And read Thee everywhere.

JOHN KEBLE (1792–1866)
The Christian Year (1827), Septuagesima

VII

The Bible tells us, not in detail, but for sure, what true religion is. It tells us to believe, and to ask to believe more and more, (i) in the creation and government of a world in time by a being himself eternal, whom we call God, (ii) in resurrection as a principle in the creation as universal as time, (iii) in an appearance in time of all the fullness of God in bodily form in the person of Jesus of Nazareth, and a shadow of the same in ourselves, (iv) in a spiritual presence to lead us through time into eternity.

43

SONS OF GOD

I

If ye live after the flesh, ye shall die: but if ye through the Spirit do mortify the deeds of the body, ye shall live. For as many as are led by the Spirit of God, they are the SONS OF GOD.

Romans 8:13

II

Let us now praise famous men, and our fathers that begat us. The Lord hath wrought great glory by them through his great power from the beginning. Such as did bear rule in their kingdoms, men renowned for their power, giving counsel by their understanding, and declaring prophecies: leaders of the people by their counsels, and by their knowledge of learning meet for the people, wise and eloquent in their instructions: such as found out musical tunes, and recited verses in writing: rich men furnished with ability, living peaceably in their habitations: all these were honoured in their generations, and were the glory of their times. There be of them, that have left a name behind them, that their praises might be reported. And some there be, which have no memorial; who are perished, as though they had never been; and are become as though they had never been born; and their children after them. But these were merciful men, whose righteousness hath not been forgotten.

Ecclesiasticus 44:1

III

It is God which worketh in you both to will and to do of his good pleasure. Do all things without murmurings and disputings: that ye may be blameless and harmless, the sons of God, without re-buke, in the midst of a crooked and perverse nation, among whom ye shine as lights in the world; holding forth the word of life.

Philippians 2 :13

IV

The Hero can be Poet, Prophet, King, Priest or what you will, according to the kind of world he finds himself born into.

THOMAS CARLYLE (1795–1881)
Heroes and Hero Worship (1841): *iii, The Hero as Poet*

V

William the Silent (1533–1584)

It was a strange, almost a unique, thing to be the idol of a nation and to remain uncorrupted, to be oneself the guardian of the people's rights sometimes against the emotional impulse of the people themselves. . . . There lies his greatest claim to recognition: he sought not to impose his own will on the embryo nation, but to let the nation create and form itself. He belonged in spirit to an earlier, a more generous and more cultured age than this of narrowness and authority, and thin, sectarian hatred. But he belonged also to a later age; his deep and genuine interest in the people he ruled, his faith in their development, his toleration, his convinced belief in government by consent—all these reach out from the mediaeval world towards a wider time. Few statesmen in any period, none in his own, cared so deeply for the ordinary comfort and the trivial happiness of the thousands of individuals who are 'the people'. He neither idealized nor overestimated them and he knew that they were often wrong, for what political education had they yet had? But he believed in them, not merely as a theoretical concept, but as individuals, as men. Therein lay the secret of the profound and enduring love between him and them. Wise, wary, slow to judge and slow to act, patient, stubborn and undiscouraged, no other man could have sustained so difficult a cause for so long, could have opposed, with so little sacrifice of

William of Orange   ADRIAEN KEY b. 1544? attr.

[Mauritshuis, The Hague]

public right, the concentrated power of a government which disregarded it. He respected in all men what he wished to have respected in himself, the right to an opinion.

There have been politicians more successful, or more subtle; there have been none more tenacious or more tolerant. 'The wisest, gentlest and bravest man who ever led a nation', he is one of that small band of statesmen whose service to humanity is greater than their service to their time or their people. In spite of the differences of speech or political theory, the conventions and complexities which make one age incomprehensible to another, some men have a quality of greatness which gives their lives universal significance. Such men, in whatever walk of life, in whatever chapter of fame, mystic or saint, scientist or doctor, poet or philosopher, and even—but how rarely—soldier or statesman, exist to shame the cynic, and to renew the faith of humanity in itself.

Of this number was William of Nassau, Prince of Orange, called the Silent.

C. V. WEDGWOOD (1910–   )
William the Silent (1944)

VI

I think continually of those who were truly great.
Who, from the womb, remembered the soul's history
Through corridors of light where the hours are suns,
Endless and singing. Whose lovely ambition
Was that their lips, still touched with fire,
Should tell of the Spirit, clothed from head to foot in song.
And who hoarded from the Spring branches
The desires falling across their bodies like blossoms.

What is precious, is never to forget
The essential delight of the blood drawn from ageless springs
Breaking through rocks in worlds before our earth.
Never to deny its pleasure in the morning simple light
Nor its grave evening demand for love.
Never to allow gradually the traffic to smother
With noise and fog, the flowering of the Spirit.

Near the snow, near the sun, in the highest fields,
See how these names are fêted by the waving grass
And by the streamers of white cloud
And whispers of wind in the listening sky.
The names of those who in their lives fought for life,
Who wore at their hearts the fire's centre.
Born of the sun, they travelled a short while toward the sun
And left the vivid air signed with their honour.

STEPHEN SPENDER (1909–　　)
Poems (1934), No. 28

VII

Son of God is a special title of Jesus Christ, but others have been called sons of God too. Such were the heroes of Greek mythology and some of the Roman Emperors, and the giving of the title to certain heroic types survives—

> Souls tempered with fire,
> Fervent, heroic, and good,
> Helpers and friends of mankind.
> Servants of God!—or SONS

and in not a few of them something of the saint. Perhaps the instinct to call them sons of God springs from the belief—and, for many, the sure knowledge—that there is something divine in all men, seen plainly for what it is in these conspicuous examples.

44

THE CHILDREN OF THIS WORLD

I

The lord commended the unjust steward, because he had done wisely: for THE CHILDREN OF THIS WORLD are in their generation wiser than the children of light.

Luke 16 :8

II

When the queen of Sheba heard of the fame of Solomon concerning the name of the Lord, she came to prove him with hard questions. And she came to Jerusalem with a very great train, with camels that bare spices, and very much gold, and precious stones: and when she was come to Solomon, she communed with him of all that was in her heart. And Solomon told her all her questions: there was not any thing hid from the king, which he told her not. And when the queen of Sheba had seen all Solomon's wisdom, and the house that he had built, and the meat of his table, and the sitting of his servants, and the attendance of his ministers, and their apparel, and his cupbearers, and his ascent by which he went up unto the house of the Lord; there was no more spirit in her. And she said to the king, It was a true report that I heard in mine own land of thy acts and of thy wisdom. Howbeit I believed not the words, until I came, and mine eyes had seen it: and, behold, the half was not told me: thy wisdom and prosperity exceedeth the fame which I heard. . . . And she gave the king an hundred and twenty talents of gold, and of spices very great store, and precious stones: there came no more such abundance of spices as these which the queen of Sheba gave to king Solomon.

1 Kings 10 :1

e Queen of Sheba   DUNCAN GRANT 1885–

[*Tate Gallery, London*]

III

Jesus said, Take heed, and beware of covetousness: for a man's life consisteth not in the abundance of the things which he possesseth. And he spake a parable unto them, saying, The ground of a certain rich man brought forth plentifully: and he thought within himself, saying, What shall I do, because I have no room where to bestow my fruits? And he said, This will I do: I will pull down my barns, and build greater; and there will I bestow all my fruits and my goods. And I will say to my soul, Soul, thou hast much goods laid up for many years; take thine ease, eat, drink, and be merry. But God said unto him, Thou fool, this night thy soul shall be required of thee: then whose shall those things be, which thou hast provided? So is he that layeth up treasure for himself, and is not rich toward God.

Luke 12 :15

IV

The world [is] the sum of created being, which belongs to the sphere of human life as an ordered whole, considered apart from God, and in its moral aspect represented by humanity. . . . It is easy to see how the thought of an ordered whole relative to man and considered *apart* from God passes into that of the ordered whole *separated* from God.

B. F. WESTCOTT (1825–1901)
Commentary on St John's Gospel (1880), 1 :10

V

The profession of a *Clergyman*, is an holy profession, because it is a ministration in *holy things*, an attendance at the *Altar*. But worldly business is to be made holy unto the Lord, by being done as a service to him, and in conformity to his divine will. . . . Men of worldly business therefore must not look upon themselves as at liberty to live to themselves, to sacrifice to their own *humours* and *tempers*, because their employment is of a worldly nature. But they must consider, that as the world and all worldly professions, a truly belong to God, as *persons* and *things* that are devoted to the *Altar*, so it is as much the duty of men in worldly business to live wholly unto God, as 'tis the duty of those, who are devoted to divine service. As the whole world is God's, so the whole world is to act for God. As all men have the same *relation* to God, as all men have all their *powers* and *faculties* from God, so all men are oblig'd to act for God with all their powers and faculties. As all things are God's, so all things are to be used and regarded as the things of God.

WILLIAM LAW (1686–1761)
A Serious Call to a Devout and Holy Life (1729), ch. IV

VI

St. Philip Neri, as old readings say,
Met a young stranger in Rome's streets one day,
And being ever courteously inclined
To give young men a sober turn of mind,
The dialogue they held comes down to us.

N.   Tell me what brings you, gentle youth, to Rome.
S.   To make myself a scholar, sir, I come.
N.   And when you are one, what do you intend?
S.   I hope to be a priest, sir, in the end.
N.   Suppose it so, what have you next in view?
S.   That I may come to be a Canon too.
N.   Assume it so.   *S.* Were it too bold to say
       That I a Bishop may become some day?
N.   What then?   *S.* Why, Cardinal's a high degree,
       And yet my lot it possibly may be.
N.   A Cardinal! What then?   *S.* Why, who shall say
       But I've a chance of being Pope one day.
N.   Well, having worn the triple crown and hat,
       And held the keys, what follows after that?
S.   Why, having held an ordinance so high
       As long as heaven shall please, then I must die.
N.   What, must you die, fine youth, and at the best
       But wish and hope, and may be all the rest?

Take my advice, whatever may betide,
For that which must be first of all provide;
Then think of that which may be, and indeed,
When well prepared, who knows what may succeed,
But you may be, as you are pleased to hope,
Priest, Canon, Bishop, Cardinal, and Pope!

Source unknown

VII

The parable of the Rich Fool has had a remarkable influence of its own. It describes the fool's folly in a very vivid way—his enormous sense of well-being, his euphoria as it is now called,—and then brings it all tumbling down. You can almost hear the crash. The parable must have helped to create a special type of Christian character, like Goldsmith's Vicar of Wakefield, or a better example still, Bunyan's Pilgrim—or rather John Bunyan himself, rich unto God, and his greatest wealth a fine collection of meaningful texts out of Scripture.

45

THE SAME SPIRIT

I

The manifestation of the Spirit is given to every man to profit withal. For to one is given by the Spirit the word of wisdom; to another the word of knowledge by THE SAME SPIRIT; to another faith by the same Spirit; to another the gifts of healing by the same Spirit; to another the working of miracles; to another prophecy; to another discerning of spirits; to another divers kinds of tongues; to another the interpretation of tongues: but all these worketh that one and the selfsame Spirit.

1 Corinthians 12 :7

II

And it came to pass, . . . that Elijah said unto Elisha, Ask what I shall do for thee, before I be taken away from thee. And Elisha said, I pray thee, let a double portion of thy spirit be upon me. And he said, Thou hast asked a hard thing: nevertheless, if thou see me when I am taken from thee, it shall be so unto thee; but if not, it shall not be so. And it came to pass, . . . that, behold, there appeared a chariot of fire, and horses of fire, and parted them both asunder; and Elijah went up by a whirlwind into heaven. And Elisha saw it, and he cried, My father, my father, the chariot of Israel, and the horsemen thereof. And he saw him no more: and he took hold of his own clothes, and rent them in two pieces. He took up also the mantle of Elijah that fell from him, and went back, and stood by the bank of Jordan; and he took the mantle of Elijah that fell from him, and smote the waters, and said, Where is the Lord God of Elijah? and when he also had smitten the waters, they parted hither and thither: and Elisha went over. And when the sons of the prophets which were to view at Jericho saw him, they said, The spirit of Elijah doth rest on Elisha.

2 Kings 2 :9

III

The very early Church

When they had prayed, the place was shaken where they were assembled together; and they were all filled with the Holy Ghost, and they spake the word of God with boldness. And the multitude of them that believed were of one heart and of one soul: neither said any of them that ought of the things which he possessed was his own; but they had all things common. And with great power gave the apostles witness of the resurrection of the Lord Jesus: and great grace was upon them all. Neither was there any among them that lacked: for as many as were possessors of lands or houses sold them, and brought the prices of the things that were sold, and laid them down at the apostles' feet: and distribution was made unto every man according as he had need.

Acts 4:31

IV

Spirit is no less real than matter, and the spiritual values of truth, goodness, and beauty no mere creations of finite minds, but abiding characteristics of that reality in the apprehension of which all minds capable of apprehending it find their satisfaction.

C. C. J. WEBB (1865–1954)
Religious Experience (1944)

V

A XVIIth century group, the Cambridge Platonists

Even as the contrast between the strife and chatter of the Agora, and the seclusion of the academic grove where Plato walked and talked, so seems to our imagination the contrast between the tumult of the outside ecclesiastical world and that little circle of choice spirits at Cambridge who 'studied to propagate better thoughts, to take men off from being in parties, or from narrow notions, from superstitious conceits and a fierceness about opinions'. What impresses one at once in these men is not so much the

214

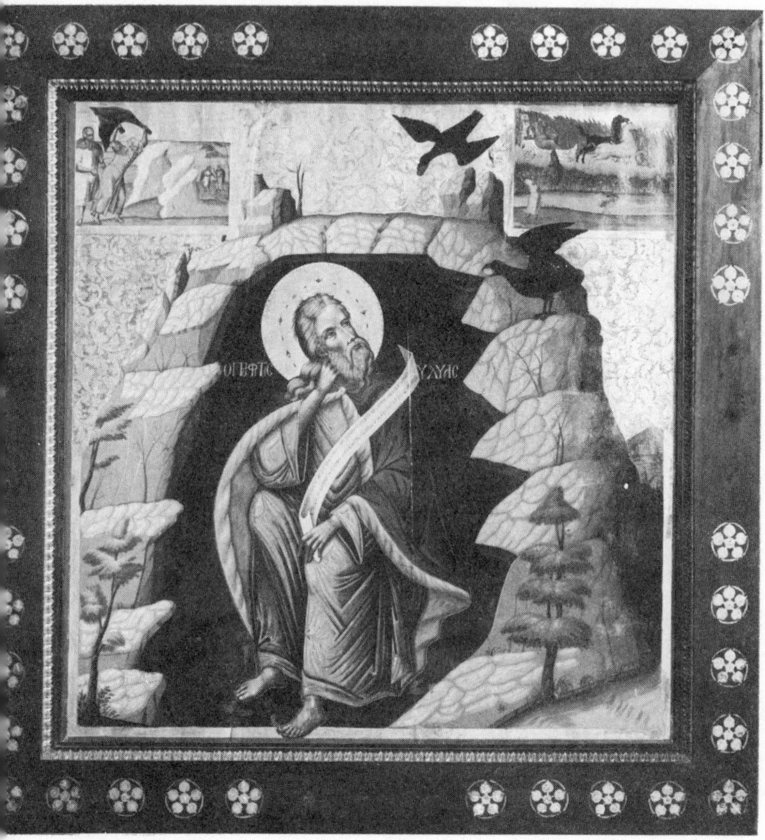

n of Elijah

[*St David's Cathedral, Pembrokeshire*]

articles of their creed—whether political or theological—as their temper. It is the temper of the Christian philosopher met with unexpectedly, and so the more welcome. They are not recluses. They are men of affairs. They are men who give free and large expression to their thoughts in speech and writing. They can give and take in controversy. Their views are definite, are deeply rooted in principle, are never lightly changed or abandoned. But, withal, their temper—as represented especially by Whichcote, Smith, Cudworth, and More—is the perfection of 'sweet reasonableness'. Bitter personalities and animosities—the generally accredited weapons of theological combatants—were abhorrent to them.

F. J. POWICKE (1854–1935)
The Cambridge Platonists (1926), Ch. 1

VI

My true Love hathe my harte, and I have his,
    By just exchaunge one for the other given,
I holde his deare, and myne hee can not misse,
    There never was a better Bargayne driven.

His harte in mee keepes mee and hym in one,
    My hart in hym his Thoughtes and sences guydes,
Hee Loves my Harte, for once yt was his owne,
    I Cherish his, bycause in mee yt bydes.

SIR PHILIP SIDNEY (1554–86)
Arcadia (1590)

VII

'Spirit is no less real than matter.' But why is it necessary to say so? The reason may be that the word 'spirit' has so many meanings. It means air and breath and breeze. It means temperament and mood. In many countries it means petrol, in England it means strong drink, in France it means wit. Even in religion it is elusive. But let us never doubt that the Holy Spirit is a fortifying presence, a Comforter, a reality essential to the life and well-being of our souls, to the conscious realization of our own *spirit*.

46

A MEASURE OF THY GRACE

I

O God, who declarest thy almighty power most chiefly in shewing mercy and pity; Mercifully grant unto us such A MEASURE OF THY GRACE, that we, running the way of thy commandments, may obtain thy gracious promises, and be made partakers of thy heavenly treasure; through Jesus Christ our Lord. Amen.

Collect

II

How was Simon the high priest honoured in the midst of the people in his coming out of the sanctuary! He was as the morning star in the midst of a cloud, and as the moon at the full: as the sun shining upon the temple of the most High, and as the rainbow giving light in the bright clouds: and as the flower of roses in the spring of the year, as lilies by the rivers of waters, and as the branches of the frankincense tree in the time of summer: as fire and incense in the censer, and as a vessel of beaten gold set with all manner of precious stones: and as a fair olive tree budding forth fruit, and as a cypress tree which groweth up to the clouds. When he put on the robe of honour, and was clothed with the perfection of glory, . . . he made the garment of holiness honourable.

Ecclesiasticus 50 :5

III

Of myself I will not glory, but in mine infirmities. . . . And lest I should be exalted above measure through the abundance of the revelations, there was given to me a thorn in the flesh, the mes-senger of Satan to buffet me, lest I should be exalted above measure. For this thing I besought the Lord thrice, that it might depart from me. And he said unto me, My grace is sufficient for thee: for my strength is made perfect in weakness. Most gladly therefore will I rather glory in my infirmities, that the power of Christ may rest upon me. Therefore I take pleasure in infirmities, in reproaches, in necessities, in persecutions, in distresses for Christ's sake: for when I am weak, then am I strong.

2 Corinthians 12 :5

IV

When it is said that somebody has the grace of God, that means that he has a certain something in him which is above and beyond nature, and proceeds from God.

ST THOMAS AQUINAS (*c.* 1225–74)
Summa Theologica (*c.* 1270), I–II, Question 110, Article 1

V

Nor was Mr *Hooker* more happy in his Contemporaries of his Time and College, than in the Pupillage and Friendship of his *Edwin Sandys* and *George Cranmer*; ... Betwixt Mr *Hooker* and these his two Pupils there was a sacred Friendship, a Friendship made up of Religious Principles, which increased daily by a similitude of Inclinations to the same Recreations and Studies; a Friendship elemented in Youth, and in an University, free from self-ends, which usually the Friendships of Age are not: and in this sweet, this blessed, this spiritual Amity they went on for many years; and, as the holy Prophet saith, so *they took sweet counsel together, and walked in the House of God as Friends* [Psalm 55:14–15]. By which means they improved it to such a degree of Amity as bordered upon Heaven; a Friendship so sacred, that when it ended in this world, it began in the next, where it shall have no end.

IZAAK WALTON (1593–1683)
The Life of Mr Richard Hooker (1665)

VI

A Parish-Priest was of the Pilgrim-Train;

218

John Keble　　　　　　GEORGE RICHMOND 1809–96

[*National Portrait Gallery, London*]

An Awful, Reverend, and Religious Man.
His Eyes diffus'd a venerable Grace,
And Charity it self was in his Face.
Rich was his Soul, though his Attire was poor;
(As God had cloath'd his own Embassador;)
For such, on Earth, his bless'd Redeemer bore. . . .
Yet, had his Aspect nothing of severe,
But such a Face as promis'd him sincere.
Nothing reserv'd or sullen was to see,
But sweet Regards; and pleasing Sanctity: . . .

    The tythes, his parish Freely paid, he took;
But never Su'd; or Curs'd with Bell and Book . . .

    Yet, of his little, he had some to spare,
To feed the Famish'd and to cloath the Bare:
For Mortify'd he was to that degree,
A poorer than himself, he wou'd not see.
True Priests, he said, and Preachers of the Word,
Were only Stewards of their Soveraign Lord,
Nothing was theirs; but all the publick Store,
Intrusted Riches to relieve the Poor.
Who, shou'd they steal, for want of his Relief,
He judg'd himself Accomplice with the Thief.

    Wide was his Parish; not contracted close
In streets, but here and there a straggling House;
Yet still he was at Hand, without Request
To serve the Sick, to succour the Distress'd;
Tempting, on Foot, alone, without affright,
The Dangers of a dark, tempestuous Night. . . .
His Preaching much, but more his Practice wrought;
(A living Sermon of the Truths he taught;)
For this by Rules severe his Life he squar'd:
That all might see the Doctrine which they heard.
For Priests, he said, are Patterns for the rest:
(The Gold of Heav'n, who bear the God Impress'd:)

JOHN DRYDEN (1631–1700)
The Character of a Good Parson
(imitated from Chaucer, 1700)

VII

Grace is by definition any free gift from God, good looks for instance, or being musical, or, more gracious still, a kind heart. But they are conditional gifts. What gifts are not? You may give your little boy a tin trumpet, but only on condition he does not madden people with it. You may have a persuasive tongue, but you may only use it for good. Every gift of grace has rules and restrictions, but these only make it more useful, and for the possessor of it more rewarding.

47

TRUST

I

And such TRUST have we through Christ to God-ward: not that we are sufficient of ourselves to think any thing as of ourselves; but our sufficiency is of God; who also hath made us able ministers of the new testament; not of the letter, but of the spirit: for the letter killeth, but the spirit giveth life.

2 Corinthians 3 :4

II

These are the words of the LORD:

> A curse on the man who trusts in man
> > and leans for support on human kind,
> > while his heart is far from the LORD!
> > He shall be like a juniper in the desert;
> > when good comes he shall not see it.
> > He shall dwell among the rocks in the wilderness,
> > in a salt land where no man can live.
> Blessed is the man who trusts in the LORD,
> > and rests his confidence upon him.
> He shall be like a tree planted by the waterside,
> > that stretches its roots along the stream.
> When the heat comes it has nothing to fear;
> > its spreading foliage stays green.
> > In a year of drought it feels no care,
> > > and does not cease to bear fruit.

Jeremiah 17 :5 NEB

III

Blessed be God, even the Father of our Lord Jesus Christ, the

222

Las Gigantillas   FRANCISCO GOYA 1746–1828

[*Museo del Prado, Madrid*]

Father of mercies, and the God of all comfort; who comforteth us in all our tribulation, that we may be able to comfort them which are in any trouble, by the comfort wherewith we ourselves are comforted of God. For as the sufferings of Christ abound in us, so our consolation also aboundeth by Christ. And whether we be afflicted, it is for your consolation and salvation, which is effectual in the enduring of the same sufferings which we also suffer: or whether we be comforted, it is for your consolation and salvation. And our hope of you is stedfast, knowing, that as ye are partakers of the sufferings, so shall ye be also of the consolation. For we would not, brethren, have you ignorant of our trouble which came to us in Asia, that we were pressed out of measure, above strength, insomuch that we despaired even of life: but we had the sentence of death in ourselves, that we should not trust in ourselves, but in God which raiseth the dead: who delivered us from so great a death, and doth deliver: in whom we trust that he will yet deliver us.

2 Corinthians 1 :3

IV

In thy word, Lord, is my trust,
    To thy mercies fast I flye;
Though I am but clay and dust,
    Yet thy grace can lift me high.

THOMAS CAMPION (*d.* 1620)
'Repentance'

V

. . . though it was too dark for Pierre to see, he felt that a suppressed smile of kindliness puckered the soldier's lips as he put these questions. He seemed grieved that Pierre had no parents, especially that he had no mother.

'A wife for counsel, a mother-in-law for welcome, but there's none as dear as one's own mother!' said he. 'Well, and have you little ones?' he went on asking.

Again Pierre's negative answer seemed to distress him, and he hastened to add:

'Never mind! You're young folks yet, and please God may still have some. The great thing is to live in harmony . . .' . . .

He seated himself more comfortably, and coughed, evidently preparing to tell a long story.

'Well, my dear fellow, I was still living at home,' he began. 'We had a well-to-do-homestead, plenty of land, we peasants lived well and our house was one to thank God for. When father and we went out mowing there were seven of us. We lived well. We were real peasants. It so happened . . .'

And Platón Karatáev told a long story of how he had gone into someone's copse to take wood, how he had been caught by the keeper, had been tried, flogged, and sent to serve as a soldier.

'Well, lad,' and a smile changed the tone of his voice, 'we thought it was a misfortune but it turned out a blessing! If it had not been for my sin, my brother would have had to go as a soldier. But he, my younger brother, had five little ones, while I, you see, only left a wife behind. We had a little girl, but God took her before I went as a soldier. I come home on leave and I'll tell you how it was, I look and see that they are living better than before. The yard full of cattle, the women at home, two brothers away earning wages, and only Michael, the youngest, at home. Father, he says, "All my children are the same to me: it hurts the same whichever finger gets bitten. But if Platón hadn't been shaved for a soldier, Michael would have had to go." He called us all to him and, will you believe it, placed us in front of the icons. "Michael," he says, "come here and bow down to his feet; and you, young woman, you bow down too; and you, grandchildren, also bow down before him! Do you understand?" he says. That's how it is, dear fellow. Fate looks for a head. But we are always judging, "that's not well—that's not right!" . . .'

LEO TOLSTOY (1828–1910)
War and Peace (1869, trans. Louise and
Aylmer Maude, 1942), Book XII, ch. 3

VI

Even such is tyme which takes in trust
Our yowth, our Ioyes, and all we have,

And payes us butt with age and dust:
  Who in the darke and silent grave
When we have wandred all our wayes,
Shutts up the storye of our dayes.
  And from which earth and grave and dust
  The Lord shall rayse me up I trust.

SIR WALTER RALEGH (1552?–1618)
The Conclusion (28 October 1618)

VII

The Christian has to take his religion on trust. Of course in this uncertain world we all have to take most things on trust, but the Christian's trust in his religion is of a special kind. He believes it can give him a sense of security and joy which others miss. It fortifies him against adversity, however threatening, for he believes that all will be well. This is because he knows that there are eternal things which cannot be shaken, and that God takes longer views than we do.

48

TRUE AND LAUDABLE SERVICE

I

Almighty and merciful God, of whose only gift it cometh that thy faithful people do unto thee TRUE AND LAUDABLE SERVICE; Grant, we beseech thee, that we may so faithfully serve thee in this life, that we fail not finally to attain thy heavenly promises; through the merits of Jesus Christ our Lord. Amen.

Collect

II

David has had to leave Jerusalem and is on the farther side of the river Jordan

And it came to pass, when David was come to Mahanaim, that Shobi the son of Nahash of Rabbah of the children of Ammon, and Machir the son of Ammiel of Lodebar, and Barzillai the Gileadite of Rogelim, brought beds, and basons, and earthen vessels, and wheat, and barley, and flour, and parched corn, and beans, and lentiles, and parched pulse, and honey, and butter, and sheep, and cheese of kine, for David, and for the people that were with him, to eat: for they said, The people is hungry, and weary, and thirsty, in the wilderness.

2 Samuel 17 :27

III

Supper being ended, the devil having now put into the heart of Judas Iscariot, Simon's son, to betray him; Jesus knowing that the Father had given all things into his hands, and that he was come from God, and went to God; he riseth from supper, and laid aside his garments; and took a towel, and girded himself. After that he poureth water into a bason, and began to wash the disciples' feet, and to wipe them with the towel wherewith he was girded. . . . So after he had washed their feet, and had taken his garments, and was set down again, he said unto them, Know ye what I have done to you? Ye call me Master and Lord: and ye say well; for so I am. If I then, your Lord and Master, have washed your feet; ye also ought to wash one another's feet. For I have given you an example, that ye should do as I have done to you. Verily, verily, I say unto you, The servant is not greater than his lord; neither he that is sent greater than he that sent him. If ye know these things, happy are ye if ye do them.

John 13:2

IV

God's service is perfect freedom (*cui servire est regnare*).

The Sacramentary of Gelasius (A.D. 494)

V

A barrister's clerk

Lovel took care of every thing. He was at once his clerk, his good servant, his dresser, his friend, his 'flapper', his guide, stop-watch, auditor, treasurer. . . . I knew this Lovel. He was a man of an incorrigible and losing honesty. A good fellow withal, and 'would strike'. In the cause of the oppressed he never considered inequalities, or calculated the number of his opponents. He once wrested a sword out the hand of a man of quality that had drawn upon him; and pommelled him severely with the hilt of it. The swordsman had offered insult to a female—an occasion upon which no odds against him could have prevented the interference of Lovel. He would stand next day bare headed to the same person, modestly to excuse his interference—for L. never forgot rank, where something better was not concerned. L. was the liveliest little fellow breathing, . . . had the merriest quips and conceits, and was altogether as brimful of rogueries and inventions as you could desire. He was a brother of the angle, moreover, and just such a free, hearty, honest companion as Mr Izaac Walton would have chosen to go a fishing with. I saw him in his old age and the

hrist washing the Disciples' Feet   FORD MADOX BROWN 1821–93

[*Tate Gallery, London*]

decay of his faculties, palsy-smitten, in the last sad stage of human weakness . . . yet even then his eye would light up upon the mention of his favourite Garrick. . . . At intervals, too, he would speak of his former life, and how he came up a little boy from Lincoln to go to service, and how his mother cried at parting with him, and how he returned, after some few years' absence, in his smart new livery to see her, and she blessed herself at the change, and could hardly be brought to believe that it was 'her own bairn'.

CHARLES LAMB (1775–1834)
The Old Benchers of the Inner Temple (1823)

VI

Horns within—Enter Lear, Knights and Attendants
Lear How now! What art thou? . . .
Kent I do profess to be no less than I seem, to serve him truly that will put me in trust, to love him that is honest, to converse with him that is wise and says little, to fear judgment, to fight when I cannot choose, and to eat no fish.
Lear What art thou?
Kent A very honest-hearted fellow, and as poor as the King.
Lear If thou be'st as poor for a subject as he's for a king, thou art poor enough. What wouldst thou?
Kent Service.
Lear Who wouldst thou serve?
Kent You.
Lear Dost thou know me, fellow?
Kent No, sir; but you have that in your countenance which I would fain call master.
Lear What's that?
Kent Authority.
Lear What services canst thou do?
Kent I can keep honest counsel, ride, run, mar a curious tale in telling it, and deliver a plain message bluntly. That which ordinary men are fit for, I am qualified in; and the best of me is diligence.

Lear How old art thou?
Kent Not so young, sir, to love a woman for singing, nor so old to
    dote on her for anything: I have years on my back forty-eight.
Lear Follow me; thou shalt serve me.

SHAKESPEARE (1564–1616)
King Lear (1606), I, iv, 9

VII

In the New Testament the same word (*doulos*) *serves* for 'servant'
and 'slave'. 'Service' (*servitium*) is simply the Latin word for
slavery. Something like half the inhabitants of Athens, where the
word 'democracy' comes from, were slaves. Today in the West
nobody can be bought or sold (except a footballer?), but millions
cannot change their situations. The kingdom of heaven which is
within us claims to make us free. God's service is perfect freedom.
We are free yet bound, servants and yet sons, called to do his will
and enjoying, if we do it, new-found liberty.

49

WALK IN THE SPIRIT

I

This I say then, WALK IN THE SPIRIT, and ye shall not fulfil the lust of the flesh. For the flesh lusteth against the Spirit, and the Spirit against the flesh: and these are contrary the one to the other: so that ye cannot do the things that ye would. But if ye be led of the Spirit, ye are not under the law. . . . But the fruit of the Spirit is love, joy, peace, longsuffering, gentleness, goodness, faith, meekness, temperance: against such there is no law.

Galatians 5 :16

II

It shall come to pass in the last days, that the mountain of the Lord's house shall be established in the top of the mountains, and shall be exalted above the hills; and all nations shall flow unto it. And many people shall go and say, Come ye, and let us go up to the mountain of the Lord, to the house of the God of Jacob; and he will teach us of his ways, and we will walk in his paths: for out of Zion shall go forth the law, and the word of the Lord from Jerusalem. And he shall judge among the nations, and shall rebuke many people: and they shall beat their swords into plowshares, and their spears into pruninghooks: nation shall not lift up sword against nation, neither shall they learn war any more. O house of Jacob, come ye, and let us walk in the light of the Lord.

Isaiah 2 :2

III

The afternoon of the first Easter Day
Behold, two of them went that same day to a village called Emmaus,

232

The Disciples at Emmaus

MICHELANGELO MERISI DA CARAVAGGIO 1569–1609

[*National Gallery, London*]

which was from Jerusalem about threescore furlongs. And they talked together of all these things which had happened. And it came to pass, that, while they communed together and reasoned, Jesus himself drew near, and went with them. But their eyes were holden that they should not know him. . . . And they drew nigh unto the village, whither they went: and he made as though he would have gone further. But they constrained him, saying, Abide with us: for it is toward evening, and the day is far spent. And he went in to tarry with them. And it came to pass, as he sat at meat with them, he took bread, and blessed it, and brake, and gave to them. And their eyes were opened, and they knew him; and he vanished out of their sight. And they said one to another, Did not our heart burn within us, while he talked with us by the way, and while he opened to us the scriptures? And they rose up the same hour, and returned to Jerusalem, and found the eleven gathered together, and them that were with them, saying, The Lord is risen indeed, and hath appeared to Simon. And they told what things were done in the way, and how he was known of them in breaking of bread.

Luke 24:13

IV

Of Courtesy, it is much less
Than Courage of Heart or Holiness,
Yet in my Walks it seems to me
That the Grace of God is in Courtesy.

HILAIRE BELLOC (1870–1953)
Verses (1910)

V

And the Bishop he was very gentle and meek man and he was devotion man too; and he likes the native people and they say of him, he is native bishop because he loves us very much and has spended his life travelling, travelling, walking walking everywhere, Nyasaland, Masasi, Newala, Magila, Misozwe, Umba, every country travelling always. And I went with him and I saw him and he is really saint and devotion man, the Lord Bishop Smythies.

(Canon) AUGUSTINE AMBALI
Thirty Years in Nyasaland (1923)

VI

After a dance :

Ere we retired,
The cock had crowed, and now the eastern sky
Was kindling, not unseen, from humble copse
And open field, through which the pathway wound,
And homeward led my steps. Magnificent
The morning rose, in memorable pomp,
Glorious as e'er I had beheld—in front
The sea lay laughing at a distance; near,
The solid mountains shone, bright as the clouds,
Grain-tinctured, drenched in empyrean light;
And in the meadows and the lower grounds
Was all the sweetness of a common dawn—
Dews, vapours, and the melody of birds,
And labourers going forth to till the fields.
Ah! need I say, dear Friend! that to the brim
My heart was full; I made no vows, but vows
Were then made for me; bond unknown to me
Was given, that I should be, else sinning greatly,
A dedicated Spirit. On I walked
In thankful blessedness, which yet survives.

WILLIAM WORDSWORTH (1770–1850)
The Prelude (1850), iv, 319

VII

St Paul uses the ordinary Greek word for walking (*peripatein*) thirty times in his Epistles, but always metaphorically, as when he urges the Galatians to walk in the Spirit. He means that they should adopt a way of life which cultivates the fruits of the Spirit, and of these he mentions nine. We might combine the literal and the metaphorical if on our walks we were thinking or talking of the fruits of the Spirit rather than of the lusts of the flesh, of which he has just mentioned seventeen varieties.

50

THE LILIES OF THE FIELD

I

Why take ye thought for raiment? Consider THE LILIES OF THE FIELD, how they grow; they toil not, neither do they spin: and yet I say unto you, That even Solomon in all his glory was not arrayed like one of these.

Matthew 6:28

II

These are the generations of the heavens and of the earth when they were created, in the day that the Lord God made the earth and the heavens, and every plant of the field before it was in the earth, and every herb of the field before it grew: for the Lord God had not caused it to rain upon the earth, and there was not a man to till the ground. But there went up a mist from the earth, and watered the whole face of the ground. And the Lord God formed man of the dust of the ground, and breathed into his nostrils the breath of life; and man became a living soul. And the Lord God planted a garden eastward in Eden; and there he put the man whom he had formed. And out of the ground made the Lord God to grow every tree that is pleasant to the sight, and good for food; the tree of life also in the midst of the garden, and the tree of knowledge of good and evil. And a river went out of Eden to water the garden.

Genesis 2:4

III

His disciples came unto him, and said, . . . They have nothing to eat. He answered and said unto them, Give ye them to eat. And they say unto him, Shall we go and buy two hundred pennyworth of bread, and give them to eat? He saith unto them, How many loaves have ye? go and see. And when they knew, they say, Five, and two fishes. And he commanded them to make all sit down by companies upon the green grass. And they sat down in ranks, by hundreds, and by fifties. And when he had taken the five loaves and the two fishes, he looked up to heaven, and blessed, and brake the loaves, and gave them to his disciples to set before them; and the two fishes divided he among them all. And they did all eat, and were filled. . . . And they that did eat of the loaves were about five thousand men.

Mark 6:35

The Greek translated 'in ranks' suggests that they were organized in oblong groups and looked like brightly coloured flower-beds.

IV

In the very act of labouring as a machine, Nature also sleeps as a picture.

J. B. MOZLEY (1813–78)
University Sermons (1871), VI

V

God *Almightie* first Planted a *Garden*. And indeed, it is the Purest of Humane pleasure. It is the Greatest Refreshment to the Spirits of Man; Without which *Buildings* and *Pallaces* are but Grosse Handy-works: And a Man shall ever see, that when Ages grow to Civility and Elegancie, Men come to *Build Stately*, sooner than to *Garden Finely*: As if *Gardening* were the Greater Perfection.

FRANCIS BACON (1561–1626)
'Of Gardens'
(*Essayes or Counsels, Civill and Morall*, 1625, No. XLVI)

VI

Or as I well remember one highday in June
bright on the seaward South-downs, where I had come afar
on a wild garden planted years agone, and fenced
thickly within live-beechen walls: the season it was

238

In Calabria   FRANK MONACO 1917–

of prodigal gay blossom, and man's skill had made
a fair-order'd husbandry of that native pleasaunce:
But had there been no more than earth's wild loveliness,
the blue sky and soft air and the unmown flowersprent lawns,
I would have lain me down and long'd, as then I did,
to lie there ever indolently undisturb'd, and watch
the common flowers that starr'd the fine grass of the wold,
waving in gay display their gold-heads to the sun,
each telling of its own inconscient happiness,
each type a faultless essence of God's will, such gems
as magic master-minds in painting or music
threw aside once for man's regard or disregard;
things supreme in themselves, eternal, unnumber'd
in the unexplored necessities of Life and Love.

ROBERT BRIDGES (1844–1930)
The Testament of Beauty, I, 19

VII

When I watch a flower growing day by day, let me think of Life:
When I find pleasure in its beauty, let me think of Love: When I
see its frailty, let me think of myself: When I see it wither, let me
remember I must die, but not forget that both my flower and I
may rise again.

51

GOD'S HELP AND GOODNESS

I

O Lord, we beseech thee, let thy continual pity cleanse and defend thy Church; and, because it cannot continue in safety without thy succour, preserve it evermore by THY HELP AND GOODNESS; through Jesus Christ our Lord. Amen.

Collect

II

The king of Syria warred against Israel, and took counsel with his servants, saying, In such and such a place shall be my camp. And the man of God sent unto the king of Israel, saying, Beware that thou pass not such a place; for thither the Syrians are come down. And the king of Israel sent to the place which the man of God told him and warned him of, and saved himself there, not once nor twice. Therefore the heart of the king of Syria was sore troubled for this thing; and he called his servants, and said unto them, Will ye not shew me which of us is for the king of Israel? And one of his servants said, None, my lord, O king: but Elisha, the prophet that is in Israel, telleth the king of Israel the words that thou speakest in thy bedchamber. And he said, Go and spy where he is, that I may send and fetch him. And it was told him, saying, Behold, he is in Dothan. Therefore sent he thither horses, and chariots, and a great host: and they came by night, and compassed the city about. And when the servant of the man of God was risen early, and gone forth, behold, an host compassed the city both with horses and chariots. And his servant said unto him, Alas, my master! how shall we do? And he answered, Fear not: for they that be with us are more than they that be with them. And Elisha prayed, and said, Lord, I pray thee, open his eyes, that he may see.

And the Lord opened the eyes of the young man; and he saw: and, behold, the mountain was full of horses and chariots of fire round about Elisha.

2 Kings 6 :8

III

And Jesus came out, and went, as he was wont, to the mount of Olives; and his disciples also followed him. And when he was at the place, he said unto them, Pray that ye enter not into temptation. And he was withdrawn from them about a stone's cast, and kneeled down, and prayed, saying, Father, if thou be willing, remove this cup from me: nevertheless not my will, but thine, be done. And there appeared an angel unto him from heaven, strengthening him.

Luke 22 :39

IV

In the Scottish rivers the salmon will leap and leap, and only after much leaping will they succeed in jumping up and into the higher reaches. Jump, Child, jump: *I* jump with you, look, we both manage it!

BARON FRIEDRICH VON HÜGEL (1852–1925)
Selected Letters (Epiphany, 1921)

V

Our Lord Jesus Christ, the Son of God, who by his Father was anointed with the Oil of gladness above his fellows, by his holy Anointing pour down upon your Head and Heart the blessing of the Holy Ghost, and prosper the works of your Hands: that by the assistance of his heavenly grace you may govern and preserve the Peoples committed to your charge in wealth, peace, and godliness; and after a long and glorious course of ruling a temporal kingdom wisely, justly, and religiously, you may at last be made partaker of an eternal kingdom, through the same Jesus Christ our Lord. Amen.

The Coronation : The Blessing after the Anointing

242

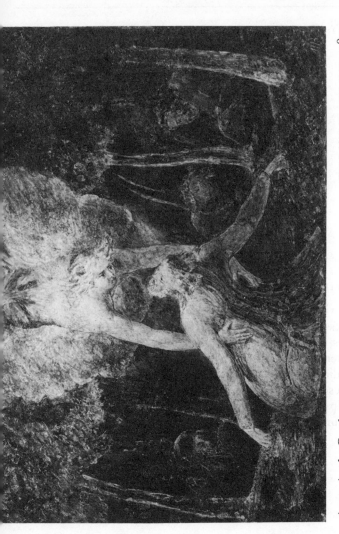

Agony in the Garden

WILLIAM BLAKE 1757–1827

[*Tate Gallery, London*]

VI

> Come, come, no time for lamentation now,
> Nor much more cause, *Samson* hath quit himself
> Like *Samson*, and heroickly hath finish'd
> A life Heroick, on his Enemies
> Fully reveng'd, . . .
>
> > To *Israel*
> Honour hath left, and freedom, let but them
> Find courage to lay hold on this occasion,
> To himself and Father's house eternal fame;
> And which is best and happiest yet, all this
> With God not parted from him, as was fear'd,
> But favouring and assisting to the end.

> > > J. MILTON (1608–74)
> > > *Samson Agonistes* (1671), 1708–1720

VII

The witness to the reality of God's help is universal, but so is the witness to the old saying that God helps those who help themselves, as also to the Bible truth that those whom the Lord loves he chastens. These are insights into the character of God's help—unfailing, co-operative, sometimes painful.

In some situations the words 'God help him' fall naturally from the lips, but too often as a cry of despair. They ought to be a cry of reassurance.

52

BAPTISM

I

There is one body, and one Spirit, even as ye are called in one hope of your calling; one Lord, one faith, one BAPTISM, one God and Father of all, who is above all, and through all, and in you all.

Ephesians 4:4

II

Joshua said unto the children of Israel, Come hither, and hear the words of the Lord your God. . . . It shall come to pass, as soon as the soles of the feet of the priests that bear the ark of the Lord, the Lord of all the earth, shall rest in the waters of Jordan, that the waters of Jordan shall be cut off from the waters that come down from above; and they shall stand upon an heap. And it came to pass, when the people removed from their tents, to pass over Jordan, and the priests bearing the ark of the covenant before the people; and as they that bare the ark were come unto Jordan, and the feet of the priests that bare the ark were dipped in the brim of the water, . . . that the waters which came down from above stood and rose up upon an heap, a great way off, at Adam,[1] the city that is beside Zaretan: and those that came down toward the sea of the plain, even the salt sea, failed, and were cut off: and the people passed over right against Jericho.

Joshua 3:9

III

They had refused obedience long ago, while God waited patiently in the days of Noah and the building of the ark, and in the ark a

[1] RV. AV says: 'very far from the city Adam'.

few persons, eight in all, were brought to safety through the water. This water prefigured the water of baptism through which you are now brought to safety. Baptism is not the washing away of bodily pollution, but the appeal made to God by a good conscience; and it brings salvation through the resurrection of Jesus Christ, who entered heaven after receiving the submission of angelic authorities and powers, and is now at the right hand of God.

1 Peter 3 :20 NEB

The feet of the priests were dipped in the water, and the people were saved ; the eight persons in the ark were saved 'by water'. These are 'figures of baptism', as also are many other uses of water.

IV

Name this Child.

Book of Common Prayer :
'Publick Baptism' (1662)

V

Extracts from Letters

Dorothy Wordsworth to Mrs Catherine Clarkson

Grasmere. 15th July [1803]

My dear Friend

Mary and I have never ceased to regret that you did not see our own darling Child before your departure from this country. It would have been very sweet to us to think that you had carried away an image of what we so dearly love. When you see him he will be a different creature and we should have liked that you had known perfectly what he is now; or rather what he was then, for he is much grown since that time, though indeed he does not appear to us to be much altered. He has blue eyes, a fair complexion, (which is already very much sunburnt) a body as fat as a little pig, arms that are thickening and dimpling and bracelets at his wrists, a very prominent nose which *will be* like his Father's and a head shaped upon the very same model. I send you a lock of his hair sewed to this letter. To-day we have all been at Church.

John the Baptist　　　　　　DONATELLO 1386–1466

[*Bargello, Florence : Mansell*]

Mary was *churched* and the Babe christened—Coleridge my Brother Richard and I were Godfathers and Godmother, old Mr Sympson answered for my brother Richard and had a hearty enjoyment of the christening cake, tea and coffee, this afternoon. . . .

About Thomas, the poet's second son, born 15 June 1806

Dorothy Wordsworth to Lady Beaumont

Grasmere, Tuesday Evening, June 17th [1806]

My dear Friend,

You will rejoice with us in my sister's safety, and the birth of a son. There was something peculiarly affecting to us in the time and manner of this child's coming into the world. It was like the very same thing over again which happened three years ago; for on the 18th of June, on such another morning, after such a clear and starlight night, the birds singing in the orchard in full assembly as on this 15th, the young swallows chirping in the self-same nest at the chamber window, the rose-trees rich with roses in the garden, the sun shining on the mountains, the air still and balmy,—on such a morning was Johnny born, and all our first feelings were revived at the birth of his brother two hours later in the day, and three days earlier in the month; and I fancied that I felt a double rushing-in of love for it, when I saw the child, as if I had both what had been the first-born infant John's share of love to give it, and its own. We said it was to be called William at first, but we have since had many discussions and doubts about the name; and Southey, who was here this morning, is decided against William; he would keep the father's name distinct, and not have two *William Wordsworths*. It never struck us in this way: . . .

Dorothy Wordsworth to Mrs Catherine Clarkson

Grasmere, July 23rd [1806]

. . . *Thomas*, so our youngest born is called, and I think you will like him the better for it, is a very fine child and thrives as well as Johnny did. I think he will be very handsome—he is like Johnny. I wish he had had hair enough on his head that we might have sent you a bit of it. He was christened the day after he was a month old,

Tom H. was Godfather and after *him* he is called, but we do not forget the two Thomas Clarksons in calling him by his name, and we are not a little proud of it, it sounds so consequential and old-fashioned. Mary Monkhouse (who came over to stand Godmother) is still here and Joanna Hutchinson. . . .

Tom H. is Mrs Wordsworth's brother

> *The Early Letters* and *The Letters* (*The Middle Years*) *of*
> *William and Dorothy Wordsworth*
> (edited by Ernest de Selincourt)

VI

Baptism

Dear be the Church that, watching o'er the needs
Of Infancy, provides a timely shower
Whose virtue changes to a christian Flower
A Growth from sinful Nature's bed of weeds!—
Fitliest beneath the sacred roof proceeds
The ministration; while parental Love
Looks on, and Grace descendeth from above
As the high service pledges now, now pleads.
There, should vain thoughts outspread their wings and fly
To meet the coming hours of festal mirth,
The tombs—which hear and answer that brief cry,
The Infant's notice of his second birth—
Recall the wandering Soul to sympathy
With what man hopes from Heaven, yet fears from Earth.

Sponsors

Father! to God himself we cannot give
A holier name! then lightly do not bear
Both names conjoined, but of thy spiritual care
Be duly mindful: still more sensitive
Do Thou, in truth a second Mother, strive
Against disheartening custom, that by Thee
Watched, and with love and pious industry
Tended at need, the adopted Plant may thrive

For everlasting bloom. Benign and pure
This Ordinance, whether loss it would supply,
Prevent omission, help deficiency,
Or seek to make assurance doubly sure.
Shame if the consecrated Vow be found
An idle form, the Word an empty sound!

WILLIAM WORDSWORTH (1770–1850)
Ecclesiastical Sonnets, Part III, xx (1827), xxi (1832)

VII

It is important to know who are married, and more still who are Christians. The growing practice for men to wear wedding-rings is useful and commendable. But baptism, which is the sign of membership of the Church, is no such visible mark. This may be because a Christian ought to be unmistakably distinguished by his attitude and behaviour. But generally speaking he is not. We who profess to be Christian need to ask ourselves often if we look like it.

53

ENRICHED BY GOD, IN ALL UTTERANCE

I

I thank my God always on your behalf, for the grace of God which is given you by Jesus Christ; that in everything ye are ENRICHED BY HIM, IN ALL UTTERANCE, and in all knowledge; even as the testimony of Christ was confirmed in you: so that ye come behind in no gift.

1 Corinthians 1 :4

II

Moses said unto the Lord, O my Lord, I am not eloquent, neither heretofore, nor since thou hast spoken unto thy servant: but I am slow of speech, and of a slow tongue. And the Lord said unto him, Who hath made man's mouth? or who maketh the dumb, or deaf, or the seeing, or the blind? have not I the Lord? Now therefore go, and I will be with thy mouth, and teach thee what thou shalt say. . . . Is not Aaron the Levite thy brother? I know that he can speak well. And also, behold, he cometh forth to meet thee: and when he seeth thee, he will be glad in his heart. And thou shalt speak unto him, and put words in his mouth: and I will be with thy mouth, and with his mouth, and will teach you what ye shall do. And he shall be thy spokesman unto the people.

Exodus 4 :10

III

These things have I spoken unto you in proverbs: but the time cometh, when I shall no more speak unto you in proverbs, but I shall shew you plainly of the Father. At that day ye shall ask in my name: and I say not unto you, that I will pray the Father for you: for the Father himself loveth you, because ye have loved me, and have believed that I came out from God. I came forth from the Father, and am come into the world: again, I leave the world, and go to the Father. His disciples said unto him, Lo, now speakest thou plainly, and speakest no proverb. Now are we sure that thou knowest all things, and needest not that any man should ask thee: by this we believe that thou camest forth from God.

John 16 :25

John uses the word for 'proverbs' (paroimiai) where the other Gospels use 'parables' (parabolai). Jesus has two kinds of utterance: (a) the hidden language of parables, (b) the plain speaking (Mark 4:11)

IV

> To me alone there came a thought of grief:
> A timely utterance gave that thought relief,
> And I again am strong.

WILLIAM WORDSWORTH (1770–1850)
'Ode on Intimations of Immortality' from
Recollections of Early Childhood (1803–6)

V

The recollections of the Head-master of Rugby [Dr Arnold] are inseparable from the recollections of the personal guide and friend of his scholars. They will at once recall those little traits, which, however minute in themselves, will to them suggest a lively image of his whole manner. They will remember the glance, with which he looked round in the few moments of silence before the lesson began, and which seemed to speak his sense of his own position and of theirs also, as the heads of a great school; . . . the well known changes of his voice and manner, so faithfully representing the feeling within; the pleased look and the cheerful 'Thank you', which followed upon a successful answer or translation; the fall of his countenance with its deepening severity, the stern elevation of the eyebrows, the sudden 'Sit down' which followed upon the reverse; the courtesy and almost deference to the boys, as to his equals in society, so long as there was nothing to disturb the friendliness of their relation; the startling earnestness with which

Kathleen Ferrier, 1951   CECIL BEATON 1904–

he would check in a moment the slightest approach to levity or impertinence; the confidence, with which he addressed them in his half-yearly exhortations; the expressions of delight with which, when they had been doing well, he would say that it was a constant pleasure to him to come into the library.

A. P. STANLEY (1815–81)
The Life and Correspondence of
Thomas Arnold D.D. (1844), Ch. III

VI

I lost the love of heaven above,
    I spurned the lust of earth below,
I felt the sweets of fancied love,
    And hell itself my only foe.

I lost earth's joys, but felt the glow
    Of heaven's flame abound in me,
Till loveliness and I did grow
    The bard of immortality.

I loved, but woman fell away;
    I hid me from her faded flame,
I snatched the sun's eternal ray
    And wrote till earth was but a name.

In every language upon earth,
    On every shore, o'er every sea,
I gave my name immortal birth
    And kept my spirit with the free.

JOHN CLARE (1793–1864)
A Vision

VII

Utterance is indeed a rich gift, and the practice of it as eloquence fraught with mighty consequences for good. It is an art of communication, of co-operation, of persuasion, of courtship, and heard best of all in well-sustained dialogue. Speech is man's special endowment, and the best description of it at its height is this: The Word became flesh and dwelt among us, full of grace and truth.

54

CORRUPT COMMUNICATION

I

Putting away lying, speak every man truth with his neighbour: for we are members one of another. Be ye angry, and sin not: let not the sun go down upon your wrath: neither give place to the devil. Let him that stole steal no more: but rather let him labour, working with his hands the thing which is good, that he may have to give to him that needeth. Let no CORRUPT COMMUNICATION proceed out of your mouth, but that which is good to the use of edifying, that it may minister grace unto the hearers. And grieve not the holy Spirit of God.

Ephesians 4:25

II

When king David came to Bahurim, behold, thence came out a man of the family of the house of Saul, whose name was Shimei, the son of Gera: he came forth, and cursed still as he came. And he cast stones at David, and at all the servants of king David. . . . And thus said Shimei when he cursed, Come out, come out, thou bloody man, and thou man of Belial. The Lord hath returned upon thee all the blood of the house of Saul, in whose stead thou hast reigned; and the Lord hath delivered the kingdom into the hand of Absalom thy son: and, behold, thou art taken in thy mischief, because thou art a bloody man. Then said Abishai the son of Zeruiah unto the king, Why should this dead dog curse my lord the king? let me go over, I pray thee, and take off his head. And the king said, What have I to do with you, ye sons of Zeruiah? so let him curse, because the Lord hath said unto him, Curse David. Who shall then say, Wherefore hast thou done so? And David said to Abishai, and to all his servants, Behold, my son, which came forth of my bowels, seeketh my life: how much more now may this Benjamite do it? let him alone, and let him curse; for the Lord hath bidden him. It may be that the Lord will look on mine affliction, and that the Lord will requite me good for his cursing this day. And as David and his men went by the way, Shimei went along on the hill's side over against him, and cursed as he went, and threw stones at him, and cast dust.

2 Samuel 16:5

III

The tongue is a little member, and boasteth great things. Behold, how great a matter a little fire kindleth! And the tongue is a fire, a world of iniquity: so is the tongue among our members, that it defileth the whole body, and setteth on fire the course of nature; and it is set on fire of hell. For every kind of beasts, and of birds, and of serpents, and of things in the sea, is tamed, and hath been tamed of mankind: but the tongue can no man tame; it is an unruly evil, full of deadly poison. Therewith bless we God, even the Father; and therewith curse we men, which are made after the similitude of God. Out of the same mouth proceedeth blessing and cursing. My brethren, these things ought not so to be.

James 3:5

IV

God be in my head,
    And in my understanding;
God be in my mouth,
    And in my speaking;
God be in my heart,
    And in my thinking.

Sarum Primer (1558)

V

This extract concerns the famous Judge Jeffreys when he was Lord Chief Justice (A.D. *1685*)

Jeffreys seemed incapable of exercising any self-restraint towards a prisoner who questioned his ruling or was not entirely submissive

Canvassing for Votes (detail)   WILLIAM HOGARTH 1697–1764

[*Sir John Soane's Museum, London*]

to his will. On the prosecution of Titus Oates for perjury the prisoner did not submit tamely to the Judge's provocative remarks, and the Judge treated him as a convicted criminal throughout the trial. Much of Jeffreys' summing up might be mistaken for a speech for the prosecution or an address to the prisoner on pronouncing sentence after his conviction. The following extracts from the summing up will serve as an illustration:

'. . . And is it not a prodigious thing to have such actions as these to-day defended in a court of justice with that impudence and unconcernedness as though he would challenge even God Almighty to punish his wickedness, and blasphemously blesses God that he has lived to do such wonderful service to the Protestant religion; and is so obstinate in his villainy as to declare he would venture his blood for the confirmation of so impious a falsehood? And indeed to speak the truth he makes no great venture in it, for when he had pawned his immortal soul by so perjured a testimony, he may very easily proffer the venturing of his vile carcass to maintain it.'

SIR JOHN C. FOX (1855–1943)
The Lady Ivie's Trial (1929: quoting from
Howell's State Trials)

VI

There used to be a custom then,
Miss Bourne, the Friend, went round at ten
To all the pubs in all the place,
To bring the drunkards' soul to grace;
Some sulked, of course, and some were stirred,
But none give her a dirty word.
A tall pale woman, grey and bent,
Folk said of her that she was sent.
She wore Friends' clothes, and women smiled,
But she'd a heart just like a child.
She come to us near closing time
When we were at some smutty rhyme,
And I was mad, and ripe for fun;
I wouldn't a minded what I done.

So when she come so prim and grey
I pound the bar and sing, 'Horray,
Here's Quaker come to bless and kiss us,
Come, have a gin and bitters, missus.' . . .

'Saul Kane,' she said, 'when next you drink,
Do me the gentleness to think
That every drop of drink accursed
Makes Christ within you die of thirst,
That every dirty word you say
Is one more flint upon His way,
Another thorn about His head,
Another mock by where He tread,
Another nail, another cross.
All that you are is that Christ's loss.'
The clock run down and struck a chime
And Mrs. Si said, 'Closing time.'
The wet was pelting on the pane
And something broke inside my brain.

JOHN MASEFIELD (1878–1967)
The Everlasting Mercy (1911)

VII

Bad language may be filthy, blasphemous, rude, at any rate disgusting to sensitive ears. It may be just vulgar abuse. It may be just a bad habit and mean less than nothing. At its worst it may serve to urge rotten arguments, whether cunning and calculated to mislead, or merely silly.

By contrast speech can edify and minister grace to the hearers, in other words it can be of great use and give great pleasure.

55

READY BOTH IN BODY AND SOUL

I

O Almighty and most merciful God, of thy bountiful goodness keep us, we beseech thee, from all things that may hurt us; that we, being READY BOTH IN BODY AND SOUL, may cheerfully accomplish those things that thou wouldest have done; through Jesus Christ our Lord. Amen.

Collect

II

Tobias is sent by his father Tobit to recover a debt from Gabael

Tobias then answered and said, Father, I will do all things which thou hast commanded me: but how can I receive the money, seeing I know him not? Then he gave him the handwriting, and said unto him, Seek thee a man which may go with thee, whiles I yet live, and I will give him wages: and go and receive the money. Therefore when he went to seek a man, he found Raphael that was an angel. But he knew not; and he said unto him, Canst thou go with me to Rages? and knowest thou those places well? To whom the angel said, I will go with thee, and I know the way well: for I have lodged with our brother Gabael. Then Tobias said unto him, Tarry for me, till I tell my father. . . . So they were well pleased. Then said Tobit to Tobias, Prepare thyself for the journey, and God send you a good journey. And when his son had prepared all things for the journey, his father said, Go thou with this man, and God, which dwelleth in heaven, prosper your journey, and the angel of God keep you company. So they went forth both, and the young man's dog with them. But Anna his mother wept.

Tobit 5 :1

Tobias and the Angel *follower of* VERROCCHIO 1435–88

[*National Gallery, London*]

III

There came down from Judæa a certain prophet, named Agabus. And when he was come unto us, he took Paul's girdle, and bound his own hands and feet, and said, Thus saith the Holy Ghost, So shall the Jews at Jerusalem bind the man that owneth this girdle, and shall deliver him into the hands of the Gentiles. And when we heard these things, both we, and they of that place, besought him not to go up to Jerusalem. Then Paul answered, What mean ye to weep and to break mine heart? for I am ready not to be bound only, but also to die at Jerusalem for the name of the Lord Jesus. And when he would not be persuaded, we ceased, saying, The will of the Lord be done. And after those days we took up our carriages, and went up to Jerusalem.

Acts 21 :10

IV

Be prepared.

Motto of The Scout Association

V

Among our Marchants here in England it is a common voyage, to trafique into Spaine: whereunto a shippe, being called The three halfe Moones, manned with eight and thirtie men, and well fensed with Munitions, the better to encounter their enemies withal, & having winde & tide, set from Portsmouth 1563, and bended her journey towarde Sivill a Citie in Spaine, intending there to trafique with them. And falling neere the Streights, they perceived themselves to be beset round about with eight Gallies of the Turks, in such wise, that there was no way for them to flie or escape away, but that either they must yeelde or else bee sunke. Which the owner perceiving, manfully encouraged his companie, exhorting them valiantly to shewe their manhoode, shewing them that God was their God, and not their enemies, requesting them also not to faint in seeing such a heape of their enemies readie to devoure them; putting them in minde also, that if it were Gods pleasure to give them into their enemies handes, it was not they that ought to shewe one displeasant looke or countenance thereagainst; but to take it patiently, and not to prescribe a day and time for their deliverance, as the Citizens of Bethulia did, but to put themselves under his mercie. And againe, if it were his minde and good will to shewe his mightie power by them, if their enemies were tenne times so many, they were not able to stande in their handes; putting them likewise in minde of the olde and auncient worthinesse of their Countreymen, who in the hardest extremities have alwayes most prevailed and gone away conquerours, yea, and where it hath bene almost impossible. Such (quoth he) hath bene the valiantnesse of our countreymen; and such hath bene the mightie power of our God.

With such other like incouragements, exhorting them to behave themselves manfully, they fell all on their knees making their Prayers briefly unto God: who being all risen up againe, perceived their enemies by their signes and defiances bent to the spoyle, whose mercie was nothing else but crueltie; whereupon every man tooke him to his weapon.

RICHARD HAKLUYT (1552?-1616)
'The Worthy enterprise of John Foxe'
(*The Principall Navigations of the English Nation*, 1560)

VI

Beatrice and her stepmother are about to be led out to execution

Beatrice   (speaking to her brother Bernardo).

                    One thing more, my child:
For thine own sake be constant to the love
Thou bearest us; and to the faith that I,
Though wrapped in a strange cloud of crime and shame,
Lived ever holy and unstained. And though
Ill tongues shall wound me, and our common name
Be as a mark stamped on thine innocent brow
For men to point at as they pass, do thou
Forbear, and never think a thought unkind
Of those, who perhaps love thee in their graves.
So mayest thou die as I do; fear and pain
Being subdued. Farewell! Farewell! Farewell!

Bernardo   I cannot say, farewell!

Camillo   (*a Cardinal*)   Oh, Lady Beatrice!

Beatrice   Give yourself no unnecessary pain,
          My dear Lord Cardinal. Here, Mother, tie
          My girdle for me, and bind up this hair
          In any simple knot; ay, that does well.
          And yours I see is coming down. How often
          Have we done this for one another; now
          We shall not do it any more. My Lord,
          We are quite ready. Well, 'tis very well.

P. B. SHELLEY (1792–1822)
The Cenci (1819), Act V, iv

VII

Having to get ready is a very frequent experience, and whether for business or pleasure, consists in providing for bodily needs, and much more in employing the mind in acquiring information, thinking over problems, adopting a line, cultivating a mood. But whatever is necessary, the purpose of it is that we may cheerfully accomplish those things that God would have us do. To keep this in mind should keep us cheerful from beginning to end.

56

THE WHOLE ARMOUR OF GOD

I

My brethren, be strong in the Lord, and in the power of his might. Put on THE WHOLE ARMOUR OF GOD, that ye may be able to stand against the wiles of the devil. For we wrestle not against flesh and blood, but against principalities, against powers, against the rulers of the darkness of this world, against spiritual wickedness in high places. Wherefore take unto you the whole armour of God, that ye may be able to withstand in the evil day, and having done all, to stand.

Ephesians 6 :10

II

And Saul armed David with his armour, and he put an helmet of brass upon his head; also he armed him with a coat of mail. And David girded his sword upon his armour, and he assayed to go; for he had not proved it. And David said unto Saul, I cannot go with these; for I have not proved them. And David put them off him. And he took his staff in his hand, and chose him five smooth stones out of the brook, and put them in a shepherd's bag which he had, even in a scrip; and his sling was in his hand: and he drew near to the Philistine. And the Philistine came on and drew near unto David; and the man that bare the shield went before him. And when the Philistine looked about, and saw David, he disdained him: for he was but a youth, and ruddy, and of a fair countenance. And the Philistine said unto David, Am I a dog, that thou comest to me with staves? And the Philistine cursed David by his gods. And the Philistine said to David, Come to me, and I will give thy flesh unto the fowls of the air, and to the beasts of the field. Then said David to the Philistine, Thou comest to me with a sword, and with a spear, and with a shield: but I come to thee in the name of the Lord of hosts, the God of the armies of Israel, whom thou hast defied. This day will the Lord deliver thee into mine hand.

1 Samuel 17 :38

III

While Jesus yet spake, lo, Judas, one of the twelve, came, and with him a great multitude with swords and staves, from the chief priests and elders of the people. Now he that betrayed him gave them a sign, saying, Whomsoever I shall kiss, that same is he: hold him fast. And forthwith he came to Jesus, and said, Hail, master; and kissed him. And Jesus said unto him, Friend, wherefore art thou come? Then came they, and laid hands on Jesus, and took him. And, behold, one of them which were with Jesus stretched out his hand, and drew his sword, and struck a servant of the high priest's, and smote off his ear. Then said Jesus unto him, Put up again thy sword into his place: for all they that take the sword shall perish with the sword. Thinkest thou that I cannot now pray to my Father, and he shall presently give me more than twelve legions of angels? But how then shall the scriptures be fulfilled, that thus it must be?

Matthew 26 :47

IV

Before Agincourt

Gloucester   I hope they will not come upon us now.

King Henry   We are in God's hand, brother, not in theirs.

WILLIAM SHAKESPEARE (1564–1616)
King Henry V (1600), III, vi, 163

V

Apollyon   *I am come out on purpose to withstand thee.*

Christian   *Apollyon*, beware what you do, for I am in the Kings High-way, the way of Holiness, therefore take heed to your self.

266

Christian and Apollyon

GEORGE BURDER 1752–1832

[*from an edition of 'The Pilgrim's Progress' published about 1790 by Alex Hogg, London*]

Then *Apollyon* strodled quite over the whole breadth of the way, and said, I am void of fear in this matter, prepare thy self to dye, for I swear thou shalt go no further, here will I spill thy soul; and with that, he threw a flaming Dart at his brest, but *Christian* had a Shield in his hand, with which he caught it, and so prevented the danger of that. Then did *Christian* draw, for he saw 'twas time to bestir him; and *Apollyon* as fast made at him, throwing Darts as thick as Hail; by the which, notwithstanding all that *Christian* could do to avoid it, *Apollyon* wounded him in his head, his hand and foot; this made *Christian* give a little back: *Apollyon* therefore followed his work amain, and *Christian* again took courage, and resisted as manfully as he could. This sore Combat lasted for above half a day, even till *Christian* was almost quite spent. For you must know that Christian, by reason of his wounds, must needs grow weaker and weaker.

Then *Apollyon*, espying his opportunity, began to gather up close to *Christian*, and wrestling with him, gave him a dreadful fall; and with that, *Christians* Sword flew out of his hand. Then said *Apollyon*, *I am sure of thee now*; . . . But as God would have it, while *Apollyon* was fetching of his last blow, thereby to make a full end of this good Man, *Christian* nimbly reached out his hand for his Sword, and caught it, saying, *Rejoyce not against me, O mine Enemy! when I fall, I shall arise*; and with that, gave him a deadly thrust, which made him give back, as one that had received his mortal wound. *Christian* perceiving that, made at him again, saying, *Nay, in all these things we are more then Conquerors*. And with that, *Apollyon* spread forth his Dragons wings, and sped him away, that *Christian* for a season saw him no more.

JOHN BUNYAN (1628–88)
Pilgrim's Progress (1678)

VI

    Not all the water in the rough rude sea
    Can wash the balm from an anointed king;
    The breath of worldly men cannot depose
    The deputy elected by the Lord.

For every man that Bolingbroke hath press'd
To lift shrewd steel against our golden crown,
God for his Richard hath in heavenly pay
A glorious angel. Then, if angels fight,
Weak men must fall; for heaven still guards the right.

WILLIAM SHAKESPEARE (1564–1616)
Richard II (*c*. 1594), III, ii, 54

VII

The Christian is perpetually at war with the flesh, the world, and
the devil. His weapons for this warfare are found to be truth,
righteousness, peace, faith, salvation, and the Word of God. He
can have none better, but must strive to make them as effective
as they possibly can be. In spite of all appearances to the contrary,
it does look as if this is what the whole world has always been after,
and is now, though in a confused and often conflicting manner.

57

THE GLORY AND PRAISE OF GOD

I

This I pray, that your love may abound yet more and more in knowledge and in all judgment; that ye may approve things that are excellent; that ye may be sincere and without offence till the day of Christ; being filled with the fruits of righteousness, which are by Jesus Christ, unto THE GLORY AND PRAISE OF GOD.

Philippians 1 :9

II

Then the three, as out of one mouth, praised, glorified, and blessed, God in the furnace, saying, Blessed art thou, O Lord God of our fathers: and to be praised and exalted above all for ever. And blessed is thy glorious and holy name: and to be praised and exalted above all for ever. Blessed art thou in the temple of thine holy glory: and to be praised and glorified above all for ever. Blessed art thou that beholdest the depths, and sittest upon the cherubims: and to be praised and exalted above all for ever. Blessed art thou on the glorious throne of thy kingdom: and to be praised and glorified above all for ever. Blessed art thou in the firmament of heaven: and above all to be praised and glorified for ever. O all ye works of the Lord, bless ye the Lord: praise and exalt him above all for ever.

The Song of the Three Holy Children, 28

III

I beheld, and I heard the voice of many angels round about the throne and the living creatures[1] and the elders: and the number of

[1] RSV.

Fireplace (detail)

DOMENICO ROSSELLI 15th century

[*Palazzo Ducale, Urbino : Mansell*]

them was ten thousand times ten thousand, and thousands of thousands; saying with a loud voice, Worthy is the Lamb that was slain to receive power, and riches, and wisdom, and strength, and honour, and glory, and blessing. And every creature which is in heaven, and on the earth, and under the earth, and such as are in the sea, and all that are in them, heard I saying, Blessing, and honour, and glory, and power, be unto him that sitteth upon the throne, and unto the Lamb for ever and ever. And the four living creatures[1] said, Amen. And the four and twenty elders fell down and worshipped him that liveth for ever and ever.

Revelation 5:11

IV

To God only be all Glory.

Motto of a City Livery Company

V

As therefore when we think of God himself, we are to have no sentiments but of praise and thanksgiving; so when we look at those things which are under the direction of God, and govern'd by his Providence, we are to receive them with the same tempers of praise and gratitude.

And though we are not to think all things right, and just, and lawful, which the Providence of God permits; for then nothing could be unjust, because nothing without his permission: yet we must adore God in the greatest publick calamities, the most grievous persecutions, as things that are suffer'd by God, like *plagues* and *famines*, for ends suitable to his wisdom and glory in the government of the world.

There is nothing more suitable to the piety of a reasonable creature, or the spirit of a Christian, than thus to approve, admire, and glorify God in all the acts of his general Providence: considering the whole world as his particular family, and all events as directed by his wisdom.

WILLIAM LAW (1686–1761)
A Serious Call to a Devout and Holy Life (1729),
Ch. XXII

[1] RSV.

VI

PRAISE above all—for praise prevails;
Heap up the measure, load the scales,
    And good to goodness add:
The gen'rous soul her saviour aids,
But peevish obloquy degrades;
    The Lord is great and glad.

For ADORATION all the ranks
Of Angels yield eternal thanks,
    And DAVID in the midst;
With God's good poor, which, last and least
In man's esteem, thou to thy feast,
    O blessed bride-groom, bidst.

For ADORATION seasons change,
And order, truth, and beauty range,
    Adjust, attract, and fill:
The grass the polyanthus cheques;
And polished porphyry reflects,
    By the descending rill. . . .

The wealthy crops of whit'ning rice,
'Mongst thyine woods and groves of spice,
    For ADORATION grow;
And, marshall'd in the fenced land,
The peaches and pomegranates stand,
    Where wild carnations grow. . . .

The chearful holly, pensive yew,
And holy thorn, their trim renew;
    The squirrel hoards his nuts:
All creatures batten o'er their stores,
And careful nature all her doors
    For ADORATION shuts.

For ADORATION, DAVID'S psalms
Lift up the heart to deeds of alms;
    And he, who kneels and chants,
Prevails his passions to controul,

> Finds meat and med'cine to the soul,
>> Which for translation pants.

CHRISTOPHER SMART (1722–71)
A Song to David (1763)

VII

We cannot increase God's glory and it sounds like an impertinence to praise him. We think too highly of ourselves when we suppose his creation of man is his highest glory, and even if it is, we tarnish it by our imperfections. We must hesitate to praise him for what seems to us so wonderful and beautiful, because, although we know something of his mind, we do not know enough. Yet praise and magnify him we must and will, not for his pleasure, but for our own deep satisfaction. We need not ask why.

58

OUR CONVERSATION IS IN HEAVEN

I

OUR CONVERSATION IS IN HEAVEN; from whence also we look for the Saviour, the Lord Jesus Christ: who shall change our vile body, that it may be fashioned like unto his glorious body, according to the working whereby he is able even to subdue all things unto himself.

Philippians 3 :20

The Greek word translated 'conversation' is politeuma, *which means a city as a place offering an organized community, life, and citizenship. 'Conversation' is used in its wider sense, now obsolete, of consorting with or having dealings with others in general, not only talking.*

II

Then went up Moses, and Aaron, Nadab, and Abihu, and seventy of the elders of Israel: and they saw the God of Israel: and there was under his feet as it were a paved work of a sapphire stone, and as it were the body of heaven in his clearness. And upon the nobles of the children of Israel he laid not his hand: also they saw God, and did eat and drink. And the Lord said unto Moses, Come up to me into the mount, and be there: and I will give thee tables of stone, and a law, and commandments which I have written; that thou mayest teach them. And Moses rose up, and his minister Joshua: and Moses went up into the mount of God. . . . and a cloud covered the mount. And the glory of the Lord abode upon mount Sinai, and the cloud covered it six days: and the seventh day he called unto Moses out of the midst of the cloud. And the sight of the glory of the Lord was like devouring fire on the top of the mount in the eyes of the children of Israel. And Moses went into the midst of the cloud.

Exodus 24:9

III

By faith Abraham, when he was called to go out into a place which he should after receive for an inheritance, obeyed; and he went out, not knowing whither he went. By faith he sojourned in the land of promise, as in a strange country, dwelling in tabernacles with Isaac and Jacob, the heirs with him of the same promise: for he looked for a city which hath foundations, whose builder and maker is God. . . . Therefore sprang there even of one, and him as good as dead, so many as the stars of the sky in multitude, and as the sand which is by the sea shore innumerable. These all died in faith, not having received the promises, but having seen them afar off, and were persuaded of them, and embraced them, and confessed that they were strangers and pilgrims on the earth. For they that say such things declare plainly that they seek a country. And truly, if they had been mindful of that country from whence they came out, they might have had opportunity to have returned. But now they desire a better country, that is, an heavenly: wherefore God is not ashamed to be called their God: for he hath prepared for them a city.

Hebrews 11:8

IV

To see a World in a Grain of Sand,
And a Heaven in a Wild Flower,
Hold Infinity in the palm of your hand,
And Eternity in an hour.

WILLIAM BLAKE (1757–1827)
Auguries of Innocence (1803)

V

Socrates is saying that the wise man will pay much more attention to his soul than to his body. Glauco assents, and Socrates continues:
Again as to honours he will keep to the same point of view. Of

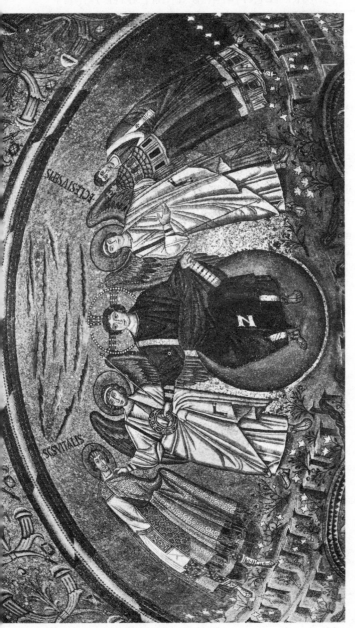

The Redeemer with two angels, S. Vitale and S. Eclesia

[*A 6th century mosaic : Church of S. Vitale, Ravenna : Mansell*]

some he will gladly take his share and have a taste, of those, that is, which he thinks will make him better; but others which he thinks will demoralize him, he will avoid both in his private and in his civic life.

If that is what he is to care about, he will be unwilling to take a part in politics, he said.

No, no, I said, he will be very willing indeed in his own city, but not perhaps in the place he is sprung from, unless by some remarkable piece of good fortune.

I understand, he said. You mean he will go in for politics in the city which we have been engaged in founding, one that is situated in the realms of thought, or at least, I think, nowhere on earth.

Perhaps, I said, there is a pattern of it laid up in heaven for anyone who has eyes to see it, and seeing it to shape the constitution within him on the same lines. But it makes no difference whether it actually exists anywhere or ever will. He would take part in the politics of this city only and of no other.

PLATO (*c.* 429–347 B.C.)
Republic (388 B.C.), IX, 592A

VI

Faire is the heaven, where happie soules have place,
In full enjoyment of felicitie,
Whence they doe still behold the glorious face
Of the divine eternall Majestie;
More faire is that, where those *Idees* on hie
Enraunged be, which *Plato* so admyred,
And pure *Intelligences* from God inspyred.

Yet fairer is that heaven, in which doe raine
The soveraine *Powres* and mightie *Potentates*,
Which in their high protections doe containe
All mortall Princes, and imperiall States;
And fayrer yet, whereas the royall Seates
And heavenly *Dominations* are set,
From whom all earthly governance is fet.

278

Yet farre more faire be those bright *Cherubins*,
Which all with golden wings are overdight,
And those eternall burning *Seraphins*,
Which from their faces dart out fierie light;
Yet fairer then they both, and much more bright
Be th' Angels and Archangels, which attend
On Gods owne person, without rest or end.

These thus in faire each other farre excelling,
As to the Highest they approch more neare,
Yet is that Highest farre beyond all telling,
Fairer then all the rest which there appeare,
Though all their beauties joynd together were:
How then can mortall tongue hope to expresse,
The image of such endlesse perfectnesse?

EDMUND SPENSER (1552?–99)
'An Hymne of Heavenly Beautie' (*Fowre Hymnes*, 1596)

VII

Plato's notion of a citizenship in heaven has come down to us with undiminished authority and influence through many channels philosophical and ecclesiastical. It makes us realize that we are somehow living in a foreign country now. Some simply feel they are foreigners. Some of us, of a happier temperament, feel we are being educated in this life for another and a better.

59

ALL PATIENCE AND LONG-
SUFFERING WITH JOYFULNESS

I

Walk worthy of the Lord unto all pleasing, being fruitful in every
good work, and increasing in the knowledge of God; strengthened
with all might, according to his glorious power, unto ALL
PATIENCE AND LONGSUFFERING WITH JOYFULNESS giving thanks
unto the Father, which hath made us meet to be partakers of the
inheritance of the saints in light.

Colossians 1:10

II

The ungodly said, reasoning with themselves, but not aright, . . .
Let us lie in wait for the righteous; because he is not for our turn,
and he is clean contrary to our doings: he upbraideth us with our
offending the law, and objecteth to our infamy the transgressings
of our education. He professeth to have the knowledge of God:
and he calleth himself the child of the Lord. He was made to
reprove our thoughts. He is grievous unto us even to behold: for
his life is not like other men's, his ways are of another fashion. We
are esteemed of him as counterfeits: he abstaineth from our ways
as from filthiness: he pronounceth the end of the just to be blessed,
and maketh his boast that God is his father. Let us see if his words
be true: and let us prove what shall happen in the end of him. For
if the just man be the son of God, he will help him, and deliver
him from the hand of his enemies. Let us examine him with des-
pitefulness and torture, that we may know his meekness, and
prove his patience. Let us condemn him with a shameful death:
for by his own saying he shall be respected. Such things they did

A Tea Party   THOMAS WEBSTER 1800–86

[*Harris Museum and Art Gallery, Preston*]

imagine, and were deceived. . . . But the souls of the righteous are in the hand of God, and there shall no torment touch them.

Wisdom 2 :1

III

Then said Jesus unto them, Nation shall rise against nation, and kingdom against kingdom: and great earthquakes shall be in divers places, and famines, and pestilences; and fearful sights and great signs shall there be from heaven. But before all these, they shall lay their hands on you, and persecute you, delivering you up to the synagogues, and into prisons, being brought before kings and rulers for my name's sake. And it shall turn to you for a testimony. Settle it therefore in your hearts, not to meditate before what ye shall answer: for I will give you a mouth and wisdom, which all your adversaries shall not be able to gainsay nor resist. And ye shall be betrayed both by parents, and brethren, and kinsfolks, and friends; and some of you shall they cause to be put to death. And ye shall be hated of all men for my name's sake. But there shall not an hair of your head perish. In your patience possess ye your souls.

Luke 21 :10

IV

. . . remember, no joy without suffering—no patience without trial—no humility without humiliation—no life without death.

BARON FRIEDRICH VON HÜGEL (1852–1925)
Letters to a Niece (Gwendolyn Greene)

V

He was an old man who fished alone in a skiff in the Gulf Stream and he had gone eighty-four days now without taking a fish. In the first forty days a boy had been with him. But after forty days without a fish the boy's parents had told him that the old man was now definitely and finally *salao*, which is the worst form of unlucky, and the boy had gone at their orders in another boat which caught three good fish the first week. It made the boy sad to see the old man come in each day with his skiff empty and he always went down to help him carry either the coiled lines or the gaff and harpoon and the sail that was furled around the mast. The sail was patched with flour sacks and, furled, it looked like the flag of permanent defeat.

The old man was thin and gaunt with deep wrinkles in the back of his neck. The brown blotches of the benevolent skin cancer the sun brings from its reflection on the tropic sea were on his cheeks. The blotches ran well down the sides of his face and his hands had the deep-creased scars from handling heavy fish on the cords. But none of these scars were fresh. They were as old as erosions in a fishless desert.

Everything about him was old except his eyes and they were the same colour as the sea and were cheerful and undefeated.

ERNEST HEMINGWAY (1898–1961)
The Old Man and the Sea (1952), The Opening

VI

'Tis forty years now since we were wed:
We are ailing an' grey needs not to be said:
But Willie's eye is as blue an' soft
As the day when he wooed me in father's croft.

Yet changed am I in body an' mind,
For Willie to me has ne'er been kind:
Merrily drinking an' singing with the men
He 'ud come home late six nights o' the se'n.

An' since the children be grown an' gone
He 'as shunned the house an' left me lone:
An' less an' less he brings me in
Of the little he now has strength to win.

The roof lets through the wind an' the wet,
An' master won't mend it with us in's debt:
An' all looks every day more worn,
An' the best of my gowns be shabby an' torn.

No wonder if words hav' a-grown to blows;
That matters not while nobody knows:
For love him I shall to the end of life,
An' be, as I swore, his own true wife.

ROBERT BRIDGES (1844–1930)
Shorter Poems (1893), Bk. V, 18

VII

The first Christians in a provincial Phrygian town like Colossae would have much to endure, and St Paul exhorts them not only to endure, but to endure with joy. He sees that they will need a special strength which he describes as 'might, according to God's glorious power'. What sort of strength is that? It is a great strength, which is elsewhere only ascribed to God, and having something of divine glory about it, what else than heroic and indomitable Courage?

60

JUDGMENT AND JUSTICE IN THE EARTH

I

Behold, the days come, saith the Lord, that I will raise unto David a righteous Branch, and a King shall reign and prosper, and shall execute JUDGMENT AND JUSTICE IN THE EARTH. In his days Judah shall be saved, and Israel shall dwell safely: and this is his name whereby he shall be called, The Lord our Righteousness.

Jeremiah 23 :5

II

God's judgment

The Lord God called unto Adam, and said unto him, . . . Hast thou eaten of the tree, whereof I commanded thee that thou shouldest not eat? And the man said, The woman whom thou gavest to be with me, she gave me of the tree, and I did eat. And the Lord God said unto the woman, What is this that thou hast done? And the woman said, The serpent beguiled me, and I did eat. And the Lord God said unto the serpent, Because thou hast done this, thou art cursed above all cattle, and above every beast of the field; upon thy belly shalt thou go, and dust shalt thou eat all the days of thy life: and I will put enmity between thee and the woman, and between thy seed and her seed; it shall bruise thy head, and thou shalt bruise his heel. Unto the woman he said, I will greatly multiply thy sorrow and thy conception; in sorrow thou shalt bring forth children; and thy desire shall be to thy husband, and he shall rule over thee. And unto Adam he said, Because thou hast hearkened unto the voice of thy wife, and hast eaten of the tree, of which I commanded thee, saying, Thou shalt not eat of it: cursed is the ground for thy sake; in sorrow shalt thou eat of it all the days of thy life; thorns also and thistles shall it bring forth to thee; and thou shalt eat the herb of the field; in the sweat of thy face shalt thou eat bread, till thou return unto the ground; for out of it wast thou taken: for dust thou art, and unto dust shalt thou return. . . . So he drove out the man; and he placed at the east of the garden of Eden Cherubims, and a flaming sword which turned every way, to keep the way of the tree of life.

Genesis 3 :9

III

Man's judgment

When Gallio was the deputy of Achaia, the Jews made insurrection with one accord against Paul, and brought him to the judgment seat, saying, This fellow persuadeth men to worship God contrary to the law. And when Paul was now about to open his mouth, Gallio said unto the Jews, If it were a matter of wrong or wicked lewdness, O ye Jews, reason would that I should bear with you: but if it be a question of words and names, and of your law, look ye to it; for I will be no judge of such matters. And he drave them from the judgment seat. Then all the Greeks took Sosthenes, the chief ruler of the synagogue, and beat him before the judgment seat. And Gallio cared for none of those things.

Acts 18 :12

IV

Justice is truth in action.

BENJAMIN DISRAELI (1804–81)
Speech in the House of Commons (11 February 1851)

V

Justice in the Law Courts
The following extracts from judgments given in the House of Lords in 1932 concern an appeal from the Court of Session in Scotland. A soft drinks manufacturer had supplied ginger-beer in an opaque bottle to a

Adam and Eve   MASACCIO (1401–28)

[*Chiesa del Carmine, Florence : Mansell*]

retailer; the retailer resold it to a lady, who, in turn, treated the appellant, a young woman of her acquaintance, to its contents, which were subsequently found to include the decomposed remains of a snail. The young woman suffered a serious illness as a result and, while there was no contractual relationship between herself and the manufacturer, a majority of their Lordships decided that he owed her a duty to take care that the contents of the bottle were not harmful and that she was consequently entitled to recover damages. The case occasioned an important clarification of the civil law of negligence.

LORD ATKIN . . . in English law there must be, and is, some general conception of relations giving rise to a duty of care, of which the particular cases found in the books are but instances. The liability for negligence, whether you style it such or treat it as in other systems as a species of 'culpa', is no doubt based upon a general public sentiment of moral wrongdoing for which the offender must pay. But acts or omissions which any moral code would censure cannot in a practical world be treated so as to give a right to every person injured by them to demand relief. In this way rules of law arise which limit the range of complainants and the extent of their remedy. The rule that you are to love your neighbour becomes in law, you must not injure your neighbour; and the lawyer's question, Who is my neighbour? receives a restricted reply. You must take reasonable care to avoid acts or omissions which you can reasonably foresee would be likely to injure your neighbour. Who, then, in law, is my neighbour? The answer seems to be—persons who are so closely and directly affected by my act that I ought reasonably to have them in contemplation as being so affected when I am directing my mind to the acts or omissions which are called in question. . . .

LORD MACMILLAN . . . In the daily contacts of social and business life human beings are thrown into, or place themselves in, an infinite variety of relations with their fellows; and the law can refer only to the standards of the reasonable man in order to determine whether any particular relation gives rise to a duty to take care as between those who stand in that relation to each other. The grounds of action may be as various and manifold as human errancy; and the conception of legal responsibility may develop in adaptation to altering social conditions and standards. The criterion of judgment must adjust and adapt itself to the changing circumstances of life. The categories of negligence are never closed. The cardinal principle of liability is that the party complained of should owe to the party complaining a duty to take care, and that the party complaining should be able to prove that he has suffered damage in consequence of a breach of that duty. Where there is room for diversity of view, it is in determining what circumstances will establish such a relationship between the parties as to give rise, on the one side, to a duty to take care, and on the other side to a right to have care taken.

M'Alister (or Donoghue) v. Stevenson [1932] A.C. 562

VI

Judgment and Mercy

Angel	Thy judgment now is near, for we are come
	Into the veiled presence of our God.
Soul of Gerontius	I hear the voices that I left on earth.
Angel	It is the voice of friends around thy bed,
	Who say the 'Subvenite' with the priest.
	Hither the echoes come; before the Throne
	Stands the great Angel of the Agony,
	The same who strengthened Him, what time He knelt
	Lone in the garden shade, bedewed with blood.
	That Angel best can plead with Him for all
	Tormented souls, the dying and the dead. ...
Soul	I go before my Judge. Ah!
Angel	Praise to His Name!
	The eager spirit has darted from my hold,
	And, with the intemperate energy of love,
	Flies to the dear feet of Emmanuel; ...
	O happy, suffering soul! for it is safe,

Consumed, yet quickened, by the glance of
God.

J. H. (CARDINAL) NEWMAN (1801–90)
The Dream of Gerontius (1865), §6

VII

Justice is ideally that system of right and wrong by which the
relations between men are regularized. The primary aim is to keep
order. In practice, there will be innumerable judgments, and
many of them will not be perfectly just, or even at all just, owing to
misconception, misdirection, or mischance. Rough justice is
probably the best we can achieve. It might be more than that if we
kept in mind that we must all appear before the judgment seat of
Christ (2 Corinthians 5:10). He sets the standard.

61

THE LORD, WHOM YE SEEK

I

Behold, I will send my messenger, and he shall prepare the way before me: and THE LORD, WHOM YE SEEK, shall suddenly come to his temple, even the messenger of the covenant, whom ye delight in: behold, he shall come, saith the Lord of hosts.

Malachi 3 :1

II

Lord, remember David: and all his trouble; how he sware unto the Lord: and vowed a vow unto the Almighty God of Jacob. I will not come within the tabernacle of mine house: nor climb up into my bed; I will not suffer mine eyes to sleep, nor mine eye-lids to slumber: neither the temples of my head to take any rest; until I find out a place for the temple of the Lord: an habitation for the mighty God of Jacob. Lo, we heard of the same at Ephrata: and found it in the wood. We will go into his tabernacle: and fall low on our knees before his footstool. Arise, O Lord, into thy resting-place: thou, and the ark of thy strength.

Psalm 132 :1

III

Then Paul stood in the midst of Mars' hill, and said, Ye men of Athens, I perceive that in all things ye are too superstitious. For as I passed by, and beheld your devotions, I found an altar with this inscription, TO THE UNKNOWN GOD. Whom therefore ye ignorantly worship, him declare I unto you. God that made the world and all things therein, seeing that he is Lord of heaven and earth, dwelleth not in temples made with hands; neither is worshipped with men's hands, as though he needed any thing, seeing he giveth to all life, and breath, and all things; and hath made of one blood all nations of men for to dwell on all the face of the earth, and hath determined the times before appointed, and the bounds of their habitation; that they should seek the Lord, if haply they might feel after him, and find him, though he be not far from every one of us: for in him we live, and move, and have our being; as certain also of your own poets have said, For we are also his offspring.

Acts 17 :22

IV

Seek, and ye shall find.

The Sermon on the Mount (Matthew 7:7)

V

Seneca, Epictetus, [Marcus] Aurelius, are among the truest and loftiest of Pagan moralists, yet Seneca ignored the Christians, Epictetus despised, and Aurelius persecuted them. All three, so far as they knew anything about the Christians at all, had unhappily been taught to look upon them as the most degraded and the most detestable sect of what they had long regarded as the most degraded and the most detestable of religions.

There is something very touching in this fact; but, if there be something very touching, there is also something very encouraging. God was their God as well as ours—their Creator, their Preserver, who left not Himself without witness among them; who, as they blindly felt after Him, suffered their groping hands to grasp the hem of His robe; . . . And His Spirit was with them, dwelling in them, though unseen and unknown, purifying and sanctifying the temple of their hearts, sending gleams of illuminating light through the gross darkness which encompassed them, comforting their uncertainties, making intercession for them with groanings which cannot be uttered. And, more than all, *our*

The Presentation

GIOTTO 1266–1337

[*Cappella Scrovegni, Padua : Mansell*]

Saviour was *their* Saviour too; . . . Yes, they too were all His off-spring.

F. W. FARRAR (1831–1903)
Seekers after God (1868), Conclusion

VI

'How hast thou merited—
Of all man's clotted clay the dingiest clot?
   Alack, thou knowest not
How little worthy of any love thou art!
Whom wilt thou find to love ignoble thee,
   Save Me, save only Me?
All which I took from thee I did but take,
   Not for thy harms,
But just that thou might'st seek it in My arms.
   All which thy child's mistake
Fancies as lost, I have stored for thee at home:
   Rise, clasp My hand, and come!'

   Halts by me that footfall:
   Is my gloom, after all,
Shade of His hand, outstretched caressingly?
   'Ah, fondest, blindest, weakest,
   I am He whom thou seekest!
Thou dravest love from thee, who dravest Me.'

FRANCIS THOMPSON (1859–1907)
The Hound of Heaven (1893) (the end)

VII

We are constantly looking around for something, from some small thing we have just mislaid to a bigger thing like a new house or a new job. But we must also be ever looking inwards, because that is when God can and will come to us, it may be quite suddenly, if he finds a place fit for him to dwell in.

62

THE MESSAGE OF AN ANGEL

I

We beseech thee, O Lord, pour thy grace into our hearts; that, as we have known the incarnation of thy Son Jesus Christ by THE MESSAGE OF AN ANGEL, so by his cross and passion we may be brought unto the glory of his resurrection; through the same Jesus Christ our Lord. Amen.

Collect

II

The children of Israel did evil again in the sight of the Lord; and the Lord delivered them into the hand of the Philistines forty years. And there was a certain man of Zorah, of the family of the Danites, whose name was Manoah; and his wife was barren, and bare not. And the angel of the Lord appeared unto the woman, and said unto her, Behold now, thou art barren, and bearest not: but thou shalt conceive, and bear a son. Now therefore beware, I pray thee, and drink not wine nor strong drink, and eat not any unclean thing: for, lo, thou shalt conceive, and bear a son; and no razor shall come on his head: for the child shall be a Nazarite unto God from the womb: and he shall begin to deliver Israel out of the hand of the Philistines. . . . And the woman bare a son, and called his name Samson: and the child grew, and the Lord blessed him.

Judges 13:1

III

There was in the days of Herod, the king of Judæa, a certain priest named Zacharias, of the course of Abia: and his wife was of the daughters of Aaron, and her name was Elisabeth. And they were both righteous before God, walking in all the commandments and ordinances of the Lord blameless. And they had no child, because that Elisabeth was barren, and they both were now well stricken in years. And it came to pass, that while he executed the priests' office before God in the order of his course, according to the custom of the priest's office, his lot was to burn incense when he went into the temple of the Lord. And the whole multitude of the people were praying without at the time of incense. And there appeared unto him an angel of the Lord standing on the right side of the altar of incense. And when Zacharias saw him, he was troubled, and fear fell upon him. But the angel said unto him, Fear not, Zacharias: for thy prayer is heard; and thy wife Elisabeth shall bear thee a son, and thou shalt call his name John. And thou shalt have joy and gladness; and many shall rejoice at his birth. For he shall be great in the sight of the Lord, and shall drink neither wine nor strong drink; and he shall be filled with the Holy Ghost, even from his mother's womb. And many of the children of Israel shall he turn to the Lord their God. And he shall go before him in the spirit and power of Elias, to turn the hearts of the fathers to the children, and the disobedient to the wisdom of the just; to make ready a people prepared for the Lord.

Luke 1 :5

IV

O be prepared, my soul!
To read the inconceivable, to scan
The myriad forms of God . . .

ALICE MEYNELL (1847–1922)
Christ in the Universe

V

. . . *two angels in white sitting one by the head and one by the feet where had lain the body of Jesus* [John 20:12] . . .

. . . It is not to be presumed that angels are physical objects reflecting rays of light upon the retina of the eye. When men 'see' or 'hear' angels, it is rather to be supposed that an intense interior

The Annunciation

DOMENICO VENEZIANO d. 1461

[Fitzwilliam Museum, Cambridge]

awareness of a divine message leads to the projection of an image which is then experienced as an occasion of something seen and heard. That divine messengers were sent and divine messages received we need not doubt; that they took physical form so that all who 'saw' anything must 'see' the same thing we need not suppose. Here they are the manifestation to Mary [Magdalene] that God was intimately active in this strange matter of the empty tomb, and was active also to comfort the sorrow of her heart.

WILLIAM TEMPLE (1881–1944)
Readings in St John's Gospel (1940)

VI

Not I, not I, but the wind that blows through me!
A fine wind is blowing the new direction of Time.
If only I let it bear me, carry me, if only it carry me!
If only I am sensitive, subtle, oh, delicate, a winged gift!
If only, most lovely of all, I yield myself and am borrowed
By the fine, fine wind that takes its course through the
                    chaos of the world
Like a fine, an exquisite chisel, a wedge-blade inserted;
If only I am keen and hard like the sheer tip of a wedge
Driven by invisible blows,
The rock will split, and we shall come at the wonder, we
                    shall find the Hesperides.

Oh, for the wonder that bubbles into my soul,
I would be a good fountain, a good well-head,
Would blur no whisper, spoil no expression.

What is the knocking?
What is the knocking at the door in the night?
It is somebody wants to do us harm.

No, no, it is the three strange angels.
Admit them, admit them.

D. H. LAWRENCE (1885–1930)
'Song of a Man Who has come Through'

VII

The Feast is called the Annunciation *of* the Blessed Virgin Mary, but our thoughts are on the annunciation *to* Mary of the coming entrance of Christ into the world. This is very proper. But we might also think of the Annunciation as something like the Proclamation of a new Queen, which in England is done with great solemnity. The angel said to Mary, *Hail thou endued with grace* (Luke 1:28 RV mg). He was claiming for her the title of 'Your Grace'. And while the world at that time was hailing the Roman Emperor with the words 'Ave Caesar', the angel was for the first time greeting Mary with the words 'Ave Maria', 'Hail Mary'.

The angel was indeed making an announcement, a unique Annunciation.

63

HE WAS TRANSFIGURED

I

Jesus taketh with him Peter, and James, and John, and leadeth them up into an high mountain apart by themselves: and HE WAS TRANSFIGURED before them. And his raiment became shining, exceeding white as snow; so as no fuller on earth can white them. And there appeared unto them Elijah with Moses: and they were talking with Jesus.

Mark 9:2

II

Transfigured through adversity
Joseph is brought out of prison to interpret Pharaoh's dream, which he does successfully.

And Pharaoh said unto Joseph, Forasmuch as God hath shewed thee all this, there is none so discreet and wise as thou art: thou shalt be over my house, and according unto thy word shall all my people be ruled: only in the throne will I be greater than thou. And Pharaoh said unto Joseph, See, I have set thee over all the land of Egypt. And Pharaoh took off his ring from his hand, and put it upon Joseph's hand, and arrayed him in vestures of fine linen, and put a gold chain about his neck; and he made him to ride in the second chariot which he had; and they cried before him, Bow the knee: and he made him ruler over all the land of Egypt. And Pharaoh said unto Joseph, I am Pharaoh, and without thee shall no man lift up his hand or foot in all the land of Egypt. And Pharaoh called Joseph's name Zaphnath-paaneah; and he gave

Transfiguration

FRA ANGELICO 1387?–1455

[*Museo di S. Marco, Florence : Mansell*]

him to wife Asenath the daughter of Potipherah priest of On. And
Joseph went out over all the land of Egypt.

Genesis 41 :39

III

Transfigured through martyrdom

There arose certain of the synagogue, which is called the synagogue
of the Libertines, and Cyrenians, and Alexandrians, and of them of
Cilicia and of Asia, disputing with Stephen. And they were not
able to resist the wisdom and the spirit by which he spake. Then
they suborned men, which said, We have heard him speak blasphemous words against Moses, and against God. And they stirred
up the people, and the elders, and the scribes, and came upon him,
and caught him, and brought him to the council, and set up false
witnesses, which said, This man ceaseth not to speak blasphemous
words against this holy place, and the law: for we have heard him
say, that this Jesus of Nazareth shall destroy this place, and shall
change the customs which Moses delivered us. And all that sat in
the council, looking steadfastly on him, saw his face as it had been
the face of an angel.

Acts 6 :9

IV

Transfigured through a cause

> In the beauty of the lilies Christ was born across the sea,
> With a glory in his bosom that transfigures you and me:
> As he died to make men holy, let us die to make men free,
>   While God is marching on.

JULIA WARD HOWE (1819–1910)
'Battle Hymn of the American Republic' (1862)

V

Transfigured through conviction

Nothing is more remarkable than the contrast between the
obscurity of Wyclif's earlier life and the fulness and vividness of

302

ıur knowledge of him during the twenty years which preceded its
:lose. Born in the earlier part of the fourteenth century, he had
ılready passed middle age when he was appointed to the master-
;hip of Balliol College, in the University of Oxford. . . . Undis-
mayed by the thunder and excommunications of the Church,
Ockham had not shrunk in his enthusiasm for the Empire from
ıttacking the foundations of the Papal supremacy or from assert-
ıng the rights of the civil power. The spare, emaciated frame of
Wyclif, weakened by study and by asceticism, hardly promised a
Reformer who would carry on the stormy work of Ockham; but
within this frail form lay a temper quick and restless, an immense
ɛnergy, an immovable conviction, an unconquerable pride. The
personal charm which ever accompanies real greatness only
deepened the influence he derived from the spotless purity of his
ife. As yet indeed even Wyclif himself can hardly have suspected
:he immense range of his intellectual power. It was only the
struggle that lay before him which revealed in the dry and subtle
schoolman the founder of our later English prose, a master of
popular invective, of irony, of persuasion, a dexterous politician,
ın audacious partisan, the organizer of a religious order, the un-
sparing assailant of abuses, the boldest and most indefatigable of
controversialists, the first Reformer who dared, when deserted and
ılone, to question and deny the creed of the Christendom around
him, to break through the tradition of the past, and with his last
breath to assert the freedom of religious thought against the dog-
mas of the Papacy.

J. R. GREEN (1837–83)
Short History of the English People (1874),
Ch. 5, Section 3

VI

Transfigured through Faith

Nothing, it seemed, between them and the grave.
No, as I looked, there was nothing anywhere.
You'd think no ground could be so flat and bare:
No little ridge or hump or bush to brave

303

The horizon. Yet they called that land their land,
Without a single thought drank in that air
As simple and equivocal as despair.
This, this was what I could not understand.

The reason was, there was nothing there but faith.
Faith made the whole, yes all they could see or hear
Or touch or think, and arched its break of day
Within them and around them every way.
They looked: all was transfigured far and near,
And the great world rolled between them and death.

EDWIN MUIR (1887–1959)
'Nothing There but Faith' (1960) in
Collected Poems 1921–1958

VII

Peter and James and John see Jesus in a new light, and ever since in the Church, if it is doing its proper work, disciples have been seeing life and all things in a new light. Truth often turns out to be the opposite to what we thought—the earth is in rapid motion while the sun stands still. The Christian way of life looks horribly hard till we see it in the right light. Christ is the Light of the world: *Lux Mundi* (John 8:12). He is the Way, the Truth, and the Life: *Via*, *Veritas*, *Vita* (John 14:6).

SELECTION OF MUSIC

Sequence

I THE HOUSE OF PRAYER
      Coronation Anthem: *I was glad*
      C. Hubert H. Parry (1848–1918)

2 DISTRESS OF NATIONS, WITH PERPLEXITY
      Libera Me (*War Requiem*)
      Benjamin Britten (1913–   )

3 STEWARDS OF THE MYSTERIES OF GOD
      March (*Die Zauberflöte* Act 2)
      Wolfgang Amadeus Mozart (1756–91)

4 THE RACE THAT IS SET BEFORE US
      Ballet: *Agon*
      Igor Stravinsky (1882–1970)

5 THE EXPRESS IMAGE OF HIS PERSON
      (a) Prelude:
          Hodie, Christus Natus Est
          Jan Pieterszoon Sweelinck (1562–1621)
      (b) *O Magnum Mysterium*
          Tomás Luis de Victoria (*c*. 1549–1611)

6 GOD WITH US
      Ihr habt nun Traurigkeit (*Requiem*)
      Johannes Brahms (1833–97)

7 JESUS CHRIST WAS MADE IN THE LIKENESS OF MEN
      Et incarnatus est (*Mass in C minor*)
      Wolfgang Amadeus Mozart (1756–91)

8 THE GENTILES SHOULD BE FELLOW-HEIRS,
    AND OF THE SAME BODY
      Carol: *The Three Kings*
      Peter Cornelius (1824–74)

9 SITTING IN THE MIDST OF THE DOCTORS
      She's leaving home (*Sergeant Pepper's Lonely
      Hearts Club Band*)
      John Lennon & Paul McCartney

10 WHATSOEVER HE SAITH UNTO YOU, DO IT
Canticle II, *Abraham and Isaac*
Benjamin Britten (1913–   )

11 STRETCH FORTH THY RIGHT HAND TO HELP AND
DEFEND US
Almighty and Everlasting God
Orlando Gibbons (1583–1625)

12 THE FRAILTY OF OUR NATURE
Fantasy: *Francesca da Rimini*
Pëtr Ilich Tchaikovsky (1840–93)

13 PSALMS AND HYMNS AND SPIRITUAL SONGS
Lord, thou hast been our refuge
Ralph Vaughan Williams (1872–1958)

14 A GREAT SOUND OF A TRUMPET
Tuba Mirum (Requiem)
Giuseppe Verdi (1813–1901)

15 HE HAD AGREED WITH THE LABOURERS FOR A PENNY A DAY
John Henry
North American Folk Song

16 THE MYSTERIES OF THE KINGDOM OF GOD
Let all mortal flesh keep silence
Edward C. Bairstow (1874–1946)

17 NOW WE SEE THROUGH A GLASS, DARKLY
Who hath believed our report?
Henry Purcell (1659–95)

18 ACKNOWLEDGING OUR WRETCHEDNESS
Miserere Mei
Gregorio Allegri (1582–1652)

19 HAVING NOTHING, AND YET POSSESSING ALL THINGS
Du bist die Ruh
Franz Schubert (1797–1828)

20 EVIL THOUGHTS WHICH MAY ASSAULT AND HURT THE SOUL
Vanne; la tua meta gia vedo . . . Credo
(Iago, *Otello* Act II, Scene ii)
Giuseppe Verdi (1813–1901)

21 AWAKE, THOU THAT SLEEPEST
Chorus: *Awake the Harp (The Creation)*
Franz Joseph Haydn (1732–1809)

306

22 JERUSALEM WHICH NOW IS—JERUSALEM WHICH IS ABOVE
The Wilderness
Samuel Sebastian Wesley (1810–76)

23 GOOD THINGS TO COME
Overture: *The Barber of Seville*
Gioacchino Antonio Rossini (1792–1868)

24 THE EXAMPLE OF HIS PATIENCE
Aria: *He was despised* (*Messiah*)
George Frideric Handel (1685–1759)

25 HE SAID, IT IS FINISHED
Aria: *Es ist vollbracht* (*St John Passion*)
Johann Sebastian Bach (1685–1750)

26 GOD, WHO THROUGH JESUS CHRIST HAST OVERCOME DEATH
(a) Prelude:
Surgens Jesus
Peter Philips (1561–*c.* 1640)
(b) *The Souls of the Righteous*
James Nares (1715–83)

27 THE FIRST DAY OF THE WEEK
Haec Dies
William Byrd (1543–1623)

28 THE SHEPHERD AND BISHOP OF YOUR SOULS
Duet: *He shall feed his flock* (*Messiah*)
George Frideric Handel (1685–1759)

29 YOUR JOY NO MAN TAKETH FROM YOU
Exultate, Jubilate
Wolfgang Amadeus Mozart (1756–91)

30 THE SUNDRY AND MANIFOLD CHANGES OF THE WORLD
Sixth Symphony in F major (*Pastoral*)
Ludwig van Beethoven (1770–1827)

31 THY MERCIFUL GUIDING
Saul, Saul, was verfolgst du Mich?
Heinrich Schütz (1585–1672)

32 HE WAS RECEIVED UP
O Clap your Hands
Ralph Vaughan Williams (1872–1958)

33 THESE THINGS HAVE I SPOKEN UNTO YOU
Noye's Fludde

Benjamin Britten (1913–   )

34   YE IN ME, AND I IN YOU
         (a) Prelude:
             Morgen
             Richard Strauss (1864–1949)
         (b) *Concerto for two violins in D minor*
             Johann Sebastian Bach (1685–1750)

35   A DOOR WAS OPENED IN HEAVEN
         Prelude, Act I: *Lohengrin*
         Richard Wagner (1813–83)

36   THE SAVIOUR OF THE WORLD
         Salvator Mundi
         John Blow (1649–1708)

37   HE LAID DOWN HIS LIFE FOR US
         Per me giunto è il di supremo . . . Io morro
         (Rodrigo, *Don Carlos* Act IV)
         Giuseppe Verdi (1813–1901)

38   AN HEARTY DESIRE TO PRAY
         Gebet (*Mörike Lieder*)
         Hugo Wolf (1860–1903)

39   THINGS TEMPORAL—THE THINGS ETERNAL
         The Burial Sentences
         William Croft (1678–1727)

40   LAUNCH OUT INTO THE DEEP
         They that go down to the sea in ships
         Henry Purcell (1659–95)

41   THE LIKENESS OF HIS RESURRECTION
         Fifth Movement, Second Symphony in C minor
         (*Resurrection*)
         Gustav Mahler (1860–1911)

42   INCREASE IN US TRUE RELIGION
         O Lord, increase our faith
         Orlando Gibbons (1583–1625)

43   SONS OF GOD
         Chorus: *Va Pensiero* (*Nabucco* Act III)
         Giuseppe Verdi (1813–1901)

44   THE CHILDREN OF THIS WORLD
         Tannhäuser Act I, Scene i

Richard Wagner (1813–83)

45 THE SAME SPIRIT
Chorus: *Then did Elijah the prophet break·forth
like a fire*; Aria: *Then shall the righteous shine
forth* (*Elijah*)
Felix Mendelssohn (1809–47)

46 A MEASURE OF THY GRACE
Veni, Creator Spiritus
Plainchant, Mode viii

47 TRUST
Credo in unum Deum (*Mass in B minor*)
Johann Sebastian Bach (1685–1750)

48 TRUE AND LAUDABLE SERVICE
Vecchia zimarra senti (Colline, *La Bohème* Act IV)
Giacomo Puccini (1858–1924)

49 WALK IN THE SPIRIT
In a Summer Garden
Frederick Delius (1862–1934)

50 THE LILIES OF THE FIELD
The Seasons
Antonio Vivaldi (*c.* 1676–1741)

51 GOD'S HELP AND GOODNESS
L'Enfance du Christ Part I, Scenes v and vi
Hector Berlioz (1803–69)

52 BAPTISM
Siegfried Idyll
Richard Wagner (1813–83)

53 ENRICHED BY GOD, IN ALL UTTERANCE
Recitative and Chorus: *And Joseph took the body*;
Solo and Chorus: *And now the Lord to rest is laid*
(*St Matthew Passion*)
Johann Sebastian Bach (1685–1750)

54 CORRUPT COMMUNICATION
Boris Godunov Act IV, Scene i (The simpleton
exploited by the crowd)
Modest Mussorgsky (1839–81)

55 READY BOTH IN BODY AND SOUL
Recitative: *Ich habe genug*; Aria: *Schlummert ein*

(Cantata 82 *Ich Habe Genug*)
Johann Sebastian Bach (1685–1750)

56 THE WHOLE ARMOUR OF GOD
Proficiscere, anima Christiana (*The Dream of Gerontius* Part I)
Edward Elgar (1857–1934)

57 THE GLORY AND PRAISE OF GOD
Gloria; *Sicut Erat* (*Magnificat, Vespers of 1610*)
Claudio Monteverdi (1567–1643)

58 OUR CONVERSATION IS IN HEAVEN
In Paradisum (*Requiem*)
Gabriel Fauré (1845–1924)

59 ALL PATIENCE AND LONGSUFFERING WITH JOYFULNESS
Turn our captivity, O Lord
William Byrd (1543–1623)

60 JUDGMENT AND JUSTICE IN THE EARTH
Dies Irae (*Requiem*)
Wolfgang Amadeus Mozart (1756–91)

61 THE LORD, WHOM YE SEEK
O Where shall Wisdom be Found?
William Boyce (1710–79)

62 THE MESSAGE OF AN ANGEL
Ave Maria
Anton Bruckner (1824–96)

63 HE WAS TRANSFIGURED
Recitative: *Behold, I tell you a Mystery;*
Aria: *The trumpet shall sound* (*Messiah*)
George Frideric Handel (1685–1759)

ILLUSTRATIONS

I THE HOUSE OF PRAYER   3
       Old Church and Steps
       L. S. Lowry 1887–
       (Private Collection, London)

2 DISTRESS OF NATIONS, WITH PERPLEXITY   9
       Guernica
       Pablo Picasso 1881–1973
       (Museum of Modern Art, New York)

3 STEWARDS OF THE MYSTERIES OF GOD   13
       Ordination by the Bishop of Rangoon
       (Society for the Propagation of the Gospel)

4 THE RACE THAT IS SET BEFORE US   19
       David Hemery
       E. D. Lacey

5 THE EXPRESS IMAGE OF HIS PERSON   23
       The Holy Family
       Peter Paul Rubens 1577–1640
       (Wallace Collection, London)

6 GOD WITH US   29
       Christ Carrying the Cross
       Stanley Spencer 1891–1959
       (Tate Gallery, London)

7 JESUS CHRIST WAS MADE IN THE LIKENESS OF MEN   35
       Christ with the High Priest
       Georges Rouault 1871–1958
       (Phillips Collection, Washington, D.C.)

8 THE GENTILES SHOULD BE FELLOW-HEIRS,
       AND OF THE SAME BODY   39
       Adoration of the Kings

Rogier van der Weyden *c.* 1399–1464
(Alte Pinakothek, Munich)

9   SITTING IN THE MIDST OF THE DOCTORS   45
     Christ among the Doctors
     Bernardino Butinone *c.* 1450–1507
     (The National Gallery of Scotland)

10   WHATSOEVER HE SAITH UNTO YOU, DO IT   49
     La Classe de Danse de M. Perrot
     Edgar Degas 1834–1917
     (Cliche Musees Nationaux Paris)

11   STRETCH FORTH THY RIGHT HAND TO HELP
     AND DEFEND US   53
     The Hand of God
     Auguste Rodin 1840–1917
     (Musée Rodin, Paris)

12   THE FRAILTY OF OUR NATURE   59
     The Scream
     Lithograph by Edvard Munch 1863–1944
     (National Gallery of Art, Washington, D.C.:
     Rosenwald Collection)

13   PSALMS AND HYMNS AND SPIRITUAL SONGS   63
     King David playing the Harp
     A late 13th century miniature in North-French style
     (Reproduced by permission of the British Library
                                              Board)

14   A GREAT SOUND OF A TRUMPET   67
     Organ Case, King's College Chapel, Cambridge
     (King's College)

15   HE HAD AGREED WITH THE LABOURERS
     FOR A PENNY A DAY   70
     Work
     Ford Madox Brown 1821–93
     (City Art Gallery, Manchester)

16   THE MYSTERIES OF THE KINGDOM OF GOD   77
     The Story of Lazarus: Martha and Mary

kneeling before Christ at the gates of Jerusalem
A 12th century carving from Chichester Cathedral
(Edwin Smith)

17 NOW WE SEE THROUGH A GLASS, DARKLY   81
     The Slanted Light
     Engraved Glass by Laurence Whistler 1912–

18 ACKNOWLEDGING OUR WRETCHEDNESS   85
     The Burghers of Calais
     Auguste Rodin 1840–1917
     (Musée Rodin, Paris © S.P.A.D.E.M.
          Paris, 1973)

19 HAVING NOTHING, AND YET POSSESSING ALL THINGS   89
     St Francis discards his secular clothing
     Giotto 1266–1337
     (The Upper Church, Assisi: Mansell)

20 EVIL THOUGHTS WHICH MAY ASSAULT
       AND HURT THE SOUL   95
         Truth beset by dark Spirits
         Francisco Goya 1746–1828
         (Sepia wash drawing: Metropolitan Museum,
              New York)

21 AWAKE, THOU THAT SLEEPEST   99
     The Agony in the Garden
     Giovanni Bellini 1430–1516
     (National Gallery, London)

22 JERUSALEM WHICH NOW IS—JERUSALEM
       WHICH IS ABOVE   103
         View of Jerusalem, 1858
         Edward Lear 1812–88
         (Tate Gallery, London)

23 GOOD THINGS TO COME   109
     Firs in Coed y Brenin Forest
     (Forestry Commission)

313

24 THE EXAMPLE OF HIS PATIENCE   113
      El Espolio
      El Greco 1541–1614
      (Museo San Vincente, Toledo)

25 HE SAID, IT IS FINISHED   119
      Christ on the Cross
      Peter Paul Rubens 1577–1640
      (Wallace Collection, London)

26 GOD, WHO THROUGH JESUS CHRIST HAST
      OVERCOME DEATH   123
      The Resurrection
      Fra Angelico 1387?–1455
      (Museo di S. Marco, Florence: Mansell)

27 THE FIRST DAY OF THE WEEK   129
      Coming from Evening Church
      Samuel Palmer 1805–81
      (Tate Gallery, London)

28 THE SHEPHERD AND BISHOP OF YOUR SOULS   133
      Il buon Pastore
      A mid 5th century mosaic
      (Mausoleum of Galla Placidia, Ravenna: Mansell)

29 YOUR JOY NO MAN TAKETH FROM YOU   139
      In the Abruzzi
      Frank Monaco 1917–

30 THE SUNDRY AND MANIFOLD CHANGES
      OF THE WORLD   143
      The Raft of the Medusa
      Théodore Géricault 1791–1824
      (Cliche Musees Nationaux Paris)

31 THY MERCIFUL GUIDING   147
      St Matthew and the Angel
      Michelangelo Merisi da Caravaggio 1569–1609
      (San Luigi dei Francesi, Rome: Mansell)

32 HE WAS RECEIVED UP   153
    The Ascension
    A 13th century window in Jerusalem Chamber,
    Westminster Abbey
    (Crown copyright)

33 THESE THINGS HAVE I SPOKEN UNTO YOU   157
    The Child Samuel
    Sir Joshua Reynolds 1723–92
    (Tate Gallery, London)

34 YE IN ME, AND I IN YOU   163
    Buttermere
    J. M. W. Turner 1775–1851
    (Tate Gallery, London)

35 A DOOR WAS OPENED IN HEAVEN   167
    Clover
    Enid Levetus

36 THE SAVIOUR OF THE WORLD   171
    St Peter healing the sick
    Masaccio 1401–28
    (Chiesa del Carmine, Florence: Mansell)

37 HE LAID DOWN HIS LIFE FOR US   177
    Death in Action
    Robert Capa d. 1954
    (Magnum Photos)

38 AN HEARTY DESIRE TO PRAY   181
    Prodigal Son
    Etching by Albrecht Dürer 1471–1528
    (Trustees of the British Museum)

39 THINGS TEMPORAL—THE THINGS ETERNAL   185
    Separation of Light and Darkness
    Michelangelo 1475–1564
    (Cappella Sistina, Rome: Mansell)

40 LAUNCH OUT INTO THE DEEP   191
    La Première Sortie
    Pierre Auguste Renoir 1841–1919
    (National Gallery, London)

41 THE LIKENESS OF HIS RESURRECTION   195
    The Resurrection of Christ
    Piero della Francesca *c*. 1420–92
    (Galleria Comunale, San Sepolcro: Mansell)

42 INCREASE IN US TRUE RELIGION   201
    The Sunday School
    Robert McInnes 1801–86
    (Leger Gallery, London)

43 SONS OF GOD   205
    William of Orange
    attributed to Adriaen Key b. 1544?
    (Mauritshuis, The Hague)

44 THE CHILDREN OF THIS WORLD   209
    The Queen of Sheba
    Duncan Grant 1885–
    (Tate Gallery, London)

45 THE SAME SPIRIT   215
    Icon of Elijah
    (St David's Cathedral, Pembrokeshire)

46 A MEASURE OF THY GRACE   219
    John Keble
    George Richmond 1809–96   .
    (National Portrait Gallery, London)

47 TRUST   223
    Las Gigantillas
    Francisco Goya 1746–1828
    (Museo del Prado, Madrid)

48 TRUE AND LAUDABLE SERVICE   229
    Christ washing the Disciples' Feet

Ford Madox Brown 1821–93
(Tate Gallery, London)

49 WALK IN THE SPIRIT   233
    The Disciples at Emmaus
    Michelangelo Merisi da Caravaggio 1569–1609
    (National Gallery, London)

50 THE LILIES OF THE FIELD   239
    In Calabria
    Frank Monaco 1917–

51 GOD'S HELP AND GOODNESS   243
    Agony in the Garden
    William Blake 1757–1827
    (Tate Gallery, London)

52 BAPTISM   247
    John the Baptist
    Donatello 1386–1466
    (Bargello, Florence: Mansell)

53 ENRICHED BY GOD, IN ALL UTTERANCE   253
    Kathleen Ferrier, 1951
    Cecil Beaton 1904–

54 CORRUPT COMMUNICATION   257
    Canvassing for Votes (detail)
    William Hogarth 1697–1764
    (Trustees of Sir John Soane's Museum, London)

55 READY BOTH IN BODY AND SOUL   261
    Tobias and the Angel
    follower of Verrocchio 1435–88
    (National Gallery, London)

56 THE WHOLE ARMOUR OF GOD   267
    Christian and Apollyon
    George Burder 1752–1832
    (from an edition of *The Pilgrim's Progress*
    published about 1790 by Alex Hogg, London)

57 THE GLORY AND PRAISE OF GOD   271
        Fireplace (detail)
        Domenico Rosselli 15th century
        (Palazzo Ducale, Urbino: Mansell)

58 OUR CONVERSATION IS IN HEAVEN   277
        *The Redeemer with two angels, S. Vitale
            and S. Eclesia*
        A 6th century mosaic
        (Church of S. Vitale, Ravenna: Mansell)

59 ALL PATIENCE AND LONGSUFFERING WITH
        JOYFULNESS   281
        A Tea Party
        Thomas Webster 1800–86
        (Harris Museum and Art Gallery, Preston)

60 JUDGMENT AND JUSTICE IN THE EARTH   287
        Adam and Eve
        Masaccio 1401–28
        (Chiesa del Carmine, Florence: Mansell)

61 THE LORD, WHOM YE SEEK   293
        The Presentation
        Giotto 1266–1337
        (Cappella Scrovegni, Padua: Mansell)

62 THE MESSAGE OF AN ANGEL   297
        The Annunciation
        Domenico Veneziano d. 1461
        (Fitzwilliam Museum, Cambridge)

63 HE WAS TRANSFIGURED   301
        The Transfiguration
        Fra Angelico 1387?–1455
        (Museo di S. Marco, Florence: Mansell)

APPENDIX

THE CALENDAR AND LESSONS FOR THE CHURCH'S YEAR
(*A Report submitted by the Church of England Liturgical Commission to the Archbishops of Canterbury and York in November, 1968*)

In taking as their framework the traditional Church's Year, the compilers of this book have not been unmindful of *The Calendar and Lessons for the Church's Year* proposed in 1968 by the Church of England Liturgical Commission for experimental use. Inevitably, however, it will be some time yet, perhaps a number of years, before a decision is reached by the Synod as to the eventual fate of these proposals. It is conceivable that they will be turned down and almost certain that they will undergo substantial modification and alteration; in any event, the use of the existing Prayer Book is unlikely to be forbidden and, if not forbidden, is likely to be continued widely for some considerable time. It is felt nevertheless that an exciting additional dimension would be lost to this book were the sequences which it contains not suitable for use with the new *Calendar and Lessons*.

The contexts from which the themes of the sequences are drawn will normally be found in the 1968 proposals, though not infrequently the relevant passages are recommended for use on entirely different occasions from those they serve in the Book of Common Prayer. Occasionally, the exact theme of a sequence does not appear in the new *Calendar and Lessons*, but in such cases a theme of almost identical meaning can be found.

The following Table is provided to enable the sequences of this book to be used with the proposed calendar, collects and lessons. It is hoped that this will add materially to the value of this book as a basis for devotional reading and that it will prove an interesting and illuminating 'bridge' between old and new. The alternative themes suggested are drawn normally from the titles, collects and Holy Communion readings provided in the new *Calendar and Lessons*, but an occasional theme has

319

been taken from the *Second Service* readings for a Sunday or Holy Day. The 1968 proposals offer a two-year cycle of readings, but this framework is considered unimportant to the purposes of this book and the following suggestions are drawn freely from both series as appropriate.

TABLE

1968 Sunday or Holy Day	Applicable Sequence	Page No.	Alternative Theme	Context of Alternative Theme
Ninth Sunday before Christmas	5 (omitting *Prelude*)	22	CHRIST IS THE IMAGE OF THE INVISIBLE GOD	*Col.* 1:15
Eighth Sunday before Christmas	37	175	HE LAID DOWN HIS LIFE FOR US	1 *John* 3:16
Seventh Sunday before Christmas	50	237	THE LILIES OF THE FIELD	*Matt.* 6:28
Sixth Sunday before Christmas	40	189	GET THEE OUT OF THY COUNTRY	*Gen.* 12:1
Fifth Sunday before Christmas	4	17	HE THAT SHALL ENDURE TO THE END, THE SAME SHALL BE SAVED	*Mark* 13:13
Fourth Sunday before Christmas	2	7	DISTRESS OF NATIONS, WITH PERPLEXITY	*Luke* 21:25
Third Sunday before Christmas	45	213	THE SPIRIT OF THE LORD	*Luke* 4:18
Second Sunday before Christmas	3	12	STEWARDS OF THE MYSTERIES OF GOD	1 *Cor.* 4:1
Sunday before Christmas	6	28	GOD WITH US	*Matt.* 1:23
Christmas Day	36 (with *Prelude* to 5)	170	THE SAVIOUR OF THE WORLD	1 *John* 4:14
Sunday after Christmas	8	38	THE GENTILES SHOULD BE FELLOW-HEIRS, AND OF THE SAME BODY	*Eph.* 3:6
Second Sunday after Christmas	9	43	SITTING IN THE MIDST OF THE DOCTORS	*Luke* 2:46
Third Sunday after Christmas	52	245	BAPTISM	Title and Collect
Fourth Sunday after Christmas	48	227	SERVICE	Collect
Fifth Sunday after Christmas	10	47	WHATSOEVER HE SAITH UNTO YOU, DO IT	*John* 2:5
Sixth Sunday after Christmas	22	102	JERUSALEM SHALL BE CALLED A CITY OF TRUTH	*Zech.* 8:3

321

1968 Sunday or Holy Day	Applicable Sequence	Page No.	Alternative Theme	Context of Alternative Theme
Seventh Sunday after Christmas	15	69	HE HAD AGREED WITH THE LABOURERS FOR A PENNY A DAY	*Matt.* 20:2
Eighth Sunday after Christmas	12	57	THE WEAKNESS OF OUR MORTAL NATURE	Collect
Ninth Sunday before Easter	16	75	THE MYSTERIES OF THE KINGDOM OF GOD	*Luke* 8:10
Eighth Sunday before Easter	55	260	READY BOTH IN BODY AND SOUL	Collect
Seventh Sunday before Easter	11	52	STRETCH FORTH THY RIGHT HAND TO HELP AND DEFEND US	Collect
Ash Wednesday	18	83	ACKNOWLEDGING OUR WRETCHEDNESS	Collect
Sixth Sunday before Easter	7	33	IT BEHOVED HIM TO BE MADE LIKE UNTO HIS BRETHREN	*Heb.* 2:17
Fifth Sunday before Easter	20	93	THE SPIRIT OF ERROR	1 *John* 4:6
Fourth Sunday before Easter	19	88	WHOSOEVER WILL LOSE HIS LIFE FOR MY SAKE SHALL FIND IT	*Matt.* 16:25
Third Sunday before Easter (*or* The Transfiguration)	63	300	HE WAS TRANS-FIGURED	*Matt.* 17:2
Second Sunday before Easter	23	107	GOOD THINGS TO COME	*Heb.* 9:11
Sunday before Easter (Palm Sunday)	24	112	THE EXAMPLE OF HIS PATIENCE	Collect
Good Friday	25	117	HE SAID, IT IS FINISHED	*John* 19:30
Easter Day	26	122	GOD, WHO HAST DELIVERED US FROM THE POWER OF THE ENEMY	Collect
Sunday after Easter	27	127	THE FIRST DAY OF THE WEEK	*John* 20:19
Second Sunday after Easter	28	132	THE SHEPHERD	Title and Collect

1968 Sunday or Holy Day	Applicable Sequence	Page No.	Alternative Theme	Context of Alternative Theme
Third Sunday after Easter	54	255	FILTHY COMMUNICATION	Col. 3:8
Fourth Sunday after Easter	14	65	A GREAT VOICE, AS OF A TRUMPET	Rev. 1:10
Fifth Sunday after Easter	29	137	YOUR JOY NO MAN TAKETH FROM YOU	John 16:22
Ascension Day	32	151	HE WAS TAKEN UP	Acts 1:9
Sixth Sunday after Easter	33	156	THESE ARE THE WORDS WHICH I SPAKE UNTO YOU	Luke 24:44
Pentecost	34	161	YE IN ME, AND I IN YOU	John 14:20
Sunday after Pentecost (Trinity Sunday)	35	166	GOD, WHO HAST REVEALED THYSELF	Collect
Second Sunday after Pentecost	38	179	OUR SUPPLICATIONS AND PRAYERS	Collect
Third Sunday after Pentecost	41	194	THE LIKENESS OF HIS RESURRECTION	Rom. 6:5
Fourth Sunday after Pentecost	43	203	SONS OF GOD	Title
Fifth Sunday after Pentecost	21	98	AWAKE, THOU THAT SLEEPEST	Eph. 5:14 (reading extended)
Sixth Sunday after Pentecost	13	61	PSALMS AND HYMNS AND SPIRITUAL SONGS	Col. 3:16
Seventh Sunday after Pentecost	17	79	NOW WE SEE THROUGH A GLASS, DARKLY	1 Cor. 13:12
Eighth Sunday after Pentecost	49	232	WALK IN THE SPIRIT	Gal. 5:16
Ninth Sunday after Pentecost	56	265	THE WHOLE ARMOUR OF GOD	Title and Eph. 6:11
Tenth Sunday after Pentecost	31	146	THY MERCIFUL GUIDING	Collect
Eleventh Sunday after Pentecost	57	270	THE GLORY AND PRAISE OF GOD	Phil. 1:11
Twelfth Sunday after Pentecost	53	251	GOD, WHO DIDST GIVE GRACE TO PREACH THY WORD	Collect

1968 Sunday or Holy Day	*Applicable Sequence*	*Page No.*	*Alternative Theme*	*Context of Alternative Theme*
Thirteenth Sunday after Pentecost	59	280	TO ACCEPT THE SUFFERINGS OF THE PRESENT TIME	Collect
Fourteenth Sunday after Pentecost	46	217	THE SPIRIT OF GRACE	Collect
Fifteenth Sunday after Pentecost	51	241	THE LORD'S HELP	Collect
Sixteenth Sunday after Pentecost	44	208	THE CHILDREN OF THIS WORLD	*Luke* 16:8
Seventeenth Sunday after Pentecost	42	199	INCREASE IN US TRUE RELIGION	Collect
Eighteenth Sunday after Pentecost	60	285	JUDGMENT	*Matt.* 5:22
Nineteenth Sunday after Pentecost	30	142	THE SUNDRY AND MANIFOLD CHANGES OF THE WORLD	Collect
Twentieth Sunday after Pentecost	58	275	OUR CONVERSATION IS IN HEAVEN	*Phil.* 3:20
Twenty-first Sunday after Pentecost	39	184	THINGS TEMPORAL— THE THINGS ETERNAL	Collect
Twenty-second Sunday after Pentecost	I	I	THE PLACE WHERE MEN WORSHIP	*John* 4:20
Twenty-third Sunday after Pentecost	47	222	TRUST	2 *Cor.* 3:4
The Presentation of Christ in the Temple	61	291	THE LORD, WHOM YE SEEK	*Mal.* 3:1
The Annunciation of the Blessed Virgin Mary	62	295	THE MESSAGE OF AN ANGEL	Collect
The Transfiguration (*or* Third Sunday before Easter)	63	300	TRANSFIGURATION	Title

INDEX OF BIBLICAL REFERENCES

INDEX OF BIBLICAL REFERENCES

OLD TESTAMENT

Genesis	Sequence	2 Samuel (*cont.*)	Sequence
1:1–5	27	17:27–29	48
1:26–28, 31	5	18:33	37
2:4–10	50	23:13–17	37
3:9, 11–19, 24	60		
3:19	15	1 Kings	
11:31–12:5	40	8:27–30	1
15:6–10, 12, 17–18	16	10:1–7, 10	44
22:1–3	10		
28:10–17	35	2 Kings	
41:39–45	63	2:9–15	45
45:3–9	31	6:8–17	51
		20:1–7	38
Exodus			
4:10–12, 14–16	53	Ezra	
20:1–17	33	3:7	15
20:18–21	14		
24:9–13, 15–18	58	Nehemiah	
		13:7–13	3
Leviticus			
19:13	15	Job	
		2:3–10	24
Deuteronomy			
8:6–10	23	Psalms	
34:1–6	32	2:1–4	2
		30:1–13	29
Joshua		39:5–9, 13–15	12
3:9, 13–16	52	46:1–11	6
		49:15–20	19
Judges		57:8–12	21
13:1–5, 24	62	102:19–27	39
		132:1–8	61
1 Samuel		137:1–6	22
16:14–18, 21–23	13		
17:38–46	56	Proverbs	
31:6, 8–13	25	2:1–6	9
2 Samuel		Ecclesiastes	
11:12–19, 21, 25, 27	20	3:1–8	30
16:5–13	54	9:10–11	4
		12:6	14

Song of Songs	Sequence
2:7–13	41
8:6–7	34

Isaiah	
2:2–5	49
11:1–10	8
41:9–13	11
63:7–9	36

Jeremiah	
14:17–21	18
17:5–8	47
22:13	15
23:5–6	60
31:31–34	42

Ezekiel	
34:11–16	28

Daniel	
7:1–2, 13–14	7

Habakkuk	
2:2	42

Malachi	
3:1	61
3:5–6	15

APOCRYPHA

Tobit	
5:1–7, 16–17	55

Wisdom	
2:1, 12–21; 3:1	59
2:23–3:5	26
9:13–17	17

Ecclesiasticus	
44:1–10	43
50:5–11	46

Song of the Three Holy Children	
verses 28–35	57

NEW TESTAMENT

Matthew	Sequence
1:20–23	6
3:13–17	35
5:1–12	33
6:28–29	50
7:7	35
	61
9:37–38	15
11:28	15
19:16–22	19
20:1–2	15
21:12–14	1
24:4–8	2
24:30–31	14
26:47–54	56
28:16–20	32

Mark	
4:35–41	12
6:35, 36–42, 44	50
9:2–4	63
10:28–30	9
13	2
14:22–26	13
14:32–34, 37–41	21
15:37–39, 42–46	37
16:9	32
16:19–20	32

Luke	
1:5–17	62
1:28	62
1:67–80	23
2:41–43, 45–51	9
5:2–6	40
8:8–10	16
9:1–6	40
12:15–21	44
12:37–44	3
15:2–7	28
16:8	44
21:10–19	59
21:25–28	2

Luke (*cont.*)	Sequence	Romans (*cont.*)	Sequence
22:39–43	51	7:18–25	18
24:13–16, 28–35	49	8:13–14	43
24:34	26	8:26	38
24:51	32	13:13–14	11

John		1 Corinthians	
2:1–5	10	1:4–7	53
4:36	15	4:1–2	3
8:12	63	9:24–27	4
11:1–3, 5, 17, 20, 21–27, 38–39, 41–44	41	12:7–11	45
12:20–26	8	13:12	17
13:2–5, 12–17	48	15:50–57	14
13:21–27, 30	20	2 Corinthians	
14:1–7	6	1:3–10	47
14:6	63	3:4–6	47
14:18–20	34	4:13–5:1	39
15:26–16:1	33	5:10	60
16:20–22	29	6:1–10	19
16:25–30	53	11:24–27, 32–33	30
19:5	7	12:5, 7–10	46
19:28–30	25	Galatians	
20:12	62	4:21–26	22
20:19	27	5:16–18, 22–23	49

Acts		Ephesians	
1:10	32	3:3–6	8
2:24	26	4:4–6	52
4:5–14	36	4:10	32
4:31–35	45	4:13–15	9
4:32	19	4:25–30	54
6:9–15	63	5:13–14	21
7:54–55, 57–60	25	5:25–32	16
8:26–35	17	6:10–13	56
12:5–12	11	6:12	4
17:22–28	61		
18:12–17	60	Philippians	
21:10–15	55	1:9–11	57
27:43–28:6	31	2:5–11	10

Romans		2:13–16	43
6:3–5	41	3:20–21	58
6:23	15	4:8	20

Colossians	Sequence	James (cont.)	Sequence
1:10–12	59	3:5–10	54
1:13–20	5	5:7–8, 10–11	24
3:16	13	5:13–16	38
1 Thessalonians		1 Peter	
1:2–3	15	1:3–8	29
4:16	14	2:25	28
		3:20–22	52
1 Timothy			
2:1–7; 3:14–15	1	2 Peter	
		1:2–8	42
2 Timothy			
1:6	38	1 John	
1:8–10	26	3:16	37
		4:10–14	36
Hebrews			
1:1–4	5	Revelation	
2:10–11, 14–18	7	1:9–18	27
9:11–12	23	4:1–2	35
11:8–10, 12–16	58	5:11–14	57
		19:6–10	34
James		21:1	13
1:27	12	21:1–5	22

INDEX OF NON-BIBLICAL SOURCES

INDEX OF NON-BIBLICAL SOURCES

	Sequence
Addison, Joseph	31
Alfred, King	28
Ambali, Augustine	49
Anon.	41, 44
Aquinas, St Thomas	46
Atkin, Lord	60
Augustine, Saint	11
Bacon, Francis	50
Barker, George	11
Barnes, William	28
Barrie, J. M.	20
Belloc, Hilaire	49
Benedict, Saint	19
Bernher, Augustine	24
Binyon, Laurence	16
Blackburn, Thomas	7
Blake, William	5, 10, 22, 29, 58
Bonhoeffer, Dietrich	10
Book of Common Prayer	3, 30, 41, 52
Bridge, A. C.	5
Bridges, Robert	50, 59
Brierly, J. L.	8
Brooke, Rupert	14
Browning, Robert	26
Bunyan, John	14, 18, 56
Butler, Bishop Joseph	17
Byrd, William	13
Campion, Thomas	47
Carlyle, Thomas	43
Churchill, Sir Winston	4
City Livery Company	57
Clare, John	53
Clayton, P. B.	25
Coronation, The	51
Crane, Stephen	29
Daily Telegraph	37
Dante Alighieri	12
Dawkins, Julia	9
De la Mare, Walter	21

333

	Sequence
Dictionary of National Biography (*s.v.* Lister, Joseph)	36
Disraeli, Benjamin	60
Donne, John	14
Dostoevsky, Fëdor	38
Dryden, John	46
Epictetus	10
Everyman	11
Farrar, F. W.	61
Fox, Sir John C.	54
Frohman, Charles	26
Froissart, Jean	18
Froude, J. A.	30
Gelasius I, Pope	48
Goldsmith, Oliver	27
Green, J. R.	63
Gregory the Great, Pope	28
Hakluyt, Richard	55
Hanslick, Eduard	13
Hare, Julius Charles and Augustus William	42
Hemingway, Ernest	59
Herbert, George	28, 34
Herrick, Robert	23
Hobbes, Thomas	2
Hodgson, Leonard	35
Hood, Thomas	15
Hopkins, Gerard Manley	30
Howe, Julia Ward	63
Hügel, Baron Friedrich von	16, 26, 51, 59
Hunt, J. H. Leigh	21
Inge, W. R.	42
Jonson, Ben	16
Keats, John	12
Keble, John	42
Kempis, Thomas a	4
Kethe, William	8
Kipling, Rudyard	15
Kitchener, Lord	24
Lamb, Charles	48
Larkin, Philip	1
Law, William	44, 57

	Sequence
Lawrence, D. H.	62
Lethaby, W. R.	17
Lightfoot, Bishop J. B.	1
Loisy, Alfred	29
Lydgate, John	33
Macaulay, Lord	23
Macmillan, Lord	60
Macneice, Louis	2
Masefield, John	4, 40, 54
Mason, A. J.	38
Matthews, W. R.	7
Meynell, Alice	62
Michelangelo Buonarroti	36
Milton, John	3, 20, 33, 51
Montrose, James, Marquess of	40
Mozley, J. B.	50
Muir, Edwin	5, 63
Newman, J. H. (Cardinal)	60
Newton, Eric	6
Owen, Wilfred	37
Palgrave, F. T.	22
Pascal, Blaise	6
Pestel, Thomas	5
Plato	25, 58
Pope, Alexander	8
Powicke, F. J.	45
Proverbial	36
Quoist, Michel	21
Ralegh, Sir Walter	47
Robinson, Armitage	32
Rossetti, Christina	31
Ruskin, John	15
Sackville-West, Vita	34
Santayana, George	39
Sarum Primer	54
Scout Association	55
Shakespeare, William	13, 18, 22, 29, 38, 48, 56, 56
Shaw, G. B.	33
Shelley, P. B.	24, 41, 55
Sidney, Sir Philip	45
Smart, Christopher	57
Smyth, Charles	31

	Sequence
Sophocles	32
Spender, Stephen	43
Spenser, Edmund	26, 39, 58
Stanley, A. P.	53
Suso, Blessed Henry	41
Symonds, J. A.	23
Teilhard de Chardin, Pierre	25, 34
Temple, Archbishop William	62
Tennyson, Lord	17, 40
Thomas, R. S.	3
Thompson, Francis	34, 61
Tolstoy, Leo	47
Vaughan, Henry	32
Waller, Edmund	12
Walton, Izaak	46
Webb, C. C. J.	45
Wedgwood, C. V.	43
Wellington, Duke of	2
Westcott, Bishop B. F.	44
Whichcote, Benjamin	39
White, J. Blanco	27
White, N. J. D.	27
Whitman, Walt	19
Wolfenden, Sir John	9
Wordsworth, Dorothy	52
Wordsworth, William	6, 9, 35, 49, 52, 52, 53
Wotton, Sir Henry	19